DATE DUE

iLLDD	3·3·15		
			PRINTED IN U.S.A.

The Victory with No Name

The Victory with No Name

The Native American Defeat of the First American Army

COLIN G. CALLOWAY

OXFORD
UNIVERSITY PRESS

OXFORD
UNIVERSITY PRESS

Oxford University Press is a department of the
University of Oxford. It furthers the University's objective
of excellence in research, scholarship, and education
by publishing worldwide.

Oxford   New York

Auckland   Cape Town   Dar es Salaam   Hong Kong   Karachi
Kuala Lumpur   Madrid   Melbourne   Mexico City   Nairobi
New Delhi   Shanghai   Taipei   Toronto

With offices in

Argentina   Austria   Brazil   Chile   Czech Republic   France   Greece
Guatemala   Hungary   Italy   Japan   Poland   Portugal   Singapore
South Korea   Switzerland   Thailand   Turkey   Ukraine   Vietnam

Oxford is a registered trade mark of Oxford University Press
in the UK and certain other countries.

Published in the United States of America by
Oxford University Press
198 Madison Avenue, New York, NY 10016

Library of Congress Cataloging-in-Publication Data
Calloway, Colin G. (Colin Gordon), 1953–
The victory with no name : the Native American defeat
of the first American army / Colin G. Calloway.
pages   cm
Includes bibliographical references and index.
ISBN 978-0-19-938799-1 (hardback : acid-free paper)
1. St. Clair's Campaign, 1791.
2. Battles—Ohio River Valley—History—18th century.
3. St. Clair, Arthur, 1734–1818.
4. Indians of North America—Wars—Ohio River Valley.
5. Indians of North America—Wars—1790–1794.   I. Title.
E83.79.C35   2014
977.004'9709033—dc23
2014007552

1 3 5 7 9 8 6 4 2
Printed in the United States of America
on acid-free paper

To Marcia, Graeme, and Meg

Contents

ACKNOWLEDGMENTS   ix

Introduction   *3*

1. *Confederations: America in 1790*   *11*

2. *Building a Nation on Indian Land*   *35*

3. *The United States Invades Ohio*   *61*

4. *The Indian Resistance Movement*   *93*

5. *The Battle with No Name*   *115*

6. *Recriminations and Reversal*   *129*

Epilogue   *153*

NOTES   165

BIBLIOGRAPHY   185

INDEX   197

Acknowledgments

AT OXFORD UNIVERSITY PRESS I am grateful to my editor, Timothy Bent, for taking up this project and helping me to bring out the story more succinctly, to Keely Latcham for her efficient editorial assistance, and to Joellyn Ausanka for guiding the manuscript through production. For readings of the manuscript, thanks to Elliott West and two anonymous readers who provided generous and helpful comments, and to Drew Cayton for casting his expert eye over chapter 2. I have depended for years on generations of historians who have written about the Old Northwest—and whose work makes the national amnesia about St. Clair's defeat the more remarkable—and I have benefited particularly from the work of scholars who have revisited the region to recover its Native American history. I am grateful to the staffs of the Chicago History Museum, the National Archives at Kew, England, the Massachusetts Historical Society, the New York State Historical Association, the Ohio Historical Society, and the Ohio State Library for assistance with archival materials and images. At Dartmouth, as always, thanks to my colleagues in the Baker-Berry Library, the History Department, and the Native American Studies Program for their support and assistance. For everything else, thanks to Marcia, Graeme, and Meg.

The Victory with No Name

Introduction

Friday, November the 4th, 1791. Moderate N.W. wind, serene atmosphere and unclouded sky; but the fortunes of this day have been as the cruellest tempest to the interests of the Country and this Army, and will blacken a full page in the future annals of America.
ADJUTANT GENERAL WINTHROP SARGENT

IN 1791 MAJOR GENERAL ARTHUR ST. CLAIR led the U.S. Army in a campaign that was intended to destroy a cluster of Indian villages along the Maumee River in northwestern Ohio and build a fort in its place. Almost within reach of their objective, St. Clair's 1,400 or so men were attacked by about one thousand Indians. The militia that composed the advance party immediately gave way and fell back upon the main body of troops, throwing them into disorder, while the Indians quickly surrounded the American encampment. The officers tried to rally their men, but they were fighting an elusive enemy who dodged from tree to tree and rained an incessant fire on the American ranks, killing the officers and gunners and silencing the artillery. After the Americans had stood their ground for three hours, those who were able fled, with the Indians in hot pursuit, cutting down both soldiers and noncombatants in flight. The retreat was so hasty that the Americans abandoned their ammunition, provisions, and baggage. They had suffered almost one thousand casualties in killed and wounded. The government investigation into the disaster cited the enemy's numerical superiority and the misconduct of the enlisted men, as well as failures in provisioning the army.

The battle and the government's findings seemed to many an echo. In 1755 General Edward Braddock led the largest British army that had ever been dispatched to North America in a campaign to seize Fort Duquesne, the French fort at the Forks of the Ohio. Almost within reach of their objective, Braddock's 1,469 men collided with a force of some nine hundred Indians, French troops, and Canadian militia. After a confused exchange of fire, the Indians took cover in the trees and quickly spread down both sides of the British line. Lieutenant Colonel Thomas Gage, commanding the advance, regrouped his troops, but they could find no enemy line to fight. The advance party then gave way and fell back upon those behind, "which very much disconcerted the Men, and that added to a manner of fighting that they were quite unacquainted with, struck a Panic" into the soldiers. The officers tried to rally their men, but, like St. Clair's army, they were fighting an elusive enemy who dodged from tree to tree and incessantly fired on the British ranks, killing the officers and gunners and silencing the artillery. After they had stood their ground for three hours, those who were able retreated, with the Indians in hot pursuit, cutting down both soldiers and noncombatants in flight. The retreat "was so hasty that we were obliged to leave the whole Train: Ammunition, Provision, and baggage to the plundering of the Indians." The British suffered almost one thousand casualties, including sixty of their eighty-six officers. Braddock, who had failed to use Indian scouts and rangers, was killed. His aide-de-camp, George Washington, managed to escape unscathed. The army's investigation into the disaster cited enemy numbers and the misconduct of the enlisted men.[1]

American writers and historians have often cited Braddock's disaster on the banks of the Monongahela River as an example of the arrogance and stupidity of British commanders. It showed that the British could be beaten and demonstrated the folly of trying to employ European battlefield tactics in the American wilderness. American colonists learned their lesson and, so the story goes, went on to win their independence by defeating ranks of British regulars with American-style guerrilla warfare. In reality the American victory in the War of Independence owed more to conventional tactics, battles between armies, and French intervention than to American farmers firing from behind trees and picking off robotic redcoats. If there were lessons to be learned from Braddock's defeat, Americans evidently did not learn them well. A number of officers in St. Clair's army had served in and survived Braddock's campaign.

Compared with bloodbaths in eighteenth-century Europe, such as Malplaquet (1709), Fontenay (1745), and Zorndorf (1758), St. Clair's defeat wasn't much of a battle. It involved only a few thousand people, lasted less than three hours, and after the first few moments the outcome was never in doubt. Most of the Americans who fought and died there were not very good soldiers, and the Indian victory was reversed three years later. Neither an epic struggle nor a clash that changed the course of history, the battle doesn't even have a name.

Yet St. Clair's Defeat, as it is usually called—occasionally the Battle on the Wabash—was hugely important in its time. "The late calamity to the Westward has produced great sensation here," wrote Thomas Jefferson three days after the news arrived in Philadelphia.[2] First accounts appearing in the press declared that it "engrosses all our thoughts." Five weeks after the battle a correspondent from Philadelphia wrote, "The Western Expedition—and its issue—occupy all our thoughts."[3] Indians fielding a multinational army, executing a carefully coordinated battle plan worked out by their chiefs, and winning a pitched battle—all things Indians were not supposed to be capable of doing—routed the largest force the United States had fielded on the frontier. The disaster generated a deluge of reports, correspondence, opinions, and debates in the press. It was memorialized in poems and in song.[4]

The battle deserves to be remembered far more than it is. It was the biggest victory Native Americans ever won and proportionately the biggest military disaster the United States ever suffered. With the British in Canada waiting in the wings for the American experiment in republicanism to fail, and some regions of the West gravitating toward alliance with Spain, the destruction of the army— what Secretary of War Henry Knox called "the sword of the republic"[5]—threatened the very existence of the infant United States. The defeat added to the growing divisions that eventually led to the creation of the first political parties. It produced the first congressional investigation in American history and in the process saw the birth of the principle of executive privilege, as the Washington administration considered whether or not to withhold documents that implicated Secretary of War Knox and Secretary of the Treasury Alexander Hamilton in the contractor fraud that had left St. Clair's troops ill fed and ill equipped. It increased the federal government's role in shaping western development and expanding the American republic.[6] It changed how Americans viewed, raised, organized, and paid for their armies and how they fought their wars. It increased the president's power to raise troops. It provided the impetus for creating a new army and for establishing that army as "the federal government's most visible agent of empire."[7]

In 1876 the Sioux and Cheyenne killed some 250 of George Armstrong Custer's Seventh Cavalry but barely slowed the march of American expansion. The Battle of Little Bighorn has generated hundreds of books and been reenacted multiple times in paintings and films. As the United States entered the final phases of its Manifest Destiny, the "Last Stand" of a flamboyant general and his gallant soldiers became an epic story of national heroism and sacrifice acted out on the sweeping plains of the West. In contrast, myth- and nation-builders found little to celebrate or commemorate in the destruction of America's first army in a slaughter pen in the woodlands of northwest Ohio. Most Americans have not even heard of St. Clair's Defeat, and only a handful of writers have covered it. Most of those have been military historians who provide excellent accounts of one side of the battle. Although it acknowledges that St. Clair's was "the worst defeat ever suffered by an American army against Native Americans," one hefty and authoritative survey of American military history devotes just one paragraph to the campaign and a single sentence to the battle itself. None of the Indian participants is identified by name or nation.[8]

The truism that history is written by the victors is not so true when indigenous people are the winners. In those instances the losers explain how they lost the battle rather than how the Natives won it. So by and large, in this Indian victory the Indians remain faceless in the forest, anonymous instruments of a battle lost by the Americans rather than a potent and organized military force with superior leadership that repulsed an enemy army that was invading their country and threatening their families.

The battle was a clash between two recently formed and fragile American confederations as well as between two American armies. The Indians living northwest of the Ohio River had formed a multitribal confederation—variously called the Northwest Confederacy, the Wabash Confederacy, and the Miami Confederacy—primarily to defend their lands against American expansion. Native American leaders exercised limited authority within their own communities; establishing and maintaining a coalition of different tribes required consensus, conciliation, and accommodation. The Indian victory was as much diplomatic as military, achieved by holding together an alliance and bringing a united force of warriors to bear at the decisive moment. The confederation remained subject to divisive strains, subordinate to the local interests of individual members. The same could be said of the other new confederation, the one that called itself the United States.

After an unsatisfactory period of government under the Articles of Confederation, the United States adopted a new Constitution in 1787, granting the federal government greater authority but still reserving significant rights of self-government to the thirteen states. The government had to deal with independently minded states and citizens. Indian leaders explaining breaches of peace frequently told American officials, "We cannot control our young men"; U.S. officials in this period could have admitted much the same. The two confederations, the United States and the Indian confederation, both in their infancy, clashed in an area each regarded as vital to its future survival. But the federal government had to establish its authority over frontier whites as well as the Indians as it extended its reach into the West.[9]

Explanations of the battle, of how a band of supposedly savage Indians could destroy an American army, have emphasized the failings of that army, not the achievements of the Indians. Although many of St. Clair's officers had served in the Revolution and some of his soldiers had seen action, the majority of his men were ill prepared for combat. Almost immediately after the defeat, officers, politicians, and disappointed land speculators placed the blame on the soldiers who died in the battle or fled from it. John Cleves Symmes, a New Jersey judge, land speculator, and promoter of settlements, whose ambitions the battle frustrated, was typical in his denunciations of the men: "Too great a proportion of the privates appeared to be totally debilitated and rendered incapable of this service, either from their youth (mere boys) or by their excessive intemperance and abandoned habits. These men who are to be purchased from the prisons[,] wheelbarrows and brothels of the nation at two dollars per month, will never answer our purpose for fighting of Indians."[10] Lieutenant Ebenezer Denny, who served as St. Clair's aide-de-camp and fought in the battle, said the bulk of the army was composed of "men collected from the streets and prisons of the cities."[11] Lieutenant Colonel William Darke, communicating "the disagreeable news of our defeat" to George Washington, heaped praise on the gallant officers but dismissed the bulk of the men killed as "as well out of the world as in it."[12] In short, good riddance to them.

Such indictments of rank-and-file soldiers were commonplace. They had been offered as explanation for Braddock's defeat in 1755 and would be offered again for the slaughter of British troops on the first day of the Somme in 1916. Blaming the troops was a convenient way to deflect criticism from generals, politicians, contractors, and land speculators whose actions or lack of action might have contributed to the disaster. But the perceived character deficiencies of the troops do not in themselves explain defeat. The Duke of Wellington routinely described his soldiers as the dregs of society, men pulled from the prisons, taverns, and whorehouses of Britain. His soldiers, most of whom were victims of economic dislocation rather than endemic vice, won impressive victories in the Peninsula campaigns and then at Waterloo, where they put to flight the battle-hardened veterans of Napoleon's elite Imperial Guard.[13]

Soldiers in modern America have often been, and continue to be, forgotten as they bear the burden of fighting unpopular wars in distant places. But the soldiers who fought and died in 1791 remain almost completely forgotten for other reasons. Not only was the battle in which they fought best forgotten, but their deaths were not heroic—and the patriotic national narrative that emerged in the late eighteenth and nineteenth century required America's citizen soldiers to be heroic.[14] Although a congressional investigation exonerated St. Clair and St. Clair himself insisted that his troops fought with honor, the disaster still bears his name, and when remembered at all it is as a rout.

Not for the last time in the history of America's Indian wars, pinning the blame for a tragedy on a commander and soldiers who were "the dregs of society" diverted attention from deeper structural issues.[15] Calling the battle "St. Clair's Defeat" not only ignores the Indian victory; by appending one man's name to the conflict it also ignores the larger deficiencies in the U.S. government and military that contributed to the defeat.

Logistical problems, lack of training and the limitations of the soldiers, and military misjudgments set up St. Clair's army to fail. But explaining the conflict only in these terms limits understanding of the battle and dismisses the experiences of most of the people who were there. The story of the battle as a military encounter must explain how the Indians won it as well as how St. Clair lost it. The story of the battle as a human tragedy—as all battles are—must include the experiences of people who died in panic, fear, and flight as well as those who stood their ground. The story of the battle as a national calamity must consider the forces and the individuals that drove the campaign ahead despite the mounting odds against it.

The winners write history, it seems, even when they lose. Although some of the Indians involved in the contest for the Old Northwest, like the Mohawk war chief Joseph Brant, were literate, and although British and American agents and observers often took down Indian speeches verbatim or close to it, the Indians generally produced few written records, and the documentation about the battle is primarily American. The documentation is also primarily the work of men in the army and in government, many of whom had a vested interest in pushing St. Clair's campaign forward and in deflecting blame for the disaster onto the voiceless—and dead—men they exposed to slaughter. The mythology of the American frontier depicts pioneer families fearlessly carving out homes in the wilderness in peril of their lives and scalps at the hands of merciless savages. Certainly the Ohio country provided homes and farms for countless emigrants, but in 1790–91 the people with the most pressing need to see Indian homelands opened up for settlement were influential men with fortunes to make.

The war against the Ohio Indians was, above all else, a war over real estate. The U.S. government, land speculators, and individual settlers all demanded that tribal homelands be transformed into American territory. It was a national project that allowed no room for the presence of tribal peoples or for the persistence of tribal homelands and the worldviews embedded in them. "Our settlements are extending themselves so fast in every quarter where they can be extended; our pretensions to the country they inhabit have been made to them in so unequivocal a manner, and the consequences are so certain and so dreadful to them, that there is little probability of there ever being any cordiality between us," St. Clair, governor of the Northwest Territory, wrote to Secretary of War Henry Knox in July 1788.[16]

Conflict over land may indeed have been inevitable, but did this particular conflict have to happen when it did? No one was in a bigger hurry to have the Indians defeated than the speculators whose investments in the rich lands of Ohio could not yield a lucrative return until the threat of Indian war was removed and settlers were willing to buy. Many of these men had friends in government, and they played on the government's fears of losing the West to advocate strong and timely measures against the Indians who stood in the way of their schemes and, they said, threatened the nation's future and security. St. Clair, with land interests himself, was under significant pressure—from President Washington, Secretary of War Knox, and others—to push his campaign forward to completion long after the optimum season for conducting the campaign had passed. In the second half of the nineteenth century the transcontinental railroad companies influenced the pace, direction, and character of American westward expansion. Powerful and well-connected men in pursuit of personal fortunes acted as agents of national expansion and sometimes dictated its pace.[17] The land companies in Ohio at the end of the eighteenth century did much the same. Their rich man's war became a poor man's fight, and when it resulted in catastrophe they blamed the levies and militia—men with lives to lose but no lands to sell.

Although the Ohio frontier, like other borderland regions, was culturally porous, the United States and the united tribes clashed head-on over a specific boundary. Perhaps at no other place and period in American history was the contest for Indian lands played out with such drama and clarity. The battle lines were drawn here in a way that lent force to the pens of those who have romanticized the struggles that decided the destiny of the continent. In their writings and in retrospect, American victory in Indian wars in the Ohio country seems inevitable. In the 1790s some politicians and land speculators even claimed it was preordained. Some Americans in the 1790s talked in those terms too. But Indian power in the early 1790s remained strong, despite the inroads of disease, dispossession, and escalating warfare, and the Indians turned back one invasion of Ohio and almost annihilated another. The Indian victory was temporary—the United States reversed the battle within a few years—but there was a time when the outcome of the struggle seemed in doubt.

As the growing nation resumed its march westward with renewed tempo, it was eager to bury the memories of St. Clair's Defeat. The men who lost the battle were dead or shamed; those responsible for it had moved on to other things. Nations build their histories and shape their identities by telling some stories from their past and forgetting others.[18] So the George Washington of popular history is the man who could not tell a lie, who crossed the Delaware in Emanuel Leutze's epic painting, and who served reluctantly but nobly as the father of his country, not the man who speculated in Indian lands, burned Indian towns, and, as commander in chief, was ultimately responsible for losing the nation's first army. The day when American Indians won their greatest victory became an aberration in the national story and a blank spot in the national memory. This book will try to fill in the blank and restore the memory.

CHAPTER I

Confederations: America in 1790

*W*INNING A REVOLUTION WAS ONE THING; building a nation was quite another. Fourteen years after the thirteen colonies had declared their independence from Great Britain, seven years after Britain had recognized that independence at the Peace of Paris, and three years after the founding fathers had met in Philadelphia to revise the Articles of Confederation and form "a more perfect union" by drawing up the Constitution, the union of states was far from perfect. "We have become a nation," declared Benjamin Rush when the Constitution was ratified. Rush, a signer of the Declaration of Independence and delegate to the Constitutional Convention, was also the country's preeminent physician, but in this case his diagnosis was premature. The Constitution created a stronger, more centralized federal government, but in 1790 it was still embryonic, an emerging construct, controversial and ill defined. As the historian Gordon Wood points out, "None of the Revolutionaries in 1776 had had any idea of making the thirteen United States anything other than a confederation."[1]

The Constitution had turned that confederation of separate states into a nation, but only on paper. It remained to be seen whether the new government could command obedience to national laws and at the same time remain true to the republican principles of the Revolution. Could it develop the resources and machinery to govern and at the same time respect local authority and protect individual liberty? Would it realize or stifle the freedoms and promises for which Americans had fought? Could commitment to democratic principles hold together a diverse array of peoples, regions, and religions? Could a republic of such size

long endure, and would western expansion cement or sunder ties between East and West? The hard work of making the new national
republic function and flourish remained to be done. North Carolina had
ratified the Constitution recently, and reluctantly, in November 1789;
Rhode Island, which had rejected the Constitution in 1788, did not ratify
it until May 1790, and then by a margin of just two votes. The government still needed to organize the nation's finances, open a mint, establish a post office and post roads, and create a national army.[2] In some
ways the United States in 1790 was no more united than the Indian
confederation it faced as it looked to expand beyond the Ohio River.

The confederation that called itself the United States was new, but
confederations were not new in North America. Long before
Europeans arrived, Indians had built relationships of cooperation, coexistence, and kinship that reached across barriers of language, distance, and culture, facilitating trade and sharing territory. In the wake
of European invasion they forged new alliances—sometimes with
European colonies—to meet new challenges. In what is now upstate
New York the League of the Iroquois—the Five, later Six, Nations of
the Mohawk, Oneida, Onondaga, Cayuga, Seneca, and then the
Tuscarora—long dominated relations between Indians and colonists
in northeastern North America, and a system of alliances known as
the Covenant Chain linked the Iroquois Confederacy and its allied
and client tribal nations to the governments of the British colonies.

At the Treaty of Lancaster in 1744 an Onondaga speaker named
Canasatego had coached colonial delegates from Virginia, Pennsylvania,
and Maryland on how to form a union. "Our wise Forefathers established Union and Amity between the Five Nations," he said; "this has
made us formidable; this has given us great Weight and Authority
with our neighboring Nations. We are a powerful Confederacy; and
by your observing the same Methods our wise Forefathers have taken,
you will acquire fresh Strength and Power."[3] Benjamin Franklin
thought it would be "a very strange Thing if six Nations of ignorant
savages should be capable of forming a Scheme for such an Union
and be able to execute it in such a manner as it has subsisted for ages
and appears indissoluble and yet that a like Union should be imprac-
ticable for ten or a Dozen English Colonies."[4] The colonies were not
quick to act on Canasatego's advice; ten years later Virginia and other
southern colonies did not even send delegates to the Albany Congress
that was called to discuss Indian relations and Franklin's Plan of
Union. But they did, in time, show that they could form "a like Union."

The Iroquois Confederacy suffered division, devastation, and loss of land during and after the American Revolution, but it continued to exert influence in the affairs of the Ohio nations and in the Indian diplomacy of Britain and the United States. In the Southeast in 1790 the Creek Confederacy, a loose coalition of some fifty semiautonomous towns, blocked American expansion and exerted influence in the Indian diplomacy of Spain and the United States.

Other Indian confederations had emerged across the continent at different times. In 1675–76 a Wampanoag chief named Metacom, known to the English as King Philip, headed an alliance of Algonquian tribes in a brutal war against New England. In 1680 Pueblo peoples in the Rio Grande Valley synchronized a united revolt against eight decades of Spanish colonial rule and in a few weeks drove the Spaniards out of New Mexico. In the Great Lakes region the Ojibwa (or Chippewa), Ottawa (Odawa), and Potawatomi, known collectively as Anishinaabeg, formed an alliance known as the Three Fires; rather than a permanent political structure, it was an extensive set of symbolic and symbiotic relationships that connected scattered communities by kinship and intermarriage. Indians who assembled at Detroit to meet the British in 1760 told the king's officers, "All the Indians in this Country are Allies to each other and as one People." The alliance bound the tribes and their multiple villages together for social, economic, and sometimes military purposes but allowed them flexibility for independent action. Allies would not fight each other, but they were not obligated to fight their allies' enemies.[5] In 1763 the Ottawa war chief Pontiac, the Seneca Guyasuta, and other leaders forged a multitribal alliance that challenged the British imperial presence in the West. Many tribes fought against the Americans during the Revolution and, as in the United States, their leaders in 1790 were veterans of that war. The Indian confederation defending the Ohio was in a long tradition of Native movements that invoked cultural and spiritual connections to forge a united struggle for autonomy and independence against a common, non-Indian enemy.[6]

Indian confederations loosely tied tribes, towns, and clans by kinship, ritual, gift exchange, and common interest rather than by institutions, laws, and constitutional authority. Their unity was often episodic, displayed in council and in conflict in response to crises and summonses, and precarious, subject to diverging agendas and multiple autonomies. Colonial powers and the United States were always ready to foment, exploit, and exacerbate divisions among the tribes.

Indian confederations were always works in progress and required a lot of work. In that respect they resembled the United States in 1790, the confederation that Indians called the "Thirteen Fires."

GEORGE WASHINGTON OUTLINED THE WORK the Thirteen Fires needed to do in the first annual presidential address to Congress—what is now called the State of the Union—on January 8, 1790. Speaking at the beginning of Congress's second session in the Senate Chamber in Federal Hall in New York City, the provisional capital at the time, he briefly reviewed the good work done in the previous session and assessed the nation's prospects looking forward: "The recent accession of the important State of North Carolina to the constitution of the United States, . . . the rising credit and respectability of our country; the general and increasing good will towards the government of the Union; and the concord, peace, and plenty, with which we are blessed, are circumstances auspicious in an eminent degree to our national prosperity." But the tasks ahead would "call for the cool and deliberate exertion of your patriotism, firmness, and wisdom."

The president focused on half a dozen topics. National defense was first on the list. "To be prepared for war, is one of the most effectual means of preserving peace," he argued. A uniform plan was necessary because "a free people ought not only to be armed, but disciplined," and they needed to develop manufacturing capability to render them "independent on others for essential, particularly for military supplies." Congress would have to give serious thought to "the proper establishment of the troops which may be deemed indispensable," and in making arrangement for it, said the commander in chief, "it will be of importance to conciliate the comfortable support of the officers and soldiers, with a due regard to economy." Washington had hoped that the "pacific measures adopted with regard to certain hostile tribes of Indians, would have relieved the inhabitants of our southern and western frontiers from their depredations," but since that was not the case, "we ought to be prepared to afford protection to those parts of the Union, and, if necessary, to punish aggressors."

Washington spent less time on the other issues in his short message. The compensation paid to public officials engaged in conducting foreign relations should be set by law and a fund established for the conduct of foreign affairs. The terms on which foreigners could become citizens "should be speedily ascertained by a uniform rule of naturalization." The United States needed to establish a uniform system of currency, weights, and measures. In addition to promoting agriculture, commerce, and industry, Congress should encourage "the introduction of new and useful inventions from abroad, as to the exertions of skill and genius in producing them at home." It must attend to the post office and post roads to facilitate communication between the distant parts of the country. It must promote education. "Knowledge is, in every country, the surest basis of public happiness," contributing to the security of a free constitution "by convincing those who are entrusted with the public administration, that every valuable end of government is best answered by the enlightened confidence of the people; and by teaching the people themselves to know and to value their own rights" and "to distinguish between oppression and the necessary exercise of lawful authority." Congress had already resolved that support of the public credit was "a matter of high importance to the national honor and prosperity." Washington concurred. The first president looked forward to working with Congress "in the pleasing, though arduous task, of ensuring to our fellow-citizens the blessings which they have a right to expect from a free, efficient, and equal government."[7]

Washington did the most to hold together the precarious unity of the United States. He was, in Joseph Ellis's words, "the core of gravity that prevented the American Revolution from flying off into random orbits." But despite his god-like status in American history, Washington was all too human and mortal, and he and his contemporaries knew it. On an official visit to New England in 1789 he had caught a cold that developed into pneumonia. "The President has been so sick as to create an alarm, but thank God he is nearly well," wrote Secretary of War Henry Knox in July. Then in the spring of 1790 he came down with influenza, developed pulmonary complications, and almost died. "You cannot conceive the public alarm on this occasion," said Thomas Jefferson. "It proves how much depends on his life." Washington reflected, "I have already within less than a year had two severe attacks, the last worse than the first. A third probably will put me to sleep with my fathers."[8] The president survived the spring, but he was still figuring out what it meant to be president, something on which the Constitution provided little in the way of detailed instructions.

Benjamin Franklin did not survive the spring; he died in April. So Franklin did not make it into the first census of the nation he had helped to create. In 1790, under the direction of Secretary of State Thomas Jefferson, recently back from France, marshals of U.S. judicial districts collected data from the thirteen states as well as from districts and territories that would later become Kentucky, Tennessee, Maine, and Vermont. They recorded the names of heads of households and categorized inhabitants as free white males age sixteen and older, free white males under sixteen, free white females, all other free persons, and slaves. In the decade before the census the population had increased dramatically, more than any other decade in American history. And it was still growing. In 1790 Comfort and Lucy Freeman of Sturbridge, Massachusetts, welcomed their ninth child into the world; their family was large but not unusual for that time and place.[9]

Both Washington and Jefferson suspected that the census undercounted the actual population. According to the official figures, the nation had a total population of slightly below 4 million, many times that of all the Indian nations within its borders. Sixty percent of America's population was of British ancestry; 18 percent came from Britain's Celtic borderlands—Scots, Irish, and Scotch-Irish; almost 9 percent were German. More than 20 percent were Africans, 90 percent of whom were slaves. Virginia was the state with the largest population, 747,610; Pennsylvania had 434,373. Only five cities—Baltimore, Boston, Charleston, New York, and Philadelphia—had populations over ten thousand. (Three years later Philadelphia had forty-five thousand, but nearly 10 percent died in the yellow fever epidemic that hit the city.) Pittsburgh had fewer than four hundred. But the rapidly growing population of the states sought land for farming, and frontier areas were growing fast. An American officer recorded more than three hundred boats and six thousand emigrants passing down the Ohio River in the first six months of 1788.[10] The population of Kentucky had been around twelve thousand in 1783; by 1790 it had surpassed seventy-three thousand, some of whom were seeping north across the Ohio into the region designated as the Northwest Territory. Virginia, Pennsylvania, and Kentucky all bordered on the Northwest Territory and pressed on the Indian lands it encompassed. The eastern frontier was growing as well: the population of Maine reached 100,000 in 1790, a threefold increase since 1775.

As population grew and pushed west, regional strains divided, or threatened to divide, the United States. The Revolution had opened up lands for settlement, but many living on the margins of the original colonies were disappointed with the distribution of those lands, and some disagreed, sometimes violently, with the governing elite and its vision of the new republic. Frontier people were the westward-facing vanguard of national expansion, but those same people also faced east, and, as they had during the colonial and revolutionary eras, they looked with resentment and suspicion toward a government that seemed unresponsive, unrepresentative, and locally impotent when it came to defending their lands, lives, and interests.[11] Separatist tendencies surfaced in Kentucky, western Pennsylvania, and Vermont, where a delegation had visited the governor of Quebec to explore the possibilities of annexation by Britain (Vermont did not become the fourteenth state until 1791.) Kentucky was pushing to join the Union, and there were fears that if it did not happen soon the territory south of the Ohio would gravitate into Spain's orbit, if not into Spain's empire. Congress in 1790 created the Southwest Territory out of western lands ceded to the federal government by North Carolina, but it would be another six years before the area achieved statehood as Tennessee. Settlers in Kentucky and Tennessee who knew that Spain could close the Mississippi to American trade might have second thoughts about remaining American. Spaniards cultivated relations with influential individuals in Kentucky who they hoped would lead a separatist movement, and James Wilkinson, who would feature prominently in the Indian campaigns of the next few years, was involved in a conspiracy to bring Kentucky under Spanish hegemony. Spaniards also courted influential southern Indian chiefs like the Creek Alexander McGillivray. In the summer of 1790 the chronically ill but diplomatically agile McGillivray and twenty-seven Creek chiefs traveled to New York and spent a month negotiating a treaty with the United States that was intended to protect Creek land from invasion by Georgia settlers and wean McGillivray from his allegiance with Spain. It did neither, but it focused the federal government's primary interest in Indian affairs that summer on New York City.[12]

While Spain was an ominous presence in the South and Southwest, the British in Canada seemed to pose a greater immediate threat. At the Peace of Paris that ended the American Revolution in 1783, Britain, without consulting or even mentioning its Indian allies, had ceded to the United States all territory south of the Great Lakes, east of the Mississippi, and north of Florida and agreed to hand over various posts along the northern frontier "with all convenient speed." Instead Britain held on to the posts for another thirteen years, citing American infringements of treaty provisions, in particular nonpayment of loyalist debts, as justification for their refusal to evacuate the forts.

By holding on to Michilimackinac in the Great Lakes, Detroit, Niagara, Oswego on Lake Ontario, Oswegatchie on the St. Lawrence, and a couple of posts on Lake Champlain, the British dominated the waterways, controlled the Indian trade, and maintained an important presence in Indian country.

With Spain controlling the Mississippi in the South, Indians posing a formidable obstacle in the West, and British garrisons in the North, the United States in 1790 had good reason to feel hemmed in, even as it looked to expand into limitless territory. Washington had written to Governor Benjamin Harrison of Virginia in 1784:

> I need not remark to you, sir, that the flanks and rear of the United States are possessed by other powers, and formidable ones, too; nor how necessary it is to apply the cement of interest to bind all parts of the Union together by indissoluble bonds, especially that part of it which lies immediately west of us, with the middle states. For what ties, let me ask, should we have upon these people? How entirely unconnected with them shall we be, and what troubles may we not apprehend, if the Spaniards on their right, and Great Britain on their left, instead of throwing stumbling blocks in their way, as they do now, should hold out lures for their trade and alliance? What, when they get strength, which will be sooner than most people conceive (from the emigration of foreigners, who will have no particular predilection toward us, as well as from the removal of our own citizens), will be the consequence of their having formed close connections with both or either of those powers, in a commercial way? It needs not, in my opinion, the gift of prophecy to foretell. The western states (I speak now from my own observation) stand, as it were, upon a pivot. The touch of a feather would turn them either way.[13]

Conflict and chaos continued in the West long after the Revolutionary War ended in the East. The Indians and their British backers had no intention of simply handing over the Ohio country to the United States. Eastern elites looked askance at frontier settlers who seemed almost as savage as the Indians, and many members of government blamed frontier whites for much of the violence and chaos on the frontier. In that they shared much in common with older Indian chiefs who struggled to restrain their own young warriors.[14] Unbridled expansion, they feared, could depopulate eastern states, depreciate eastern land values, and sever connections between East and West before the union had a chance to form. Western expansion must be controlled. But before western lands could be surveyed, sold, and settled, peace between the Indians and the frontiersmen was necessary. Bringing order to the West, protecting western citizens against the Indians (and the British), securing access to the Mississippi, and integrating the West into the new nation were major tests of the new government in 1790.

For whites on the Ohio frontier, peace meant ridding the region of Indians. Indian raids threatened settlers' lives and land speculators' profits. One surveyor found it "impossible to proceed in surveying" because the Indians were "dispersed through almost every Part of the Country where *our* Land lies" (emphasis added). Settlers, squatters, land speculators, and frontier officials insisted that only the state could deliver them from the horrors of continuing Indian war.[15] Indians must be defeated or removed, and westerners looked to the federal government to do it. For men and women on the frontier, it often seemed that the federal government lacked the will to protect their interests and even their lives.

In reality the American government lacked the means. It threatened Indians who resisted with destruction, but its military arm remained feeble. The Continental Army had been disbanded at the end of the Revolutionary War, all troops discharged except twenty-five men at Fort Pitt and Captain John Doughty's garrison of fifty-five men at West Point. Many in Congress feared that a standing army in peacetime was "inconsistent with the principles of republican government, dangerous to the liberties of a free people."[16] The day after it dissolved the Continental Army in June 1784, the Confederation Congress had formed the First American Regiment. Intended primarily for frontier defense, the regiment was to comprise eight infantry and two artillery companies totaling seven hundred soldiers, one-year recruits to be furnished from the militias of four states: Connecticut, New Jersey, New York, and Pennsylvania. The actual number of men never exceeded five hundred. Because Pennsylvania contributed most men (260—the only state that met its quota), it was permitted to select the commanding officer, Josiah Harmar, who had had an undistinguished record as a brigadier general in the Revolution. In 1785 Congress authorized increasing the size of the army and then increased the enlistment term to three years. Even then the actual strength of the army remained stuck at around five hundred soldiers.

Dispersed among frontier posts, the army was ineffective at anything other than local police action.[17]

Henry Knox recognized the limitations. In his report to Congress in July 1787, the secretary of war explained that it was unlikely Indians and whites could ever be good neighbors: "The one side anxiously defend their lands which the other avariciously claim." Troops were needed to defend the frontiers and hold the West, but there were insufficient funds and they would have to make do with careful disposition of existing troops. Then, with prescience, he added:

> In the present embarrassed state of public affairs and entire deficiency of funds an Indian war of any considerable extent and duration would most exceedingly distress the United States. The great distance by land by which the stores and supplies must be transported would render the expences intolerable. If in the event it should be found necessary to commence with an attack on the Wabash Indians it will be very difficult if not impracticable to prevent the other tribes from joining them. The Officers or traders at the British posts would use every art and intrigue for that purpose.[18]

Knox was forty-two and a big man, over six feet tall and about 280 pounds. (His wife was evidently of similar build; the Reverend Manasseh Cutler uncharitably described her in his journal as "very gross," although he was apparently more concerned with her "disgusting" hairstyle.)[19] A former Boston bookseller who became chief of artillery during the Revolution, Knox had served Washington with an energy that belied his bulk, hauling heavy guns over the snow from Ticonderoga to Boston in 1776, fighting at Trenton and Princeton, and enduring the hard winter at Valley Forge, and he was in at the kill at Yorktown. Appointed secretary of war in 1785 under the Articles of Confederation, he continued in that position, at a salary of $3,000 a year, when the new Constitution went into effect in 1789 and established the War Department as one of the executive branches of government. The Constitution authorized Congress to raise armies, declare war, and call out the militia of the several states but balanced that power by making the president commander in chief of the army and navy and of the militia "when called into the actual service of the United States." The new Congress authorized funding for the War Department to maintain a minimal federal military establishment and retained authority to determine the size of the nation's armed forces.

Henry Knox by Charles Willson Peale, from life, ca. 1784. Courtesy of Independence National Historic Park.

Suspicion of standing armies went back to colonial times and to England, and the new nation—a nation born in war—debated what kind of military force a republican government should be able to call upon.[20] The militia tradition also originated in England, and many Americans deemed "a well-regulated militia" the best defense against both aggression from without and tyranny within. Congress was reluctant to take measures that would strengthen a national army. But the militia system had proved most effective in colonial wars, when its members rallied to defend their own homes, less so when called to fight on distant frontiers.[21] Men like Washington, Knox, and Arthur St. Clair, all of who had served in the Continental Army, now held positions of political power and knew that a national government required a national military. Responding to a proposal in the Constitutional Convention to limit the standing army to three thousand men,

Washington is reputed to have offered the tongue-in-cheek counter-proposal that "no foreign enemy should invade the United States at any time, with more than three thousand troops."[22] Even so, in January 1790 Knox felt that "a small corps of well-disciplined and well-informed artillerists and engineers, and a legion for the protection of the frontiers and the magazines and arsenals, are all the military establishment which may be required for the present use of the United States." Knox advised Congress to reject a standing army and establish a "well-constituted militia" because "an energetic national militia is to be regarded as the *capital security* of a free republic, and not a standing army forming a distinct class in the community." In the end the federal government exercised its authority under the Constitution to raise a national army, and the states retained their own militias. In April 1790 Congress authorized a further increase in the regular army to 1,273 officers and men for a term of three years and added four more companies of infantry. Privates' pay was $3 per month, minus $1 for clothing and medical expenses. The United States was already at war with the Indians in the Northwest Territory before the troops were raised.[23]

Lack of money, low pay, poor morale, desertions, ideological opposition to standing armies, quarreling between individual states, state appointments of their own officers, and a corrupt and inefficient contract system that provided substandard arms, equipment, food, and clothing, all hampered efforts to build a federal army. Army suppliers and congressmen had acquired what the late military historian and collector William Guthman called "bad habits" with regard to the army, and Americans had come to accept the army's plight—"starvation and survival"—as part of life.[24]

Funding the military required revenue, and raising revenue depended on the military: the government would have difficulty selling western lands unless it could protect prospective settlers from Indian raids. The nation's other institutions and endeavors had to be financed as well. The head of the new Treasury Department was Alexander Hamilton. Thirty-five years old in 1790, Hamilton was the illegitimate son of a Scottish merchant in the West Indies ("the bastard brat of a Scottish pedlar," as John Adams put it). He was brilliant and flamboyant and had displayed reckless personal courage at the siege of Yorktown. He set about putting the nation's finances in order and mapping out its future prosperity with his usual boldness, tackling first of all the huge national debt. The foreign debt—the amount owed to France, Spain, and Dutch bankers—amounted to $12 million. The domestic debt—the amount owed by the federal and state governments to their own citizens—was about $42 million and $25 million, respectively.

In January 1790, five months after he took office, Hamilton presented Congress with a forty-thousand-word report on public credit, laying out his proposals for paying off the debt. They included the controversial plan for the federal government to assume the states' debts and consolidate them into the kind of permanent national debt that Britain had, thereby relieving the states of the need to raise taxes, giving investors a stake in the new national government, and binding states and citizens to the national government. In May 1790, as part of his plans for centralizing public finances, Hamilton introduced to Congress his proposed tax on whiskey, the first federal tax on an American product. (It was passed the following March.) In December 1790 he followed up with a second report outlining his plans for a national bank, modeled in part on the Bank of England, which had proved an effective engine of national growth. Hamilton and his fellow Federalists believed the new nation needed a strong central government and centralized financial institutions and economic policy.[25] Others, Thomas Jefferson among them, worried that such measures threatened the gains of the Revolution and the principles on which the nation was founded.

Hamilton's plans threatened to divide rather than cement the new union. Three states—Massachusetts, Connecticut, and South Carolina—owed nearly half the total state debts and were eager for the federal government to assume those debts. Virginia, Maryland, and Georgia, on the other hand, had paid off much of their debts and were not anxious to pay federal taxes to help retire the debts of those states that had not. Congress became deadlocked on the issue until, at a dinner arranged by Jefferson, Hamilton and James Madison agreed to a compromise: southern states would accept the national assumption of state debts in return for moving the capital to the Potomac after it had been at Philadelphia for ten years. (The capital moved to Philadelphia in August 1790).[26] Hamilton's plan to charter a national bank further divided the regions: southern agriculturalists saw no need for it and feared it was an instrument for northern merchants and speculators. After a difficult passage through Congress early in 1791, Washington signed the bank bill into law.[27]

If the national government's inability to defeat the Indians and to secure free navigation of the Mississippi disgruntled western settlers, its tax on whiskey infuriated them. Distilling corn and grain into whiskey for easier transportation, sale, and bartering was an important component of western farmers' economy. The whiskey excise aggravated existing divisions that pitched East against West, city against country, settled against frontier regions, mercantile against agricultural interests. No sooner had the U.S. government quelled resistance in Indian country than it would call up an army to crush a tax rebellion among its own citizens on the frontier.

Even more divisive was the issue of slavery. The Constitution was a series of compromises that left slavery intact south of the Potomac. In February 1790 two Quaker delegations presented petitions to the House of Representatives calling on the federal government to end the slave trade. Discussion broadened to include gradual emancipation and ending slavery itself, not just the trade in human flesh. With slavery entrenched and expanding in the South, the issue threatened to tear the union asunder before it had properly formed. Congress balked at the prospect, resolved that it had no authority to interfere in the emancipation of slaves, and lost the opportunity to finish the major piece of "unfinished business" from the Revolution.[28]

Much of the discussion over these issues took place in newspapers, of which there were many in the United States in 1790, as well as monthly magazines like the *American Museum*, a literary magazine established in Philadelphia by Mathew Carey, which ran from 1787 to 1792. Typically they were newssheets that freely reprinted news from other papers, reproduced government documents, carried advertisements—including notices for runaway slaves—and opened their pages to contributors and correspondents on any number of topics. By conveying news across regions and providing a forum in which to debate the issues of the day, newspapers, magazines, pamphlets, and broadsheets played a critical role in forging national identity and national unity. In the wake of St. Clair's campaign, as we've seen, they reported and debated the first national disaster. They reprinted correspondence that passed between St. Clair and Knox during the campaign, and between St. Clair and Washington in the aftermath of the campaign; they printed lists of the casualties, paeans to the fallen, and the report of the congressional committee that investigated the causes of the catastrophe. After November 4, 1791, the issues that Americans debated and contested in their newspapers turned on the government's Indian policy.

The Indian policy of the new nation was essentially land policy. The nation's security, prosperity, and future depended upon converting

Indian country into American real estate, creating a national market in Indian lands, and turning Indian homelands and hunting territories over to commercial agriculture and economic development. Indian policies implemented the process. Managed properly, some hoped, it could be a relatively bloodless process. The Indians "will ever retreat as our Settlements advance upon them, and they will be as ready to sell, as we are to buy," George Washington wrote to New York senator James Duane in 1783. "That is the cheapest, as well as the least distressing way of dealing with them, none who is acquainted with the nature of an Indian warfare, and has ever been at the trouble of estimating the expense of one, and comparing it with the cost of purchasing their Lands, will hesitate to acknowledge." Instead of driving the Indians from their country by force, gradually extending American settlement would, as Washington put it, "as certainly cause the Savage as the Wolf to retire; both being beasts of prey tho' they differ in shape. In a word there is nothing to be obtained by an Indian War but the Soil they live on and this can be obtained by purchase at less expence, and without that bloodshed, and those distresses which helpless Women and Children are made partakers of in all kinds of dispute with them."[29] Nevertheless—and indicative of the new nation's expectations—conduct of Indian affairs was lodged in the War Department (where it remained until 1849, when it was transferred to the Department of the Interior).

The Confederation Congress had passed a series of land ordinances, culminating in the Northwest Ordinance of 1787 that committed the nation to a policy of territorial expansion while at the same time pledging its intention to deal justly and honorably with the Indians it dispossessed in the process. The Constitution affirmed congressional authority over Indian affairs in the commerce clause and in the requirement that Indian treaties, like treaties with other nations, be ratified by the Senate. Congress reaffirmed its authority in 1790, passing the Indian Trade and Intercourse Act, which prohibited trading in Indian country without license from Congress and declared illegal any transfers of Indian land that did not secure congressional approval. With new authorities granted in the Constitution and an increased army, Washington and Knox were now in a position to pursue a more aggressive Indian policy, to turn from a policy of frontier defense, using garrisons to police and protect white settlers, to one of frontier offense, launching military strikes against the Indians who raided frontier communities and resisted opening the Northwest Territory to American expansion.[30] The United States would spend $5 million, almost five-sixths of the total federal expenditures for the period 1790-96, fighting the Indian confederation, and it needed land sales to foot the bill.[31]

THE INDIAN PEOPLES WHO WERE THE OBJECT of these policies and assaults defied uniform description. Their relationship with the United States was multisided, involving many tribal nations that each conducted its own foreign policies with other tribes, foreign powers, and sometimes even individual states. The Ohio country, inhabited by Native people for thousands of years before Europeans arrived, was heavily depopulated in the seventeenth century by the ripple effects of European epidemics and escalating indigenous warfare. But it became a gathering place in the eighteenth century as tribal nations and displaced peoples regrouped there. Though battered and decimated after generations of contact with Europeans, Indian nations were still the major powers in the Ohio country, although the heart of Indian settlement had shifted westward, away from the Allegheny Valley, where it had once been located.[32]

The Shawnee had left their Ohio Valley homelands and scattered to Illinois, Pennsylvania, and the Southeast, but most were back in the Ohio country by the middle of the eighteenth century, their villages clustered along the Muskingum, Scioto, and Miami rivers.[33] The Delaware attempted to consolidate their people after years of dispossession and diaspora. Some Delaware lived close to the Wyandot at Sandusky in northern Ohio; others moved up the Maumee River, establishing a town on the east bank of the St. Joseph River and two towns on the St. Marys. One report said that the Miami and also Ottawa had "given the Delawares land from the Miami to the Wabash, so that now again they have their own land to live on." Some Delaware settled on the White River in Indiana. For Shawnee and Delaware, movement and relocation had become practically a way of life, and as they rebuilt their communities they drew on their long experience mediating and forming alliances to forge new alliances with the other tribal nations with whom they now shared territory and resources.[34] Westward-moving Seneca and Cayuga— known to the English and Americans as Mingo, from the Delaware word *mingwe*—also took up residence in the Ohio country and, like the Delaware and Shawnee, increasingly asserted independence from the dominance of the Iroquois League. Miami and others from farther west were drawn to the area by the increasing presence of European traders who followed the migrant Indians into Ohio.

Having reoccupied the Ohio country, the Indians fought to preserve it during the colonial wars in the second half of the century. In the French and Indian War most Indians in the Great Lakes and Ohio country initially sided with the French. Many withdrew their support when the tide of the war turned and the British offered assurances that their homelands would be protected, but British garrisons and postwar policies seemed to threaten rather than protect Indian lands and independence. After Pontiac's War broke out in 1763 the British government placed the trans-Appalachian West off-limits to British settlers and required that future land cessions be negotiated by the crown's representatives in open treaties. But at the Treaty of Fort Stanwix in 1768 the Iroquois ceded thousands of square miles of land south of the Ohio River to Sir William Johnson, Britain's superintendent of Indian affairs, and his associates. It was land the Iroquois claimed but did not own; they diverted the tide of settlement away from their own lands by selling other peoples' lands. The Shawnee resisted the subsequent invasion of the ceded territory. Defeated by Virginia in at the Battle of Point Pleasant in 1774, the Shawnee made peace and grudgingly reaffirmed the Ohio River as their boundary. Kishkalwa, a chief who had fought in the battle, led his band south to live with the Creek. He later returned to the Ohio, but the American Revolution brought renewed raids back and forth across the river, and Kentucky militia targeted and burned Shawnee villages. Kishkalwa and part of the Shawnee migrated west of the Mississippi to escape the conflict.[35] Those who remained moved farther from the Ohio River. As they moved they rebuilt their villages in new locations but kept old names like Piqua and Chillicothe. "All these Chillicothys," wrote General Josiah Harmar, who burned one of them in 1790, "are Elegant situations—fine water near them & beautiful prairies. The savages knew how to take a handsome position as well as any people upon Earth."[36]

By 1790 most Ohio Indians were living in Miami territory along the Maumee River in northwestern Ohio and where the Eel River meets the Wabash in what is now northeastern Indiana. Displaced peoples joined those indigenous to the region at Kekionga, a cluster of villages where the St. Marys and St. Joseph rivers join to form the Maumee River flowing northeast to Lake Erie. It was often called "the Great Carrying Place," a major portage between the Great Lakes

KISH-KAL-WA.

. A SHAWANOE CHIEF

Kishkalwa. From Thomas L. McKenney and James L. Hall, *History of the Indian Tribes of North America, with Biographical Sketches and Anecdotes of the Principal Chiefs* (Philadelphia, 1854). Courtesy of the Ohio Historical Society (OHS-AL02779).

and the Ohio River, and it was a crossroads, a key point of commerce, communication, and diplomacy between the Indians of the Ohio country and Detroit, the center of British military power and trade in the Great Lakes area.[37] The Miami chief Little Turtle later described Kekionga as "that glorious gate…through which all the good words of our chiefs had to pass from the north to the south, and from the east to the west."[38] Amid the movement and upheaval flexible networks of clan, kinship, and marriage maintained and linked societies. Henry Hay, a trader from Detroit who spent ninety-nine days at Kekionga in the winter of 1790, kept a diary that described a mixed and multiethnic community. Indians came and went, often from their hunting and wintering grounds, and they sometimes brought in scalps and captives from raiding the American frontier. They also regularly visited the French traders' village nearby. Indian chiefs sat down for breakfast with traders, drank tea with traders' wives, attended dances, and enjoyed fiddle music. Indians and traders drank together and sometimes got drunk together. Little Turtle and the Miami head chief, Le Gris, "drank tea, also Madeira," and on New Year's Day "came to visit us & breakfasted with us *as usual*" (emphasis added).[39] Extensive cornfields stretched beyond the villages. After American attacks in 1790, communities withdrew from Kekionga and relocated downriver to an area known as the Glaize, at the junction of the Maumee and Auglaize rivers.

The regrouping of refugee populations in the Ohio country created fertile ground for building a new multitribal confederation. But

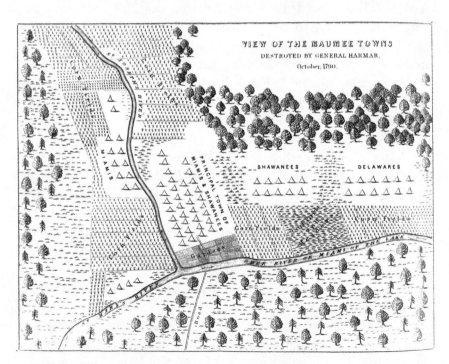

Map of the Indian towns at Kekionga in 1790. From *The Military Journal of Major Ebenezer Denny: An Officer in the Revolutionary and Indian Wars* (Philadelphia: J. B. Lippincott, 1859).

old enemies visited their new homes. Imported epidemics had dev-astated Indian populations since first contact and continued to plague the peoples of the Ohio country. In the fall of 1786 Indians were suffering from "a severe fever," and there was sickness "every-where." Smallpox raged at Sandusky during the next two years; in one town everyone died except two families, who burned the old town and removed to another site. Disease and hunger worked hand in hand to reduce Indian numbers; a "very great famine" was re-ported in the Maumee Valley in 1787, which left children wasting away from hunger. Hard frosts in the fall of 1789 left the people at Sandusky with "no harvest."[40] The influx of migrant populations offset losses and may even have increased the Indian population of the Ohio country during the mid-eighteenth century, but by 1790, while the non-Indian population in America soared, Indian popula-tions were a fraction of what they had been four hundred or even one hundred years before. Many of the people fighting to defend their lands were hanging on.

They were acutely aware of their position between two expanding settler societies: the United States to the east and south and the British in Canada to the north. The Moravian missionary John Heckewelder heard Indians compare the Americans and the British to the blades of a pair of scissors: when they closed they did not cut each other but only the Indians who were caught between them, and "by this means they get our land."[41] Few Indian leaders harbored any illusions about British commitment to their interests, but they recog-nized that British presence, population, and policy in Canada posed the lesser of the two threats and represented a potential source of support against the American expansion across the Ohio. Increasingly preoccupied with events in Europe after the French Revolution, the British continued to court the Indians as potential allies and Canada's best defense in the event of renewed war with the United States. Britain also promoted the idea of setting aside the Northwest as a permanent Indian country, which would preserve Indian lands and serve as a buffer zone between Canada and the aggressive young republic to its south.

Late in the summer of 1783, a few months after British diplomats in Paris transferred their homelands to the United States, delegates from thirty-five Indian nations met at Lower Sandusky in northwestern Ohio and issued a call for all Indians "to join in the Defense of their Country."[42] The Mohawk war chief Joseph Brant (Thayendanegea) played a prominent role in the congress. Brant had been born in the Ohio country in 1743 but grew up in his mother's town at Canajoharie in New York. He had fought alongside the British in the border warfare of the Revolution on the New York frontier, where alleged atrocities earned him a reputation among American settlers as "monster Brant." But John Heckewelder described him as a "distinguished-looking & very modest" man who spoke English well. Educated, literate, and articulate, Brant offered the nations assembled at Sandusky a wampum belt and called for unity: "Brothers and Nephews, you the Hurons, Delawares, Shawanese, Mingoes, Ottawaas, Chippeweys, Poutteawatomies, Creeks & Cherokees, We the Six Nations with this Belt bind your Hearts and minds with ours, that there may be never hereafter a Separation between us, let there be Peace or War, it shall never disunite us, for our Interests are alike, nor should anything ever be done but by the Voice of the whole, as we make but one with you."[43]

Americans in 1790 and later often depicted the struggle as a clash between hunters and farmers, but Indian and American subsistence cycles, farming techniques, and lifestyles shared many similarities, which threw them into competition for the same lands and made that competition deadly. Indians and Americans alike depended on extensive fields of corn cultivated on fertile lands, and growing numbers of American hunters adopted Indian hunting techniques, going after the same game in the same territories. The Indians traditionally inhabited semipermanent villages, moved with the seasons, and practiced a mixed economy. As they had for centuries, women planted corn, beans, and squash in the spring and harvested the crops in the fall, and they supplemented their diet by gathering herbs, roots, berries, and various wild plants and nuts. After the crops were gathered in, families dispersed. The men hunted deer, elk, bear, turkey, and buffalo. In the winter, when the animals' pelts were thickest, they hunted for the fur trade. During late winter and early spring people reassembled in the villages, tapped the sap from maple trees, and boiled it into sugar. Men assisted in clearing fields for planting, and the annual cycle began again. Like white settlers, and like Indian women, the Moravian Indian community at New Salem near the Huron River in 1789 cleared bottom lands at river bends, where they planted "Indian corn, beans, tobacco, & all kinds of garden stuff."[44]

By 1790 Indian villages in the Ohio country increasingly resembled those of the Americans: some Indians lived in log cabins instead of (or as well as) traditional bark houses; some families raised cattle and other livestock. Many Indians also enjoyed a material standard of living equal to, and often above, that of American frontier families. John Brickell, who was captured in the winter of 1791 by Indians he knew well, as "they had been frequently about our house," lived for four years with the Delaware chief Big Cat and his family and described their home as similar to the log cabins of the first American settlers except that it had a bark roof and no floor. "It consisted of a single room with a French made chimney of cat-and-clay" (a wooden chimney plastered with clay, commonly used in frontier cabins).[45] Participation in the fur trade provided Indian people with iron and brass kettles, steel knives, axes, and traps, awls, guns, gun flints, lead shot, gunpowder, woolen blankets, beads, ribbons, thread, linen shirts, dresses made of Stroud (course woolen cloth, often traded as blankets), silk handkerchiefs (which men often wore as turbans), ceramics, brooches and other jewelry made of trade silver, and a host of other manufactured goods and hardware. Such things had become an essential part of the tribes' material culture.

Indians fought to keep settlers out of the Ohio country, but they needed to let traders in. Traders lived with Indians, often had Indian families, and traded with everyone they could; they inhabited an intercultural world where kinship and cooperation were as important as conflict and violence. Old French trading centers—Vincennes on the Wabash, Kaskaskia and Cahokia in the Illinois country, Detroit—remained, reminders of a French Empire that had depended on Indian alliances, and Indian villages existed close by. French frontier inhabitants largely ignored the international agreements that made them British after 1763, then American after 1783, and French-Indian kinship networks permeated Indian country. Traders were not the only non-Indians living beyond the Ohio. Many captives, abducted by Indian raiding parties from frontier settlements, whether they returned to white society or continued to live in Indian villages, moved in similar spheres and operated in similar ways. Men like Simon Girty, who had been captured by Indians in his youth and fought alongside the Indians and the British in the Revolution, functioned as culture brokers. William Wells, taken captive in 1784 when he was thirteen and adopted by a Miami chief named Kaweahatta or The Porcupine, now fought with his Indian relatives against Americans. Isaac Zane lived for more than twenty years with the Wyandot, but in 1788 he was ready to return to Virginia.[46] People who moved into Indian country, in the eyes of eastern and foreign observers, became imbued with Indian characteristics and lived "more like Indians than the Indians themselves." Such comments reflected eastern or European snobbery, fears, and myopia, but they also convey the subtle transformations brought about by contact with Indians. It was a world that the Indians and men like Girty wanted to preserve and that American expansion threatened to destroy.

"Indian" and "white" were not the only criteria determining the nature of relations between peoples, and conflict and cooperation did not divide or unite people along strictly racial lines. But the war for the land cut through the multicultural mosaic, pitting Indians against Americans in dramatic confrontations that placed neutral people and interethnic communities in peril.

AMERICANS IN 1790 DISAGREED ABOUT MANY THINGS: the nature of society; how to preserve the gains and realize the promises of the Revolution; the role of government; the relative powers of state and national governments; the need for taxation; the role of women and slaves in a democratic republic; whether the republic should be agricultural or commercial; and whether westward expansion would unite the states or divide the nation. But most agreed that, one way or another, their nation would be built on Indian land.

Native Americans in 1790 also disagreed about many things, including whether, to what extent, and at what pace they should change their way of life. But they agreed that the states were united in their hunger for Indian land.[47] In defending their land, the Indians of the Northwest Confederacy were defending their relationship with the land, the meaning of the land, and their own vision of America. As articulated by Joseph Brant and other confederacy leaders, Indian land was shared space, extensive hunting territories laced with a network of rivers, riverside villages, and relationships; as envisioned by American speculators, settlers, and government, land was property, divided into small plots and individually owned.[48] Defending Indian land was an endeavor that united divided Indian nations.

In 1790 the American plan for national expansion onto Indian land was in place; the process was already under way in the territory beyond the Ohio River. Blood was already being spilled. In his second annual message to Congress, in December 1790, Washington declared that the raids committed by "certain banditti of Indians from the North West side of the Ohio" made the dispatch of military force to punish their crimes "essential to the safety of the Western Settlements."[49] Turning tribal homelands into American real estate was becoming costly and bloody.

CHAPTER 2

Building a Nation on
Indian Land

*T*HE NEW REPUBLIC FIRST EMBARKED on a program of national westward expansion and launched its first national offensive in the region north and west of the Ohio River. The lands beyond the Ohio thus became the testing ground for "a new kind of empire, linked to a new kind of state" that originated in the American Revolution.[1] Jefferson called it an "empire of liberty," one in which individual citizens would be free to pursue their interests and rewarded for doing so by settling western land. But the government feared that simply opening up the new territory to a flood of squatters in a chaotic scramble for land would threaten the social order of the young republic before it was properly established. "To suffer a wide-extended country to be overrun with land jobbers, speculators, and monopolizers, or even scattered settlers is inconsistent with that wisdom and policy which our true interest dictates, or which an enlightened people ought to adopt," Washington declared in 1783. Unless the U.S. government acted to establish its authority in the West, the Ohio country would fall into the hands of "banditti" who would "bid defiance to all authority."[2]

The federal government envisioned building the empire of liberty in an orderly process that would hold individual squatters in check while lands were systematically surveyed, sold, and settled in townships. That process would involve coordinating national and private interests, Congress collaborating with land speculators in their pursuit of profits, and forging a reciprocal relationship between the national government and the men, many of them former Continental Army officers, who organized land companies.[3] Unlike the frontier riffraff and squatters who so alarmed eastern elites and members of government, law-abiding, town-dwelling citizens would settle the territory north and west of the Ohio—and some members of the eastern elite and government would get rich getting them settled.

In 1783 the U.S. government had debts amounting to an estimated $40 million. Under the Articles of Confederation it lacked the power to impose taxes. Its only source of revenue was the land ceded to it by Britain at the Peace of Paris, but its claim to sovereignty over the area and its inhabitants was shaky at best. The question of who owned the western land, in particular the land in the Ohio Valley, inflamed passions and threatened to turn states against one another. Congress issued a proclamation prohibiting the settlement or purchase of Indian lands without its express authority.[4] The first president himself, however, had established a precedent for defying distant governments and speculating in Indian lands; hence his fellow Americans had few qualms about continuing the tradition. The United States tried to enforce the rules and to obtain Indian lands by treaty, but U.S. commissioners found themselves competing with state agents, land companies, and individual speculators. Various states had prerevolutionary and sometimes overlapping claims to these western lands. Maryland had insisted that cession of these claims to Congress—in effect making the land "public land"—was a condition of its ratifying the Articles of Confederation, and the states gradually agreed. Massachusetts and New York ceded their claims. Virginia ceded all its territory north and west of the Ohio, with the exception of a tract of more than 4 million acres between the Scioto and Little Miami, which became known as the Virginia Military District. Virginia reserved that territory in order to honor the land bounties it had promised its soldiers in the Revolution, and it was opened in 1790. Connecticut, which had competing claims with Pennsylvania, relinquished its claims except for 3,250,000 acres in northern Ohio that became known as the Western Reserve.[5] The states' cessions of the lands northwest of the Ohio afforded Congress the opportunity to pay off its debts and generate much-needed revenue by selling those lands to its citizens.

The rich lands and rivers of Ohio were the key to settlers' hopes, land speculators' fortunes, and the nation's future. "The Fate of the American Empire calls the Eastern Emigrants from the barren Mounts of the North to these Luxuriant Fields," wrote Captain Jonathan Heart of Connecticut, who, like many others, pinned his hopes for the future on the rich lands of Ohio.[6] One land company agent described the Ohio River as the "grate Vein that Conducts the Waters of a thousand big and Little Rivers to Missippia [*sic*] which receive and conveys it to the Mighty Ocian."[7] Manasseh Cutler, a Congregationalist minister and land speculator, claimed in 1787 that the river bottoms in Ohio "afford as rich soil as can be imagined, and may be reduced to proper cultivation with very little labor." Orderly settlement by Congress and American citizens would make the region between the Ohio River and Lake Erie a center of agriculture, commerce, and manufacturing and provide "a wise model for the future settlement of all the federal lands." With a mixture of hyperbole and prescience, Cutler announced, "Not many years will elapse before the whole country above Miami will be brought to that degree of cultivation which will exhibit all its latent beauties, and justify those descriptions of travelers which have so often made it the garden of the world, the seat of wealth, and the center of a great empire."[8] The New Jersey judge and land speculator John Cleves Symmes agreed: "The extent of country spreading for many miles on both sides of the G[reat] Miami, is beyond all dispute equal, I believe superior in point of soil, water, & timber, to any tract of equal contents to be found in the United States. From this Egypt in Miami, in a very few years will be poured down its stream to the Ohio, the products of the country, from two hundred miles above the mouth of G. Miami."[9] Cutler, Symmes, and hundreds of others could barely wait to get their hands on the land and fill their pockets by providing homes for military veterans and settlers.

Washington "took a decided interest" in promoting schemes for settling Ohio. He was a seasoned speculator in the region and held lands there; he sympathized with former soldiers whose service and sacrifices in the Revolution had been inadequately rewarded, if at all; he was associated, often as a comrade-in-arms, with many of the men who were promoting the settlement; and he was anxious to bind the West to the East, especially Virginia, by ties of land and commerce. Who better to settle the West than "the disbanded Officers and Soldiers of the Army, to whom the faith of Government hath long since been pledged, that lands should be granted at the expiration of the War?" They would "connect our government with the frontiers, extend our Settlements progressively, and plant a brave, a hardy and respectable Race of People" there who "would give security to our frontiers."[10]

After the Iroquois and British negotiated away Shawnee and Cherokee hunting territories at the Treaty of Fort Stanwix in 1768, the area south of the Ohio River witnessed interracial bloodshed, squatting, and a confusion of overlapping and competing individual land claims. As the United States set its sights on the area north of the Ohio, it intended that things would be different there. The federal government laid out a plan for filling the nation's coffers and paying off its crushing war debt while the nation grew in an orderly fashion as territories were settled, townships grew, and new states joined the union.[11] It was, as the historian Peter Onuf remarks, a vision for the West that "was nothing like the West that already existed."[12]

The government set in motion a system of measuring out the West. The idea that land was a commodity that could be divided up, owned, bought, and sold as individual property was a relatively recent phenomenon in Europe and had taken shape in colonial America. However, only after independence did transforming the so-called wilderness into property become a national policy. In 1784 the Confederation Congress set up a committee, chaired by Jefferson, to consider plans for distributing the national domain and formulate a blueprint for the future development of the territory west of the Ohio. Congress had prohibited individuals from squatting on public lands, but when Washington toured the western land that summer he found to his irritation that in defiance of Congress's proclamation intruders were roaming "over the Country on the Indian side of the Ohio," marking out, surveying, and settling land. There was, he said, "a rage for speculating" in the lands northwest of the Ohio and hardly a valuable spot without a claimant. "Men in these times, talk with as much facility of fifty, a hundred, or even 500,000 Acres as a Gentleman formerly would do of 1,000 acres."[13] Washington wanted "compact and progressive settling" that would strengthen the Union and "admit law and good government"; sparse settlement scattered across several states or large territory would "have the directly contrary effects; and, whilst it opens a large field to land jobbers and speculators, who are prowling about like wolves in many shapes, will injure the real occupiers and useful citizens, and consequently the public interest." Fearful of the risk that a country too rapidly on the move might fly apart, he wanted an orderly national advance in which one "tract of country, of convenient size for a new state, contiguous to the present settlements on the Ohio," would be surveyed, divided, and at least partially settled "before any other state is marked out, and no land is to be obtained beyond the limits of it."[14]

The 1785 Land Ordinance again prohibited illegal intrusions and ordered the squatters to depart. It also provided for the surveying and sale of the territory northwest of the Ohio as and when the United States acquired title from the tribes. Unlike the method of metes-and-bounds surveys in place south of the Ohio, by which settlers claimed irregular areas of lands and marked their boundaries by landscape features, such as streams and rocks, the country north of the Ohio would be surveyed and divided up into squares before it was occupied. The ordinance stipulated that "the surveyors shall proceed to divide the said territory into townships of 6 miles square, by lines running due north and south, and others crossing these at right angles, as near as may be." The western boundary of Pennsylvania, running north to Lake Erie, provided the first north-south line; the first east-west line began where the Pennsylvania borderline intersected with the Ohio River. Townships were to be further divided into thirty-six sections of one square mile, or 640 acres. Townships were arranged in north-south rows called ranges; ranges, townships, and sections were all systematically numbered. The surveyors were to measure the lines by chains, mark them on trees, and describe them exactly on charts. Thomas Hutchins, the U.S. geographer, and surveyors from the various states surveyed the first tracts of land in eastern Ohio, known as the Seven Ranges. The secretary of war was to choose by lot one-seventh of the land to compensate veterans of the Continental Army. The rest of the lots were to be sold at auction. The ordinance established a pattern of land settlement and landownership by which the United States surveyed, measured, and divided land into squares as it marched across the continent.[15]

The fact that the ordinance established 640 acres as the minimum purchase, at $1 an acre, suggests that Congress did not envision selling much land to the "common man." Jefferson envisaged land as America's salvation and the basis for his empire of liberty, in which individual American citizens would own and farm their own property in a landowning democracy. The reality soon became somewhat different. Gentlemen speculators exerted their financial and political influence to get first dibs on the Ohio country.[16] They purchased vast parcels of land on credit, in anticipation that they could quickly resell them to settlers and generate the cash for future payment. They also bought up at a fraction of their face value the unpaid notes of the Continental Congress, veterans' land bounties, and military warrants and used them to buy land. Military "warrants"—scrip for claims to western

land—had been used as war bounties and incentive payments to encourage soldiers to reenlist during the Revolution. The Continental
Congress had offered bounties in land—1,100 acres for a major general,
850 for a brigadier general, 500 for a colonel, 400 for a major, 300 for a
captain, 200 for a lieutenant, and 100 for noncommissioned officers and
privates—but at the time Congress had no land to give. After the war
many veterans lacked the interest or the means to move west and sold
their warrants, often for a pittance, to men who offered ready cash.

Buying and selling thousands of acres of land became big business.
Despite the intention of government ordinances, "it was the speculators in Philadelphia, New York, and Boston who reaped the harvest."[17]
The Northwest Territory was a land of opportunity for the nation, for
settlers, but above all for the land companies. "Free enterprise was
born out of land dealing," wrote the late Andro Linklater, author of
Measuring America, "and long before the first business corporation
existed, land companies issued shares and created many of the financial and legal structures that the nineteenth-century stock-dealing,
capitalist economy used to finance the railroads and industrialization
of the United States." As in years to come, matching private interests
to the national agenda provided a powerful engine for growth, but the
majority of the resources ended up in the hands of a few.[18]

Two sets of people stood in the way of Congress and the land companies getting control of lands in the Northwest Territory and setting
the nation on the path to orderly westward expansion: the Indians
who lived there and the squatters who settled there illegally. Samuel
H. Parsons, a Harvard graduate, officer in the Continental Army, and
Indian treaty commissioner from Connecticut who hoped to make a
fortune selling lands pledged to veterans, denounced the unruly frontier population as "our *own* white Indians of no character," who were
motivated only by their private interests and paid no regard to the
public good.[19] Before former Continental Army officers invaded
Indian country in the war of 1790–91, they led expeditions across the
Ohio to burn and destroy squatters' cabins and order the squatters
back across the river. Expelling squatters would help preserve peace
with the Indians and reserve the land for settlement under the aus-
pices of the federal government and the land companies. But the
army was too small to patrol such a large country, and there were too
many frontier people for the government to prevent illegal squatting
beyond the Ohio.[20]

The Indians presented a more serious obstacle.

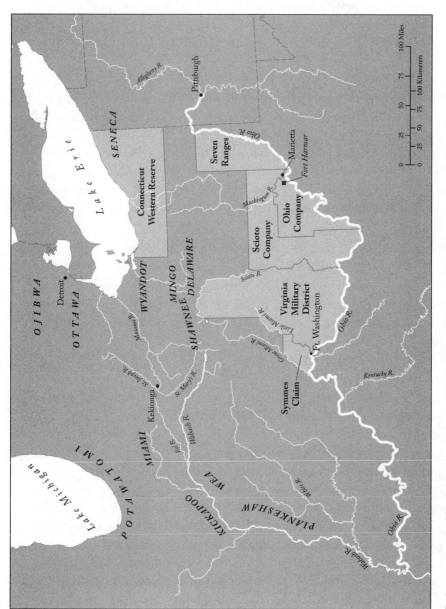

Indian nations and land company claims in the Northwest Territory. (Map drawn by Meg Calloway.)

Whatever the British and American diplomats had agreed to at the Peace of Paris, Ohio was Indian country. As settlers and land speculators saw their dreams deferred by Indian raids, they looked to the federal government to protect them and deal with the "Indian problem."[21] The first land pledges had been made to the army, and it was the army that would be called upon to secure the lands from the Indians.[22]

The government spoke of offering the Indians a "reasonable" peace, but in American eyes any reasonable peace still involved the Indians giving up their land. In 1785 and 1786 the United States dictated treaties to most of the Ohio tribes, claiming their lands by right of conquest. At Fort McIntosh (present-day Beaver, Pennsylvania) the American treaty commissioners Richard Butler, George Rogers Clark, and Arthur Lee told the Indians that the English king had made no provision for them; they were "therefore left to obtain peace from the U. States, & to be received under their government and protection, upon such conditions as seem proper to Congress, the Great Council of the U. States." They brushed aside the Indians' objections that these lands had been handed down to them by their ancestors: "The detail of these claims and title may appear to be of consequence among yourselves. But to us…they have no relation; *because* we claim the country by conquest; and are to give not to receive."[23] The commissioners demanded southern and eastern Ohio as the price of peace.

A Shawnee chief called Kekewepelethy or Captain Johnny denounced the American tactics. "We see your intentions," he said; "you are drawing so close to us that we can almost hear the sound of your axes felling our trees & settling our country. According to the lines settled by our forefathers, the Ohio is the boundary, but you are encroaching on the grounds given to us by the Great Spirit…. It is clear to us that your design is to take our country from us." The Indians had no objection to American traders coming into their country, but they warned the Americans to keep their settlers out, "or we will whip them back to your side of the Ohio." All the Indians were "strong, unanimous, & united in determination to defend this country," Captain Johnny declared, "as one man, with but one heart & mind."[24]

Captain Johnny may have articulated an emerging Indian sentiment, but the realities did not yet match his vision of tribal unity: the next year a division of the Shawnee, the Mekoche, made a treaty at

Richard Butler (1743–1791). Butler sat for this oil-on-wood portrait by John Trumbull the year before he was killed at St. Clair's defeat. Courtesy of Yale University Art Gallery (Trumbull Collection 1832.78).

Fort Finney at the mouth of the Great Miami River. The three American commissioners were Butler, Clark, and Parsons. Butler had been a trader among the Shawnee, spoke their language, and had two children by a Shawnee woman, but he had also fought against the Shawnee in 1764. Clark had made a name for himself as an Indian fighter during the Revolution, had burned Shawnee villages, and operated on the belief that the only thing Indians understood or respected was force. The Americans demanded that the Shawnee cede all land east of the Great Miami and give hostages as a guarantee of compliance. Captain Johnny balked at the terms and insisted on the Ohio River as the boundary. "God gave us this country, we do not understand measuring out the lands, it is all ours," he said and handed the commissioners a wampum belt. Strings and belts of wampum—white and purple shells or beads woven into graphic designs—conveyed messages, emphasized the significance and truth of spoken words, and served as records of diplomatic agreements. The commissioners refused to accept Captain Johnny's belt. Butler picked it up "and dashed it on the table." Taking his cane, Clark pushed it off the table and "set his foot on it," grinding it into the dirt his boot. The Americans then "threw down a black and white string" of wampum and walked out of the meeting. White beads represented life, peace, and well-being; purple or "black" beads represented death, war, and mourning. Clark and Butler were forcing the Shawnee to choose between war and peace, and threatened to destroy their villages, women, and children if they failed to comply with the American demands.

An old chief named Moluntha urged his people to reconsider. When the council reconvened the Shawnee gave the commissioners a white wampum belt and grudgingly accepted the American terms.[25] The Shawnee brought in their prisoners, as required by the treaty, although some succeeded in escaping and returning to the Indians. The Shawnee war chief Blue Jacket came in with his son, whom he offered to leave as a hostage as a sign of their good intentions.[26] But many Shawnee resisted, and before the year was out Colonel Benjamin Logan and eight hundred Kentucky militia invaded Shawnee country, up the Miami River. They burned Moluntha's village and left Moluntha lying dead, a Kentuckian's axe in his skull and his fingers still clutching a copy of the treaty he had persuaded his people to sign. The old chief "was tomahawked after he had delivered himself up," Ebenezer Denny heard. Logan's militia had "found none but old men, women and children in the towns; they made no resistance; the men were literally murdered."[27] Any hope of peace evaporated. Most Shawnee pulled away from the danger zone and resettled close to the cluster of Miami villages at Kekionga in northwestern Ohio.

Denny was present at both the Fort McIntosh and Fort Finney treaties. He made the usual disparaging comments about Indians, describing those who came to Fort McIntosh in January 1785 as "an ugly set of devils." But he also was interested in Indians, spent time in the Indian camps, and recorded a vocabulary of Delaware and Shawnee languages. In fact he may have had more interest than his journal reveals and found Indian women less ugly than he professed: the Delaware vocabulary he compiled at Fort McIntosh included the phrases for "I love you," "I must sleep with you," and "Will you sleep with me?"[28]

Many Indians did not attend the treaty meetings, denounced those who did, and refused to accept the terms. In December 1786 delegates from the Iroquois, Shawnee, Delaware, Huron, Ojibwa, Potawatomi, Ottawa, Piankeshaw, Wea, Miami, and Cherokee gathered in council at Brownstown, a Wyandot town near Detroit, and sent Congress a forceful message, denouncing the divisive policies of making treaties with individual tribes. Since "landed matters are often the subject of our councils with you, a matter of the greatest importance and of general concern to us," they said, any cessions of their lands "should be made in the most public manner, and by the united voice of the confederacy." All previous "partial treaties" they declared "void and of no effect."[29] They "expressed the highest disgust" at the treaties the United States made based on "the doctrine of conquest," which was "so repugnant to their feelings, that rather than submit thereto, they would prefer continual war."[30] Further, they asked the United States government to meet with them in the spring and settle a reasonable boundary line, and requested that in the meantime they prevent their surveyors and settlers from crossing the Ohio. The Indians then held a second council, on Christmas Eve. Speaking for the confederated tribes, Joseph Brant asked the British Indian agent Alexander McKee what assistance they could expect from Britain in the event the United States refused them a reasonable peace.[31] By the time the Indians' message reached Philadelphia, Congress was implementing the Northwest Ordinance.

ON MARCH 1, 1786, A GROUP OF NEW ENGLANDERS convened at the Bunch of Grapes tavern in Boston. They described themselves as "reputable, industrious, well-informed men" of "wealth, education, and virtue." Most of them were veterans of the Revolutionary War who had not been adequately paid for their wartime services. They were there to form the Ohio Company of Associates, a syndicate that sold stock to speculators and then petitioned the federal government for enormous grants of land. Today we might call them venture capitalists. They intended to raise up to $1 million in Continental notes and then purchase 1.5 million acres of land from Congress, ostensibly with the goal of settling New England veterans in the territory northwest of the Ohio River. The Company offered one thousand shares at $1,000 in Continental paper currency (and $10 in gold or silver to defray agents' fees and other expenses in purchasing the land) to raise the capital. In effect the Ohio Company would buy the land the United States had won during the war by giving back to Congress the nearly worthless paper it had issued to finance that war. The Company elected as secretary Winthrop Sargent, who had been one of the surveyors of the Seven Ranges and sent back glowing reports about the Ohio country.[32] A week later, this time at Brackett's Tavern, the associates appointed as company directors General Samuel Parsons, the Reverend Manasseh Cutler, and General Rufus Putnam.[33]

Rufus Putnam from Massachusetts was the driving force. He had learned to make his way in the world after his father died when he was seven. During the French and Indian War he served as an engineer in the British army's 60th Foot, known as the Royal American Regiment. After the war he married well, produced a large family, and turned to a career as a surveyor and land speculator. His military engineering skills proved invaluable to Washington during the Revolution; his connection to Washington proved invaluable to Putnam in building a fortune in western land after the Revolution. He would consistently present his own interests and the national interest as compatible if not identical. "I am *Sir*," he had told Washington while promoting a petition of army officers for lands between the Ohio and Lake Erie a couple of months after the Peace of Paris, "among those who consider the *Cession* of so grate a tract of Territory to the United States in the Western World as a very happy circumstance; and of grate consequence to the American Empire." And he was impatient to get at that territory: "The Settlement of the Ohio Country Sir ingrosses many of my thoughts, and much of my time," he had told Washington in April 1784.[34]

Manasseh Cutler, a former lawyer, doctor, and merchant, as well as a chaplain in the revolutionary army, was now pastor of the Congregationalist church in Ipswich, Massachusetts. According to Cutler's grandchildren, Cutler and his associates "were a power in the land," which is true, "and their power was always exerted in the line of the highest attainments of a Christian civilization," which is debatable.[35] Cutler and company immediately began to promote their scheme as an opportunity for orderly settlement of the West and a down payment of the national debt that the government could not afford to miss and that Congress must support.[36] Cutler also sold shares in the Company to leading government officials, including the president of Congress Arthur St. Clair and the secretary of the Confederation's Treasury Board, William Duer.[37]

Manasseh Cutler. Courtesy of the Ohio Historical Society (OHS-AL07015).

William Duer was born in England in 1747 and had served in India as an aide to Robert Clive. He came to America in 1768, purchased land in the Hudson Valley, took the American side in the Revolution, and was a member of the Continental Congress. "He is a gentleman of the most sprightly abilities, and has a soul filled with the warmest benevolence and generosity," wrote Cutler. "He is made both for business and the enjoyments of life, his attachments strong and sincere, and diffuses happiness among his friends, while he enjoys a full share of it himself."[38] Duer was a political and business crony of Alexander

Hamilton, and after the Constitution was adopted became assistant secretary in the Treasury Department under Hamilton, an appointment that did little to curb his financial shenanigans. He was also a business partner of Secretary of War Henry Knox, who owned stock in the Ohio Company. In Gordon Wood's words, Duer "seemed to have little or no sense that his public responsibilities ought to precede his private interests."[39]

In July 1787, in one of its last acts—the Constitutional Convention was meeting in Philadelphia at the same time—the Confederation Congress issued another land ordinance, commonly known as the Northwest Ordinance. Arthur St. Clair was away in Pennsylvania at the time on "pressing business," but he was well aware of what was going on. The negotiations surrounding the Ordinance and the Ohio Company's land purchase proposal were intertwined, and the weave was pretty tight. Acting as agent for the Company, Cutler went to New York carrying more than forty letters of introduction to prominent and influential people and kept a journal of his activities as he negotiated with Congress and the Treasury Board.[40] Cutler persuaded Congress to disregard the provisions of the 1785 Ordinance relating to the survey and division of land into squares before it was sold. He worked closely with St. Clair and the chairman of the Land Committee, Edward Carrington, to purchase a large tract of land in the Northwest Territory on which to form settlements. Carrington's committee recommended to Congress that "the board of treasury be authorised and empowered to contract with any person or persons for a grant of land which shall be bounded by the Ohio from the Mouth of the S[c]ioto to the intersection of the western boundary of the seventh range of townships." The price was "to be not less than one dollar per acre for the contents of the said tract excepting the reservations and gifts aforesaid payable in specie loan office certificates reduced to specie value or certificates of liquidated debts of the United States, liable to a reduction by an allowance for bad land and all incidental charges and circumstances whatever provided that such an allowance shall not exceed in the whole one third of a dollar per acre." Purchasers who possessed "rights for bounties of land to the late Army" were "to be permitted to render the same in discharge of the contract, acre for acre, provided that the aggregate of such rights shall not exceed one seventh part of the land to be paid for." The purchasers would pay $500,000 when the contract was executed, the balance paid once the surveys were completed.[41]

On July 20, during the negotiations, wrote Cutler, "Colonel Duer came to me with proposals from a number of principal characters in the city, to extend our contract, and take in another Company, but that it should be kept a profound secret. He explained the plan they had concerted, and offered me generous conditions, if I would accomplish the business for them. The plan struck me agreeably."[42] Cutler cut a deal with Duer that would give the Scioto Company an option on an additional 3.5 million acres, and Duer agreed to serve as a liaison between the Ohio Company and Congress. At dinners and in private conversations Cutler and his friends solicited the support of key members of Congress. He threatened—or gave the impression of threatening—to abandon his land purchase proposal if his terms were not met. "This I found had the desired effect." He told Congress that if it would agree to his terms, he would extend the purchase to the Scioto, "by which Congress would pay off near four millions of national debt; that our intention was an actual, a large, and immediate settlement of the most robust and industrious people in America; and that it would be made systematically, which must instantly enhance the value of federal lands, and prove an important acquisition to Congress."[43]

Cutler got the support of Samuel Osgood, president of the Board of Treasury. "No gentleman has a higher character for planning and calculating than Mr. Osgood," he noted in his journal, but "such is the intrigue and artifice which is often practiced by men in power, that I felt very suspicious, and was as cautious as possible." But Cutler's suspicions were overcome, and before long they "entered into the true spirit of negotiations with great bodies; every machine in the city that it was possible to set to work we now put in motion."[44] Cutler's personal influence and maneuvering secured the necessary votes and political alignments. On July 27 Congress passed the Ordinance and directed the Board of Treasury to complete the contract. The Ohio Company obtained a grant of 5 million acres of land. It retained 1.5 million and held the remaining 3.5 million "for a private speculation, in which," wrote Cutler, "many of the principal characters in America are concerned. Without connecting this speculation, similar terms and advantages could not have been obtained for the Ohio Company."[45] The "private speculation" was that of William Duer and his cronies, who acquired title to the land and then formed the Scioto Company.

Manassah Cutler had pulled off "the nation's first large-scale real-estate deal."[46] He had managed to hustle it through Congress in just over two months, and most of the time Congress was not even in session.[47] The fact that the Ohio Company's purchase and the Ordinance were both completed in July 1787 does not mean there was a conspiracy, says the historian Andrew Cayton, "but it was no coincidence either." The men who wrote the Ordinance and associates of the Ohio Company "were like-minded men. Indeed, they were often the same men."[48]

The Northwest Ordinance both established a blueprint for national expansion and offered a vision of a more harmonious, prosperous, and powerful nation, in which the potentially centrifugal forces of western expansion would be harnessed and directed. As the thirteen American colonies had grown, they had come to resent their colonial status and had taken up arms to cast off Britain's authority. How could the new nation prevent history from repeating itself as western territories grew in the same way? The Northwest Ordinance provided the solution. Unlike Britain's colonies, U.S. territories would not suffer permanent inferior status. In time they would take their place in the union on an equal footing with the other states. The Northwest Territory, some 220,000 square miles of it, would be surveyed, divided into districts and lots, sold, and settled. The Ordinance stipulated that lands be surveyed into six-by-six-mile townships before sale, but it also cleared the way for selling large areas of land to private interests, which would promote settlement and at the same time help bring in much-needed revenue. The territory would have its own territorial government, with a governor and, once the population reached five thousand, an elected assembly and a court. As well the Ordinance provided for proportionate representation of the people in a territorial legislature, freedom of religion, trial by jury, habeas corpus, and judicial proceeding according to common law. It encouraged education and schools; it prohibited slavery and involuntary servitude. Once its population reached sixty thousand the territory could petition to become a state. The Ordinance stipulated that "not less than three nor more than five States" should be formed in the territory. Eventually Ohio, Indiana, Illinois, Michigan, and Wisconsin entered the Union as states carved from the Northwest Territory, and ultimately more than thirty states entered the Union through the process outlined in 1787.

At the same time as the Ordinance committed the nation to expansion into Indian lands, however, and to the chagrin of many frontier settlers, it also pledged that the United States would observe the "utmost good faith" in its dealings with the Indians. Their lands would not be taken from them without their consent, and they would not be attacked except "in just and lawful wars authorized by Congress."[49] Since the Indians insisted on keeping the Ohio River as a boundary to white settlement and wanted to keep the Northwest Territory free of surveyors and settlers, there clearly would be "just and lawful wars authorized by Congress."

Back at the Bunch of Grapes at the end of August, Cutler reported to the members of the Ohio Company the conditions of the contract he had agreed upon with the Board of the Treasury. The government's price for the land was nominally $1 an acre, he told them, "from which price is to be deducted one third of a dollar for bad lands, and defraying the expenses of surveying &." The Company would therefore pay $1 million—in other words, 66 cents per acre—half immediately and the balance when the surveying was completed.[50] But because Cutler got Congress to agree to accept payment for the land in depreciated government securities and devalued military warrants, the real cost to the company was more like 8.5 cents per acre.[51] The members of the company then got to work promoting the scheme and raising the money. Cutler's journal entries, normally much fuller, reflected the ensuing flurry of activity:

> Aug. 31, Fri. Met again at Bracket's. Determined to send men this fall into the Ohio country.
> Sept. 1, Sat. Met again in the morning....
> Sept. 10–15. House full of Ohio people all the week.
> Sept. 21, 22. Ohio people here....
> Oct. 1, 2. Taking money for the Ohio Company.
> Monday, Oct. 8. Left Ipswich for New York, in order to complete the contract of the Ohio Company for lands in the Western Country....
> Wed. Oct. 10. Spent the day in Boston on Ohio business.[52]

Money was scarce, but the shares were selling. "The rage for going into the Country from this part of Massachusetts and New Hampshire has astonished me," Cutler told Sargent.[53]

On October 27, 1787, Cutler and Sargent as agents of the Ohio Company completed their contract with the Board of Treasury (Samuel Osgood, Arthur Lee, and Walter Livingston). They signed the agreement "on parchment in two distinct contracts; one for the

Ohio Company, and the other for the Scioto Company." Cutler pronounced it "the greatest private contract ever made in America." That evening he dined with Henry Knox and a group of former officers in the Continental Army.[54] Before long "almost every army officer owned shares in the Ohio Company."[55]

Whereas the Ohio Company intended to sell land to American settlers, the Scioto Company planned to sell land—lots of it—to foreign capitalist interests. Hundreds of European emigrants purchased acreage from agents of the company, but the Scioto Company never paid the government for the land, and when the emigrants arrived in the Northwest Territory they were unable to obtain clear title to their purchases.[56] Duer abandoned the Scioto scheme soon after it started, turning his attention to land speculations in Maine (then part of Massachusetts; Maine did not become a state until 1820) with Henry Knox.[57] Duer would be appointed the contractor for St. Clair's campaign in 1791.

Cutler had originally supported Samuel Parsons for governor of the territory, but when it looked as if Parson's appointment might impede progress, he agreed to accept St. Clair, so long as Parsons was made first judge and Winthrop Sargent was appointed secretary. Sargent would be St. Clair's adjutant general on the campaign. Parsons apparently preferred to be a judge rather than governor, but he did not long enjoy the position; he drowned descending the rapids on the Big Beaver River in November 1789. Rufus Putnam was appointed to fill the vacancy in March 1790.[58]

The new governor of the Northwest Territory owned more than one thousand Ohio Company acres.[59] Arthur St. Clair was born in Scotland in 1734 or 1736 and attended the University of Edinburgh. (At a time when England had only two universities, Oxford and Cambridge, providing education for the sons of the aristocracy and for clerics, Scotland had five and made higher education available to the sons of middle-ranking families like St. Clair's.) At twenty-three St. Clair purchased a commission in the Royal American Regiment. Dispatched with his regiment to fight in the French and Indian War, he served in two campaigns that were key to wresting Canada from French control: Jeffery Amherst's capture of Louisburg in 1758 and James Wolfe's capture of Quebec in 1759. In his own words, he "took up the profession of arms" at an early age "and served through the whole of the war of 1756, under some of the first generals of the world."[60] He never returned to Britain. After the war he married the niece of the wealthy James Bowdoin, governor of Massachusetts, and settled in western Pennsylvania. There he became an important member of the frontier community, serving as a clerk, judge of probate, surveyor, and recorder of deeds, among other positions, and gained some experience dealing with the Indian tribes of the region. During the Revolution he joined the American cause and fought at Trenton, Princeton, Ticonderoga, Brandywine Creek, and Yorktown, besides marching a command to South Carolina in 1781. Although his abandonment of Ticonderoga in 1777 prompted an inquiry, he was exonerated and ended the war a major general. He developed a close relationship with Washington and enjoyed Washington's continued confidence. After the war he served in Congress and as its president in 1787.

Now in his fifties by the time of his appointment in the Northwest Territory, corpulent and afflicted with gout, St. Clair seemed qualified for the position of territorial governor thanks to his experiences as a soldier, administrator, and politician and his interests in western lands. As governor he had the authority to command the militia, appoint magistrates, establish new counties and townships, and, with the territorial judges, enact laws (until the population reached five thousand free inhabitants, at which time local landowners would elect a legislature).[61] St. Clair formally moved west with his three daughters, Louisa, Jane, and Margaret, and his twenty-one-year-old son, Arthur, in 1788 (his wife joined them later) and inaugurated the territorial government in Marietta in July.

Rufus Putnam of the Ohio Company established Marietta as a community of fifty-two families and 157 single men across the Muskingum River from Fort Harmar, named it in honor of Marie Antoinette, the queen of France, America's ally during the Revolution, and built a stockade fort to protect it. There was an extensive complex of earthwork mounds in the area; Samuel Parsons made a map of them and sent a copy and description to Ezra Stiles, president of Yale College, who in turn forwarded it to Thomas Jefferson in Paris, and Major Jonathan Heart wrote an account of them that was published by the American Philosophical Society, although Heart did not live to see it.[62] Despite the surrounding evidence of an ancient Indian civilization, the members of the Ohio Company saw themselves establishing civilization in the Ohio country. They envisioned Marietta as a model community of republican virtue and discipline, laid out like a New England town, with a church and schoolhouse and streets in a regular pattern. But many of

Arthur St. Clair by Charles Willson Peale, from life, 1782. Courtesy of Independence National Historical Park, Philadelphia.

the people who settled there had other ideas about law and life on the frontier, and Marietta resembled a backwoods settlement more than a New England town.[63] Nevertheless, for Manasseh Cutler, who preached a sermon in Marietta in August, such a state of affairs was temporary; his and the nation's plans for the West were part of something bigger: "The sun, the glorious luminary of the day, comes forth from his chambers of the East, and rejoicing to run his course, carries light and heat and joy through the remotest parts of the West, and returns to the place from whence he came. In like manner divine truth, useful knowledge, and improvements appear to proceed in the same direction, until the bright day of science virtue, pure religion, and free government, shall pervade the western hemisphere." In Cutler's vision, Marietta's first settlers were "the advance guard of the American Empire."[64]

The lands to which the Ohio Company had a grant were in the Muskingum Valley; the district between the Scioto and the Little Miami was set aside to satisfy the military warrants issued by Virginia; the next desirable tract of land lay between the Little Miami and the Great Miami rivers. John Cleves Symmes made a tour down the Ohio in the spring and summer of 1787 to identify the best land for his planned colony. He and his associates persuaded Congress that year to sell them 2 million acres between the Great and Little Miami rivers for $1 an acre. Unable to raise the money for the first payment, Symmes asked Congress to reduce the grant to 1 million acres.[65] One-seventh of the amount was paid in military warrants and the rest in debt certificates. Congress reduced the price per acre by one-third to compensate for poor lands, and, as with the Ohio Company, debt certificates and military warrants acquired at huge discount reduced the actual cost to between 8 and 9 cents an acre. Symmes and his partner Elias Boudinot set aside for themselves forty thousand acres on the Ohio River. Thanks in part to the influence of his friend and agent Jonathan Dayton, who "spoke to several of the most influential characters in the Senate,"[66] Symmes was appointed one of the three judges for the Northwest Territory in 1788. (The judges exercised final jurisdiction over land disputes, of course.) Symmes was able to come up with only $83,330 in certificates and military warrants and could not close the deal, but being "naturally of an impetuous disposition,"[67] he moved to Ohio, built a home at a place he called North Bend, and placed advertisements in New Jersey newspapers promoting settlement in the Miami Purchase.[68]

Symmes sold eight hundred acres opposite the mouth of the Licking River. The first group of settlers arrived at the site in the final days of 1788 and began to lay out a small town they called Losantiville. Symmes kept a close eye on political developments in the East (especially the adoption of the Constitution) and on the prospects of an Indian treaty or an Indian war in the West. There was no question in his mind that the Indians would have to go; land sales and settlement could not proceed until the way was cleared. It was just a matter of how they were to be removed. "I hope the Government will not forever bear their insults," he wrote in 1788. "I know they may be easily chastised."[69] But while Symmes had no doubt the United States could defeat the Indians, his frontier settlements, his settlers, and his investment were in jeopardy so long as there were no troops in the area. Why were there no troops at the settlements on the Miami

Purchase? he asked in November 1788. "Is it a matter of no moment to the United States whether we are saved or destroyed by the savages?" "We are in three defenceless villages along the banks of the Ohio," he wrote in May 1789, as people were leaving in fear of Indian attack. "I fear I shall be stripped of settlers and left with one dozen soldiers only." Two months later there were reports that Indians were preparing to strike settlements on the Miami and Limestone rivers: "What will be the issue, God only knows." Symmes asked Dayton to use his influence with Secretary of War Knox. Dayton lobbied Knox hard, and Knox made the necessary arrangements.[70]

In 1789 Josiah Harmar, who was also a proprietor in the Ohio Company, built a fort at Losantiville to protect the settlers in the Miami Purchase as well as across the river in Kentucky. He named it Fort Washington. In January 1790 St. Clair renamed Losantiville, calling it Cincinnati. With a garrison of more than three hundred men and a regular traffic of soldiers, civilians, hunters, traders, and contractors, Fort Washington and Cincinnati, with its taverns and brothels, were to feature prominently during St. Clair's campaign.[71]

It soon became apparent that Symmes was a bigger deterrent to settlement than were the Indians. He sold lands to other speculators from the original 2 million–acre grant; sold lands before he actually acquired title from Congress; sold lands on credit and then neglected to pursue payment; and because he was not careful in surveying and the boundaries of deeds often overlapped, sometimes sold the same lands to more than one settler. St. Clair was astonished to find that Symmes "had given out, and published indeed to the World" that he had contracted for all the lands between the Great and Little Miami rivers, whereas in fact his purchase did not extend more than twenty miles up the Ohio from the mouth of the Great Miami. "It could never have entered into my Head that any Person, much less one invested with a respectable public Character, had published a falsehood—was persisting in it, and availing himself of the pecuniary advantages flowing from it."[72]

The governor tried to remove Symmes's settlers as illegal squatters. Jonathan Dayton, for one, felt the heat of the "torrents of abuse" against Symmes and felt compelled to tell him. Every New Jersey man who had returned from Miami complained about him; Kentuckians hated him; and his reputation for nefarious dealings, "especially in promising & disposing of lands one day to one person, and selling

FORT WASHINGTON.

Print depicting Fort Washington in 1790, based on a drawing by Major Jonathan Heart the winter before he was killed at St. Clair's defeat. Courtesy of the Ohio Historical Society (OHS-AL02875).

them the next day to another," put a damper on "the spirit & rage" for emigrating and buying land in the Miami Purchase. Symmes vociferously denied charges of profiteering. "The insidious reports which have been spread abroad of my selling the same lands several times over," he replied to Dayton in January 1790, "are really vexatious to me." In time many settlers sued him, and he had to give up lands to meet judgments that went against him.[73]

Land speculation was a risky business. Any number of factors could frustrate the eastern speculators' goals. What if the federal government opened western land offices and reduced the price of lands? When Alexander Hamilton proposed such a plan to Congress in 1790, it set alarm bells ringing. "The moment the bill for establishing the land office is passed & made known, you may bid adieu to any further disposal of your lands," Dayton warned Symmes.[74] Time was also a threat. Speculators needed to resell their lands quickly in order to pay off their creditors. Delay could bring ruin. Speculators' timetables for realizing a tidy return on their investments therefore depended on speedy resolution of "the Indian problem," which meant getting Indians out of the way, by treaty or by war.

WHEN ST. CLAIR WAS APPOINTED GOVERNOR
of the Northwest Territory, his instructions included making a treaty
with the Indians if "the welfare of the frontiers and the settlements
forming in that country" required it. Congress authorized and financed
St. Clair to convene the tribes in a general council and get them to
confirm their earlier land cessions. In other words, the United States
was now prepared to pay for the lands it had earlier demanded as the
price of peace. But St. Clair was not to depart from the treaties that
had already been made "unless a change of boundary beneficial to the
United States" could be obtained. And while purchasing Indian land
was not the primary object of making a treaty at this point, the new
governor should "not neglect any opportunity that may offer of extin-
guishing Indian rights to the westward, as far as the river Mississippi."
In addition he was to do his utmost "to defeat all confederations and
combinations among the tribes."[75] St. Clair promised to take advantage of every opportunity "to sow the seeds of discord among them."[76]

Most of the Indians stayed away from St. Clair's treaty. Their chiefs
warned them that American treaty commissioners employed "pen
and ink witch-craft" that put words in their mouths and tried "to
make dogs of all the nations who have listened to them."[77] Alexander
McKee apparently told them that the treaty would accomplish nothing: St. Clair might promise peace, but "the Kentuck[y] people would
brake it immediately."[78]

About two hundred Indians met St. Clair at Fort Harmar in
December 1788. The land speculators watched from the wings in anticipation. "A successful termination of the Indian treaty now seems
to be almost the only thing wanted to make your settlement the most
flourishing upon the Ohio, & the seat of western government,"
Dayton wrote Symmes in the middle of the month. "I wait with anx-
iety to hear the result of it, knowing well that in case of failure, the
other alternative is war."[79] At first the Indians demanded the Ohio
River be restored as the boundary, but St. Clair took the same tone
employed by American commissioners in earlier treaties, telling the
Indians that Britain had given up their lands and that the United
States was generous in its restraint. In January 1789 St. Clair signed
two treaties, one with the Seneca chief Cornplanter and representatives of the Six Nations (although his rival Brant and the Mohawk
stayed away), the other with Wyandot, Delaware, and some Ottawa,
Ojibwa, and Potawatomi. The Indians confirmed earlier treaties and
land sales. Again Ebenezer Denny was present at the treaty. After

some half-hearted resistance on the part of the Indian delegates, St. Clair browbeat them into signing; the United States wanted peace, he said, "but if the Indians wanted war they should have war." The Indians signed. "This was the last act of the farce," Denny commented in his journal. For his part, St. Clair found the negotiations "both tedious and troublesome" but was more than satisfied with the outcome.[80]

By dealing with the Six Nations and the western tribes separately, St. Clair felt he had forestalled any incipient union between them: "I am persuaded their general confederacy is entirely broken, indeed, it would not be very difficult, if circumstances required it, to set them at deadly variance."[81] Noting that "none of the western Indians attended it"—there were no Shawnee, Miami, or Wabash—Harmar agreed that the treaty was likely "to divide the savages in their councils, and to prevent the General Confederacy taking place."[82] The proceedings at Fort Harmar did expose divisions among the tribes, but St. Clair's uncompromising stance only convinced the Indians of the futility of negotiating with the United States. In fact, the British noted, those nations that refused to attend St. Clair's treaty meeting now seemed determined to prevent all American settlements northwest of the Ohio and sent war pipes to the different tribes, announcing "their determination for war."[83] Many of those who signed the treaty quickly disavowed it. St. Clair and Harmar underestimated the tribes' political capacities, as they were about to underestimate their military capacities.

The Treaty at Fort Harmar brought no peace. In the spring of 1789 a group of Shawnee came down the Miami to see Symmes. They asked if the United States had sent him there. Symmes replied in the affirmative and showed them a flag and the seal of his commission bearing the American arms. He explained that the eagle held a branch of a tree as an emblem of peace in one claw, and a bundle of arrows, symbolizing the power to punish enemies, in the other. The Shawnee chief examined the seal and replied via an interpreter:

That he could not perceive any intimations of peace from the attitude the Eagle was in; having her wings spread as in flight; when folding of the wings denoted rest and peace. That he could not understand how the branch of a tree could be considered as a pacific emblem, for rods designed for correction were always taken from the boughs of trees. That to him the Eagle appeared from her bearing a large whip in one claw, and such a number of arrows in the other, and in full career of flight, to be wholly bent on war & mischief.[84]

The New England speculators and settlers who pushed into the Northwest Territory saw themselves bringing order and civility and conducting even-handed relations with the Indians. To the Indians, an invasion was an invasion.[85] As the Shawnee chief indicated, it was difficult to see the pacific intent in American empire building. The Indians prepared to attack the New England settlements and made it known that they "were resolved to fight for their land, and then if they lost it they would lose it like men."[86]

The presence of troops reinforced the Indians' apprehensions about American intentions. The First American Regiment was stationed on the frontier not only to protect settlers but also to facilitate the surveying and selling of land.[87]

A detachment from the First Regiment patrolling the Wabash Valley in June 1789 found the body of a soldier who had been killed a few hours earlier: "He was shot in two places with balls, had two arrows sticking in his body, was skalped, his heart taken out and his privates cut off." Such tactics had generated fear and hatred during the French and Indian and Revolutionary wars, and they had similar effects now.[88] Soldiers, settlers, and speculators called on the state to deploy its military resources to prevent its citizens from being murdered and mutilated. Providing protection was vital if the territories were to remain part of the nation, Rufus Putnam argued to Fisher Ames, member of Congress from Massachusetts in 1790 (and to just about everyone else); neglecting to do so might "prove an infinite mischief to the United States." The Ohio, Scioto, and other companies had contracted for lands in full confidence that those lands would be protected; unless that protection was provided, "these contracts must all fail (to the loss of many Millions of dollars to the United States) *for of what value are lands without inhabitants, and who will wish to inhabit a country where no reasonable protection is afforded*[?]"[89] If the Indians could not be subdued by treaty, the United States would have to use force.

CHAPTER 3

The United States
Invades Ohio

PRESIDENT WASHINGTON ORDERED GOVERNOR ST. CLAIR to make war on the Indians of the Northwest Territory only as a last resort. But, he added, should the Indians continue to be hostile despite American efforts to preserve peace, the United States would "be constrained to punish them with severity."[1] What the United States regarded as a necessary application of force to bring order to its territory, of course, the Indians regarded as an illegal invasion of their homelands by an aggressive foreign power. The Indian nations living in Ohio had not agreed to the Peace of Paris and did not feel bound by it; they fought to defend their territorial boundaries as set by colonial treaties, in particular the Ohio River boundary established by the Treaty of Fort Stanwix in 1768. "These people," Governor Frederick Haldimand of Quebec wrote, "have as enlightened Ideas of the nature & Obligations of Treaties as the most Civilized Nations have, and know that no Infringement of the treaty in 1768...Can be binding upon them without their Express Concurrence and Consent."[2] The Indians would fight to halt American expansion at the Ohio River.

By 1790 Indians and Americans had had plenty of experience with each other's ways of waging war, and each had adapted to new conditions. Confronted, and then armed, with guns, Indians had abandoned old ways of fighting by ranks of warriors and developed more lethal tactics of hit-and-run guerrilla warfare that Europeans both feared and disparaged as treacherous and cowardly. The English had also adopted Indian tactics. During King Philip's War in New England in 1675–76, wrote the Puritan missionary John Eliot, "God pleased to shew us the vanity of our military skill, in managing our arms, after the

61

European mode. Now we are glad to know the skulking way of war."[3] During the French and Indian War, Robert Rogers's New Hampshire Rangers and Gorham's Rangers successfully incorporated Indian ways of fighting.[4]

Nevertheless colonial and American militia and armies continued to drill and train for battles fought by ranks of soldiers on open fields, and armies conducting European-style campaigns rather than frontiersmen taking advantage of forest cover determined the outcome of the war between France and Britain and the war between Britain and the United States.[5] When Europeans and Americans defeated Indians they usually did so by wars of attrition. French expeditions against the Iroquois in the seventeenth century, British expeditions against the Cherokee in 1760–61, and General John Sullivan's scorched-earth campaign through Iroquois country in 1779 had all demonstrated that the most effective strategy for waging war against mobile warriors fighting in their own terrain was to burn Indian crops and villages. Striking in late summer or fall, when the corn was ripe and there was not enough time for replanting before the first frosts, rendered Indian families homeless and hungry in the coming winter. Americans forged unlimited war and irregular war into their own way of war, which included, and justified, killing noncombatants, burning villages, and destroying crops.[6] The American forces that invaded Ohio in 1790–91 intended to wage this kind of total war and to defeat Indian men by targeting fields and homes, the domain of women.

FINANCIAL AND FAMILY WORRIES weighed on Arthur St. Clair's mind as he readied for war. His wife, Phoebe, suffered from mental instability. Worse, in May 1790, St. Clair had had no news from his family for some time and was "very much alarmed at the account of my little Peg's situation." He had heard that his daughter, Peg, or Margaret, the youngest of his seven children, had contracted smallpox and measles simultaneously. She had had smallpox before (which would have given her immunity), "but if any other eruptive fever came with the measles, there is very little probability that she would overcome." "I wish to God I knew the worst, if it has happened," he confided to Josiah Harmar, "for then I should be easy."[7] Peg died that year. She was nine years old.[8]

Following Washington's instructions, as St. Clair prepared for war he also held out the prospect of peace, although he had limited expectations. He felt he could count on the friendly disposition of the

Wyandot but feared that "the Miamis, and the renegade Shawanese, Delawares, and Cherokees, that lay near them" were "irreclaimable by gentle means." Still it was worth a try, if only to buy time while St. Clair gathered his forces: "At any rate, I do not think we are yet prepared to chastise them."[9] Like much of American Indian policy, St. Clair's strategy aimed to foment and exacerbate divisions among the tribes and to try to isolate those he and Henry Knox called "banditti."

In the spring of 1790 St. Clair sent an Indian agent and trader, Antoine Gamelin, to the western tribes. Gamelin met with the Piankeshaw, Wea, and Kickapoo in April, but they told him they could make no answer without consulting their elder brothers the Miami. They also took offense at the tone of St. Clair's speech and his ultimatum: "I do now make you the offer of peace, accept it or reject it as you please." Gamelin omitted it in future translations. He spoke with the Miami and Shawnee at Kekionga, but they said they could do nothing without consulting their British father at Detroit and the Indians who lived nearer the Great Lakes. The Shawnee chief Blue Jacket told Gamelin in private that the Indians distrusted the Big Knives, as they referred to the United States, having been deceived before; the peace offers were just a precursor to taking their lands "by degrees." Unless the settlers were removed from the north side of the Ohio, Blue Jacket said, there could be no peace.[10] The Six Nations sent wampum belts to the Miami advising them to "sit still," but the Miamis replied, "We have been preparing ourselves this spring to gather all our people together and make them all look one way." The western nations were united and strong, they said.[11]

St. Clair was convinced there was "not the smallest probability" of reaching an accommodation with the Indians and that things were nearing a crisis point.[12] Indian attacks on boats traveling down the Ohio demonstrated the ineffectiveness of defensive measures against "the banditti Shawanese and Cherokees, and some of the Wabash Indians" who were causing the trouble. Henry Knox agreed. He thought "the whole amount of these bad people may not exceed two hundred," but their raids were enough to alarm the entire Ohio frontier "and in a considerable degree injure the reputation of the Government." It was time to launch a punitive expedition. Knox anticipated a short and swift campaign, which, he reminded Washington, would "be highly satisfactory" to the people on the frontiers.[13] The United States had made offers of peace "on principles of justice and humanity to the Wabash Indians" and been rebuffed.[14] The expedition was fully justified; in the words of the Northwest Ordinance, it would be "a just and lawful war." The expedition, Knox told St. Clair, was "intended to exhibit to the Wabash Indians our power to punish them for their hostile depredations, for their conniving at the depredations of others, and for their refusing to treat with the United States when invited thereto." This power would be demonstrated by "a sudden stroke" against their towns and crops.[15] Many people, especially on the western frontiers, believed that mounted Kentucky militia had the best record in delivering "sudden strokes" against the Indians and were most likely to do so again, but Washington insisted upon combined operations that involved both the regular army and militia under the overall command of a federal officer.[16]

Thirty-seven-year-old General Josiah Harmar was confident of victory. Three years before he had declared that he was "determined to impress upon the minds of the Indians as much as possible the majesty of the United States" and "let them know that if they persisted in being hostile that a body of troops would march to their towns and sweep them off the face of the earth."[17] Before Harmar set off to do the sweeping, Knox sent him a secret letter of caution. A report had reached the president—and Knox wrote with Washington's knowledge but no one else's—"that you are too apt to indulge yourself to excess in a convivial glass." Harmar must guard against any suspicion of such conduct in the coming campaign.[18]

Harmar left Fort Washington on the last day of September with 320 regulars and about 1,100 militia from Pennsylvania and Kentucky. It was a larger army than most of the Indians had ever seen, but many in the militia were old men and young boys hardly able to bear arms, carrying an "indifferent" assortment of muskets. They were "not such as might be expected from a frontier country," admitted Major William Ferguson, "viz. the smart active woodsman, well accustomed to arms, eager and alert to revenge the injuries done them and their connections. No—there were a great many of them *substitutes*, who probably had never fired a gun." Lieutenant Ebenezer Denny agreed: they "were not of that kind which is calculated for Indian Expeditions; they were drafts & substitutes, many of them had never fired a rifle in their lives."[19] So much for the myth of pioneer forebears defending their freedom with unerring marksmanship as they exercised their Second Amendment rights. Winthrop Sargent had already made

Josiah Harmar. Photographic reproduction of an engraved portrait by John Sartain based on a painting by Raphael Peale. Courtesy of the Ohio Historical Society (OHS-AL02989).

clear his views on militia and their elected officers. In the unlikely event that the Indians stood and fought instead of running away, he warned St. Clair in August, "it appears to me, from the past Conduct of the Kentuckey militia that they will absolutely take themselves off— We know how their Officers are appointed & from repeated Experiments how little Dependence can be placed in them."[20]

Harmar's orders were to destroy the Miami villages on the Maumee River and kill any Indians who opposed him. At the same time Major John Hamtramck left Vincennes on the lower Wabash with three hundred regulars and three hundred Kentucky militia, invading Miami country in the west while Harmar struck in the east. To avoid sparking an unintended international conflict, Knox ordered St. Clair to inform the British commander at Detroit that the campaign was directed only against hostile Indians, not the British posts. The post commander replied that Britain was unconcerned, although he promptly sent messages warning British traders in the Miami villages, and the British Indian department observed and encouraged the Indians' preparations.[21] At the same time, St. Clair sent messages to the Wyandot, Seneca, and Ottawa, assuring them that the forthcoming campaign was directed only against the "foolish nations" that were committing hostilities; the Americans would not harm those tribes who sat quietly and kept their warriors at home.[22] The chiefs of the "foolish nations" sent runners in all directions calling for help and prepared to move noncombatants to safety.

Hamtramck reached an abandoned Piankeshaw village at the mouth of the Vermilion on October 11, burned its lodgings and crops, and then turned for home. He attributed his decision to shortage of supplies and the unreliability of his militia. It would not be the last time he would have to explain his actions in turning back rather than engaging the enemy.

Harmar reached Kekionga around noon on October 17, a Sunday. The village was "beautifully situated between the Rivers Miami & St. Joseph," but the occupants had abandoned it "in the utmost consternation, leaving behind them vast quantities of corn & vegetables, supposed 10,000 bushels in ears." Harmar ordered it all put to the torch. "It will be a great stroke," he wrote to St. Clair on the 18th, "the next thing to killing of them." In addition to the principal town at Kekionga, there were several smaller towns on both branches of the rivers, some log houses said to have been occupied by British traders, "a few pretty good gardens with some fruit trees, and vast fields of corn in almost every direction." The next day Harmar's men rode about two miles to Chillicothe, a Shawnee village of about eighty cabins and wigwams, with "a vast quantity" of corn and vegetables hidden in caches. The soldiers killed and, as was common practice on the frontier, scalped two Indians that day and another that night. Harmar's column spent three days destroying villages and "everything that could be of use: corn, beans, pumpkins, stacks of hay, fencing and cabins, &c." On the 21st the army began its return march to Fort Washington, "having burned five villages, besides the capital town, and destroyed twenty thousand bushels of corn in ears."[23]

Meanwhile, on the 19th Colonel John Hardin and a force of three hundred men went in pursuit of the Indians. The Indians ambushed them, the militia fled, and the regulars had to cover the retreat back to the main body. Harmar blamed Hardin's loss on "the shameful conduct of the militia." When Harmar began his return march on the 21st he split his force again and sent Major John P. Wyllys and four hundred men, of whom sixty were regulars, to attack the Indians as they returned to Kekionga. Wyllys then split *his* force. The Indians lured the militia into giving chase and caught and killed most of regulars at the village. Wyllys "received a shot through his heart which dismounted him." Once again, said Harmar with dripping sarcasm, the militia "behaved themselves charmingly." Harmar's army regrouped and limped back to Fort Washington, having suffered more than two hundred casualties and the loss of a third of the packhorses and abandoning much equipment.[24]

At first Harmar claimed a victory. St. Clair sent Knox glowing reports of "the entire success" of the expedition and assured Winthrop Sargent that Harmar had conducted "a very successful campaign," despite "the loss of our friend, Major Wyllis, who was sacrificed by the militia." But it quickly became clear the campaign was a humiliating defeat.[25] Writing to Hamtramck on November 29, Harmar expressed surprise that the major had not sent him "a single line" since the expedition and requested a detailed account of his operations. As for his own command, Harmar stated, he had "completely burned and destroyed the Miami Village and all the Omee towns with about 20,000 bushels of corn & a vast abundance of vegetables & slain upwards of 100 of their prime warriors, but not without considerable slaughter upon our side. The loss of Major Wyllys & Lieut. [Ebenezer] Frothingham is greatly to be regretted. Our total loss was 180—73 of whom were federal troops. The savages fought desperately."[26]

"I expected *little* from the moment I heard he was a drunkard," Washington fumed to Knox. "I expected *less* as soon as I heard that on *this account* no confidence was reposed in him by the people of the Western Country. And I gave up *all hope* of success, as soon as I heard that there were disputes with him about command."[27] Knox informed Harmar, "It would be deficiency of candor on my part were I to say your conduct is approved by the President of the United States, or the public."[28] A court of inquiry consisting of Major General Richard Butler and Lieutenant Colonels George Gibson and William Darke concluded that Harmar's conduct was irreproachable, the organization of the army order of march and battle were effective, and the detachments of forces on the 14th, 19th, and 21st were "made of good principles." The problem lay in the fact that Harmar's orders "were not properly executed." Witnesses reported no evidence of drunkenness.[29] The blame fell on the militia, and Harmar retired to civilian life. A campaign that was supposed to quash Indian resistance only intensified it. Another expedition would be required.

ST. CLAIR BLAMED THE BRITISH. No fort, no matter how strong, could sufficiently overawe the Indians to prevent every depredation, "especially when there is another nation in their neighborhood who court them, and who instigate them to those depredations," he wrote Knox in November. And it was not only British traders who encouraged them. Alexander McKee and the British Indian department were at work. "Mr. McKee's being among them distributing ammunition and stores at the moment they were to be attacked, looks so like the support of Government, that it is impossible they should view it in any other light."[30] American aggression and Native American resistance to it, not British intrigue, caused the war, but St. Clair nonetheless accurately assessed both McKee's role and how the Indians interpreted it.[31]

Hamtramck, who had burned the Piankeshaw village and crops, said it was not enough to march into Indian country, burn houses and corn, and return the next day, "for it is no hardship to an Indian to live without, they make themselves perfectly comfortable on meat alone, and, as for houses, they can build them with as much facility as a Bird do his nest." Indians would not stand and fight unless they had a clear advantage and could always retreat deeper into the country to avoid fighting a battle on unfavorable terms. The only way to "chastise" Indians was to surprise them in their towns or camps.[32] Hamtramck was right about the Indians' strategies of withdrawal. They rebuilt their homes and began to move to safer locations downriver at the area known as the Glaize.[33] But he was off the mark in his assessment of their stomach for a fight. It was an almost unquestioned assumption among American military men that, confronted by disciplined regular soldiers in battle, Indians would not stand and fight. Such thinking missed the point that in such circumstances Indians never intended to stand and fight.[34] In the next campaign the Indians decided otherwise.

Harmar's campaign was a blow to speculators who had had great expectations of success. "But for the repulse of the army I should have had several new stations advanced further into the purchase [the Miami Purchase] by next spring," Symmes wrote in early November.

Now he would be lucky just to maintain the three he already had, and the settlers living there were alarmed. There "never had been fairer prospects of speedy sales and settlements of lands in the Purchase than were about the time the army marched," he lamented, "but the strokes our army got seems to fall like a blight upon the prospect." Symmes expected "the panic running through the country" to reach New Jersey and deter emigration. The Indians were ruining his prospects. He hoped the president would "have at them again in the spring."[35]

That winter, in a departure from the tradition that tended to limit warfare to particular seasons, war parties left the villages at the Glaize to raid the settlements on the north side of the Ohio. In January 1791 a raiding party of Wyandot and Delaware struck a new settlement on the east bank of the Muskingum, about thirty miles upriver from Marietta, killing eleven men, a woman, and two children in what became known as "the Big Bottom Massacre."[36] Several days later Indians attacked Dunlap's Station, a blockhouse on the east bank of the Great Miami River garrisoned with a dozen soldiers to protect the settlers clearing land on the Symmes Purchase. Indians were not thought capable of mounting and sustaining a siege, but they seemed to come prepared for one at Dunlap's Station, with heavily laden packhorses. They captured a surveyor named Abner Hunt and tortured him to death in sight of the garrison. The inhabitants decided to retreat down the Miami.[37]

Indian raids spread. Benjamin Van Cleve said the Indians near Cincinnati became "so daring as to skulk thro the streets at night & through the gardens around Fort Washington." John Van Cleve and his family had migrated down the Ohio and settled in Cincinnati in January 1790, and he had set up shop as a blacksmith. The following year he was killed and scalped by Indians, leaving eighteen-year-old Benjamin to support his widowed mother and three siblings. Since Fort Washington was the headquarters for the expeditions against the Indians, Benjamin got a job working for his uncle, an army contractor. In that capacity he accompanied St. Clair's expedition as a pack horseman at $15 a month.[38]

New Englanders, who had envisioned their settlement of Ohio as an orderly process marked by harmonious relations with the Indians, now faced a full-blown Indian war. At Marietta the agents of the Ohio Company saw "all our Settlements in the utmost danger of being swallowed up."[39] Rufus Putnam fired off letters to Washington, Knox, and congressman Fisher Ames. "Our prospects are much

changed," he wrote in January 1791; "in stead of peace and friendship
with our Indian neigbours a hored Savage war Stairs us in the face[;]
the Indians in stead of being humbled by the Destruction of the
Shawone Towns & brought to beg for peace, appear determined on
a general War, in which our Settlements are already involved." The
Indians apparently "threatened there should not remain a Smoak
[white settler's cabin] on the ohio by the time the Leaves put out." The
government, in Putnam's view, must send troops to protect the settlements and do it quickly because, after all, the government was at least
partly to blame for the situation. The Ohio Company had bought
their lands on the assumption that they had been fairly obtained
from the Indians, but when they arrived the Indians told them this
was not true and, looking at the treaties that were made, even Putnam
agreed "that the lands were rather wrested from them than fairly
purchased." He had hoped that because of St. Clair's treaty at Fort
Harmar the whole situation would have been "pritty well patched up."
Many chiefs remained dissatisfied, however.[40] The Indians who came
to Fort Harmar to trade in the winter of 1791 all reported "that a great
many Indians are going to war." Putnam reminded Washington that
the crisis was of crucial importance not only to the inhabitants of the
frontiers (and, though he did not say so, to speculators like himself)
but also to the United States:

> for Should Government take effectual measu[res] to bring the na-
> tives to Submission, & for the protection of those who have Settled
> under her authorety, She may fairly calculate on a rapid sale of
> her lands, by which She may Sink many millions of her National
> Debt—but on the Contrary Should She leve her Citizens to be
> insulted & murdered by the Savages, I think it dos not require the
> Spirit of prophecy to foretell the consequence. No more lands will
> be purchased but will probably be Seized on by privit adventurers
> who pay little or no reguard to the laws of the United States or the
> rights of the natives.

Once it became known that the government had given up protecting
the region, adventurers and squatters would "return like a flood &
Seize the country to them Selves." If that happened the United States
would incur greater expense reducing these people "to obedience"
than it would defeating the Indians.[41] In other words, it was in the
national interest to protect Putnam's interests.

Bombarded with petitions from frontier settlers, concerns from land speculators in Congress, and fears of western separatism, the government moved decisively to deal with the crisis. Knox requested expansion of the regular army to three thousand—1,200 regulars, 1,300 volunteer levies enlisted for four months, and five hundred rangers—at a cost of $100,000, in preparation for a new offensive in the summer.[42] Volunteer levies were raised and officered by the federal government, but, like the militia, they were short-term enlistments. On March 3, 1791, Congress passed into law An Act Raising a Second Regiment to the Military Establishment of the United States, and for Making Further Provision for the Protection of the Frontiers. The law authorized a second regiment of 912 men and authorized the president to raise two thousand levies and a body of militia for six months.

The next day Washington appointed fifty-five-year-old Arthur St. Clair as major general to command the army. "Your knowledge of the country north-west of the Ohio, and of the resources for an army in its vicinity, added to a full confidence in your military character, founded on mature experience, induced my nomination of you to the command of the troops on the frontiers," the president wrote him.[43] After the debacle with Harmar, Washington apparently felt St. Clair was a safe bet. Most of the officers who were appointed had seen service in the Revolution, although finding and commissioning willing and able men took time. Newspaper advertisements called for veterans of the Revolution to return to "honorable service" and encouraged young men who had an ambition for military life to sign up with the promise of western land on easy terms and a generous bounty.[44] The two thousand levies were to be raised from the various states, assemble at Fort Pitt, and then move downriver to Fort Washington to prepare for the start of the campaign. St. Clair would have an army of about three thousand men.

In March 1791 Ebenezer Denny wrote Josiah Harmar from Philadelphia. Denny enjoyed good relations with his former commander. After his campaign Harmar had recommended Denny for "some mark of honor" in recognition of his "long and faithful services."[45] The respect was mutual. Denny wrote with news: "The great people here have at length determined to carry on another campaign against the savages upon a more extensive plan than the last. In the meantime they have thought it necessary to order a temporary expedition, entirely of militia, for the purpose of amusing the Indians and to prevent them from committing any further depredations on the frontiers." Denny very much wanted to be back on the Ohio frontier with Harmar, "for I am perfectly sick of the court and all courtiers." He then turned his attention to the appointments for the new campaign: "Major—— [Butler] is appointed Lieut.-Col. Commanding of the second regiment. Some reasons which will operate very forcibly upon him, make me think that it is uncertain whether he will accept or not. Some people are troubled with the *cannon fever*, and if I was not much mistaken, he was very subject to it—a feather bed would be a fitter place than the field." He hoped Harmar would be reconciled to St. Clair's being appointed commander for the summer campaign, citing the long friendship between the two of them.[46]

Knox maintained that the United States wanted peace with the Indians. Unfortunately it must first wage war to make peace. The Indians considered themselves victorious, so a campaign that would impress them with the power of the United States and convince them of the futility of further resistance was necessary "as the ground work of that system of justice and mercy, which it will be the glory of the general government to administer to all the Indians, within its limits." Knox's orders to St. Clair repeated that the U.S. government and the majority of the American people wanted "to establish a just and liberal peace with all the Indian tribes," but if, as seemed increasingly likely, that proved impossible, St. Clair was to employ "coercive means." Knox authorized St. Clair to dispatch mounted militia units against Indian villages, which would divert warriors from attacking the frontiers to protecting their women and children at home. Meanwhile he was to prepare the main expedition to march to Kekionga and build a permanent fort there. A strong post erected right in the middle of the Miami villages and garrisoned by a thousand men "would curb and overawe not only the Wabash Indians, but the Ottawas and Chippewas, and all others who might be wavering, and disposed to join in the war." A post there would protect the Ohio frontier more effectively than one at any other location. Knox was confident that a disciplined army could triumph over undisciplined Indians.[47] He overestimated the discipline of the former and underestimated the discipline of the latter.

Thomas Jefferson was optimistic. "I hope we shall give the Indians a thorough drubbing this summer, and then change our tomahawk into a golden chain of friendship," he told Washington in April. Jefferson would have preferred to "bribe" the Indians into peace with gifts and feared that recurrent campaigns would entrench the national army and the national debt. "The least rag of Indian depredation will be an excuse to raise troops for those who love to have troops, and for those who think a public debt is a good thing," he wrote.[48] Washington, a veteran of Braddock's defeat, was more cautious about prospects for victory, although his words of warning to St. Clair to beware of surprise appear to be later attributions.[49]

Meanwhile the government continued to work through the Six Nations. The Ohio Company in 1788 had granted the Seneca chief Cornplanter one square mile of land because of his service to the United States and "the Friendship he has manifested to the Proprietors of Land purchased by the Ohio Company."[50] The government wanted to keep the Seneca from joining the Indian resistance and to employ Cornplanter as an emissary to the western tribes. St. Clair hoped that some of Cornplanter's Seneca might even accompany him on his expedition.[51] Cornplanter, together with two other Seneca chiefs, Half Town and Big Tree, traveled to Philadelphia. Washington assured them that the Iroquois lands were safe now that the government had the sole authority to negotiate sales, and that the war preparations were a last resort; the western Indians had refused peace offers and continued their hostilities. Cornplanter assured the United States of his people's pacific intentions, and the government made arrangements for him to go on a peace mission to the Miami and Wabash villages, a mission, Washington said, that would "render those mistaken people a great service, and probably prevent their being swept from the face of the earth."[52]

Colonel Thomas Proctor, who had been an artillery officer during the Revolution and served in Sullivan's campaign into Iroquois country, was to accompany Cornplanter. Knox told him to stress "the candor and justice" of the federal government and tell the Indians that all they had to do to obtain peace was be peaceful. If they refused, they would "be liable for the evil which will fall upon and crush them." Proctor carried with him a message from the secretary of war. "The United States are powerful, and able to send forth such numbers of warriors as would drive you entirely of the country," the message declared; "it would be absolute destruction to you, your women, and your children." The United States required nothing from the Indians but peace. Indeed as proof of their good intentions, the Americans wanted to teach Indians to cultivate the earth. (How Knox explained the hundreds of acres of Indian crops burned by Harmar's soldiers the previous fall if the Indians needed instruction in agriculture is not clear.) It was much better "for human kind to have comfortable houses, to have plenty to eat and drink, and to be well clothed, than to be exposed to all the calamities belonging to a savage life." What the United States was offering the Indians was for their own good, "and the Great Spirit above will approve it." It was the final offer: "If you do not embrace it now, your doom must be sealed for ever." To try to distance the Delaware from the Miami and Shawnee, St. Clair sent a message to Captain Pipe (Hopocan) and other Delaware chiefs telling them to receive Proctor as a messenger of peace; if the Miami and Shawnee refused to listen to him, their blood would be upon their own heads and the United States would "be justified before the Great Spirit... and to all the world, in bringing that destruction upon them which they have merited long ago." With or without peace, Proctor was to be back at Fort Washington by May 5. Knox stressed the importance of this, informing Proctor that it was connected with "collateral arrangements."[53]

Proctor traveled to the Iroquois in New York and set off for the Miami villages. But Cornplanter stayed home, the British commander at Fort Niagara refused Proctor's request for a boat to carry his party across Lake Erie, and the peace embassy fizzled out.[54] Meanwhile Colonel Timothy Pickering embarked on another diplomatic mission to try to ensure the neutrality, if not secure the aid, of the Six Nations and to isolate western tribes. In April St. Clair sent another message to the Wyandot, scolding them for not responding to his earlier messages and warning them to remain at peace with the United States.[55]

The chances of peace were not great. As John Hamtramck had pointed out, even were a peace treaty made, those living on the frontier would without doubt be the first to break it. "The people of Kentucky will carry on private expeditions against the Indians and kill them whenever they meet them, and I do not believe there is a jury in all Kentucky who would punish a man for it."[56] Nor did Washington see much hope of peace with the Indians "so long as a spirit of land jobbing prevails, and our frontier Settlers entertain the opinion that there is not the same crime (or indeed no crime at all) in killing an Indian as in killing a white man."[57]

The "collateral arrangements" Knox referred to were the preparations for war that were going ahead while the United States sent out peace feelers. Brigadier General Charles Scott and the mounted Kentucky militia were ready on May 10 to set out against the Wea towns on the Wabash River. The expedition was delayed a couple of weeks, waiting for word of Proctor's peace mission.[58] A Virginian by birth, Scott had served as a private in Braddock's defeat and had fought and been captured in the Revolution. After the war he had migrated to Kentucky. Indians killed and scalped his son Samuel on the Kentucky River in the spring of 1787; a second son, Captain Merritt Scott, was killed in Harmar's expedition. Scott had good reason to carry the war into Indian country.[59]

Scott kicked off St. Clair's campaign in late May, leading eight hundred Kentucky mounted militia across the Ohio and against the Indian villages in the Wabash Valley. According to Scott's report, his men advanced through torrents of rain, blasts of wind, and thunderstorms. When they appeared on the banks of the Wabash, overlooking the group of Wea villages known as Ouiatenon, the Indians, in great confusion, tried to escape in canoes across the river. Lieutenant Colonel James Wilkinson and the first battalion quickly seized the riverbank, and, despite "a brisk fire" from a Kickapoo town on the opposite bank, "they, in a few minutes, by a well directed fire from their rifles, destroyed all the savages with which five canoes were crowded." He did not specify how many women and children were in the canoes. Scott then sent Wilkinson upriver to other towns, including Kethtippecanunk, or Tippecanoe. "Many of the inhabitants of this village were French," reported Scott, "and lived in a state of civilization; by the books, letters, and other documents, found there, it is evident that place was in close connexion with, and dependent on, Detroit; a large quantity of corn, a variety of household goods, peltry, and other articles, were burned with this village, which consisted of about seventy houses, many of them well finished."

Scott reported he killed thirty-two people, "chiefly warriors of size and figure," and took fifty-eight captives. The Americans suffered only five wounded. Freeing some of the elderly and incapacitated captives to carry messages to the tribes, Scott compiled a list of the names of forty-one Indian prisoners, a remarkable document; Indian prisoners of war were a rarity. Equally remarkable—so much so that Scott reported it with "much pride and pleasure"—was the fact that "no act of inhumanity has marked the conduct of the volunteers of Kentucky on this occasion; even the inveterate habit of scalping the dead, ceased to influence."[60] Some Indian warriors later came to Fort Washington to see their captured families.[61] The destruction of Ouiatenon and Kethtippecanunk further distanced these Wea Miami bands from the tribal leadership at Kekionga.[62]

Land speculators complained that Indian hostilities, and Harmar's failure to end them, were destroying their business.[63] So Manasseh Cutler, for one, was delighted to hear of Scott's "astonishing success" against the Indians and hoped St. Clair's campaign would be equally successful. Emigration would immediately revive if the settlers could be assured of safety, he wrote Winthrop Sargent, and shares in the Ohio Company had risen sharply, with speculators paying "from one to two hundred pounds ye Share in specie." Confident of the outcome and eager to reap the rewards, he asked Sargent to send him an account of the expedition when he had time.[64]

HAD ST. CLAIR'S CAMPAIGN PROCEEDED on schedule, the army would have advanced into Indian country on the heels of Scott's campaign. St. Clair had left Philadelphia on March 23, two days after he received Knox's formal orders for the campaign, but, delayed by illness, he did not reach Fort Washington and assume command until mid-May. At that point he had barely one hundred men present and fit for duty. The start date of July was abandoned. Instead, on August 1, St. Clair dispatched Lieutenant Colonel James Wilkinson and five hundred mounted troops on a second raid into the Wabash Valley.

Wilkinson left Fort Washington, feinted a move against Kekionga, and then turned west against the Wea towns in the Wabash. He attacked and burned the complex of villages stretching for three miles along the Eel River at L'Anguille. His attack killed six men and, "in the hurry and confusion of the charge," two women and a child. He took thirty-eight prisoners, including the wife and baby of William Wells, who now lived as a Miami. The next day he burned the corn and pushed on toward the Kickapoo towns, leaving two old women and a child with a "talk" to the Indians on the Wabash River: "The arms of the United States are again exerted against you, and again your towns are in flames, and your wives and children made captives; Again you are cautioned to listen to the voice of reason, to sue for peace." But losing his way in swamps and prairies, with many of his horses lame and his men reluctant to push deeper into Indian country, Wilkinson gave up on the Kickapoo towns. Instead he destroyed a village and cornfield just west of Ouiatenon, and then moved on to the Ouiatenon villages previously destroyed by Scott. The Indians had already rebuilt their villages and replanted their corn, which "was now in high cultivation, several fields being well ploughed, all which we destroyed." Consoling himself that the Wea "left without houses, home or provision, must cease to war," Wilkinson headed home.[65]

Congress had appointed General Richard Butler as St. Clair's second in command. Butler had experience fighting and negotiating with, or at least dictating terms to, Indians. He was responsible for raising the officers and men for the Second Levy Regiment and for coordinating recruiting in New Jersey, Maryland, Virginia, and Pennsylvania, his home state. Two of Butler's younger brothers, Thomas and Edward, both of whom had served in the Revolution, received commissions in the Pennsylvania battalions.[66] Winthrop Sargent was appointed adjutant-general. Sargent, a Harvard graduate with an aristocratic New England pedigree, had served with the artillery in the Revolution. Sargent's wife, Rowena, had died in childbirth, along with the baby, the year before, a tragedy that did little to ease Sargent's stiff demeanor, what St. Clair acknowledged as "an austerity in his manner."[67] His impatience and frustration as he watched the campaign flounder did little to endear him to fellow officers and soldiers, with whom he was already unpopular. Lieutenant Colonel George Gibson commanded the Second Regiment of levies; Lieutenant Colonel William Darke, a veteran of Braddock's defeat, commanded the Virginia, Maryland, and North Carolina troops of the First Regiment of levies; Lieutenant Colonel William Oldham commanded the Kentucky militia, and Major William Ferguson commanded the artillery battalion. Major Hamtramck commanded the First Infantry Regiment; Major Jonathan Heart the Second.[68] Troops were to assemble at Hagerstown in Maryland and Winchester in Virginia and then join troops from the northern states at Fort Pitt.

From the outset preparations for supplying the campaign were beset by delay, incompetence, and corruption. During the Revolutionary War the quartermaster's department had operated under the Board of War, but after Robert Morris became superintendent of finance in 1781 he replaced the system of requisitions on the states with the European practice of using private contractors; Congress "privatized" its duties, and the government accepted bids from individuals and companies on contracts to supply the military. Although civilians, contractors were granted the rank and salary of lieutenant colonel. Morris's system produced some improvements but also opened up new opportunities for profiteering.[69] Army contractors in Europe were notorious for their corruption.[70]

The provisions contract for St. Clair's campaign was made in October 1790 with a New York merchant named Theodosius Fowler, who transferred the contract to William Duer in January 1791 and later claimed that he had acted as Duer's agent.[71] Duer had resigned from his position as assistant secretary of the treasury to pursue a career in contracting and speculating. The cash advances he received from the government—more than $75,000—for purchasing army supplies allowed him to fend off some of his creditors, and he also invested some of it in land speculations. He loaned $10,000 to his friend Henry Knox, and they formed a secret partnership speculating in land in Maine. The Maine land speculations diverted much of Duer's attention—and cash—from the business of supplying the army and organizing an effective supply system to sustain it during the coming campaign.[72]

In March Knox had appointed as quartermaster general another friend and business associate, Samuel Hodgdon, formerly a colonel in the Continental Army, in which he had considerable quartermaster experience, and then a successful merchant in Philadelphia. The secretary of war handled most of the clothing purchases himself, awarding contracts to the lowest bidders, but the quartermaster general was supposed to deal with contracts and inspection in Philadelphia, buy boats and horses, arrange for the manufacture of artillery shells at Pittsburgh, and have everything sent downriver, and then proceed to Fort Washington. He was provided with "ample funds" to do so. Hodgdon's chief assistant was William Knox, the secretary of war's younger brother.

Although Henry Knox kept insisting that Quartermaster Hodgdon was "amply furnished with the means of obtaining every thing that shall be wanting for the campaign" and that everything would be made good, there were recurrent deficiencies and problems. Clothing and canteens were slow to arrive at Fort Pitt. Sheet iron was sent so that camp kettles could be fashioned at the fort. Knapsacks that had been sent from Philadelphia split and leaked. The knapsacks arrived "neither painted nor strapped," and the quartermaster had to forward paint and straps. The shoes provided by Duer were too small and split after a few days' wear. Clothing was shoddy. Packsaddles, manufactured in Philadelphia and transported across the mountains at great expense, were too big, and new ones had to be made. General Butler complained about the tents, which, as Knox explained to him, were lightweight and suitable for a summer campaign.[73] Many of the firearms were in poor repair and some unfit for use. Major Ferguson, commanding the artillery, was to be furnished with three 5 1/2-inch brass howitzers, three brass three-pounders, and three brass six-pounders. But, he complained, the casks in which the gunpowder was sent were "very slight" and not tightly secured, and the cartridge paper for the muskets was "not of the proper sort, being too easily torn, and of course the cartridges made of it will not bear much carriage."[74] Other officers complained later that the powder was defective, probably because it had been damaged by moisture. Knox had to get after Duer about what he called "embarrassments relative to the Beef."[75]

Hodgdon was supposed to reach Fort Pitt before the middle of June, but he did not leave Philadelphia until June 4, and even his friend Knox had to send him a strongly worded message to get a move on. Hodgdon did not join St. Clair until a week into September. St. Clair had to resort to employing local workmen—coopers, carpenters, wheelwrights, and gunsmiths—in Cincinnati, while he and his troops waited for the quartermaster and supplies to arrive.[76] Things got so bad that even Knox got worried. "For God's sake, put the matter of provisions on the frontier in perfect train," he wrote Duer privately in June, and then the next month, "I hope in God you have made other and more effectual [arrangements] or you will suffer exceedingly."[77] Knox remained adamant that "the public service must be neither delayed nor injured for want of provisions," but, not for the last time in America's wars, the men appointed and contracted to carry out the business of provisioning America's soldiers did not share such concerns.[78]

St. Clair continued to have problems with the contractors even after the quartermaster arrived at Fort Washington. St. Clair's orders and strategy required establishing a supply route from Fort Washington to the Miami towns, with a series of garrisoned posts at intervals along the route. The army's advance into Indian country required coordinating the movement of troops and supplies:

That forty-five thousand rations of provisions should move with the army; that twice every ten days forty-five thousand rations should move from Fort Washington to the next post, until three hundred and sixty thousand rations were sent forward; that forty-five thousand rations should again move with the army from the first post to a second, and an equal number twice in every ten days until the residue of the three hundred and sixty thousand were carried forward, and so on from post to post, still moving with forty-five thousand rations.

Instead, St. Clair informed Hodgdon, the contractors "have failed entirely in enabling me to move with forty-five thousand rations."[79] The army was constantly delayed in its progress as it waited for supply trains to catch up.

Troops trickled in during the summer. In July Washington was "exceedingly anxious" that the campaign should begin as soon as possible, and Knox ordered Butler to descend the Ohio immediately with all the troops at his command. By August Washington considered it "an unhappy omen" that the troops had not yet descended the Ohio. In late August troops that should have been at Fort Washington were still detained on the upper Ohio by low waters. Washington was now "extremely anxious" that the delay was jeopardizing the campaign and that "unless the highest exertions be made by all parts of the army to repair the loss of the season, that the expenses which have been made for the campaign will be altogether lost, and that the measures from which so much has been expected will issue in disgrace."[80]

Captain Samuel Newman's journal records his difficulties dealing with discipline, drink, and camp followers. Newman had served as an ensign and lieutenant in the Revolution and returned to service as a captain in the newly formed Second Regiment. He recruited his men from the farms and villages of the Connecticut Valley in western Massachusetts, assembled them at Springfield, Massachusetts, and then proceeded with them to Brunswick Barracks in Philadelphia.[81] From there they marched to Pittsburgh and headed by boat down the Ohio to Fort Washington. He left Philadelphia at the end of July with eighty-three men and four women, but ten men were already confined for desertion and other crimes. On August 1 Newman received an order from the secretary of war "to permit Mary Hastings to join my Company!" He was not happy about it: "She's a d—d Bitch & I intend to Drum her out the first time she gets drunk." The next day, "the Men getting drunk, & becoming refractory," he had "four of the most impudent" flogged. A week later, near Elizabeth Town, eighteen miles from Lancaster, he dismissed a Mrs. Graham for repeatedly bringing canteens of rum to the men, despite his orders and repeated warnings against it. He hoped it would serve as an example to the others, but four days later he "drummed Mr. Willaghan out of the Camp for bringing rum into it, and dismiss'd Mrs. Brady for her Insolent language" during the punishment of two soldiers whom he flogged for getting drunk. The next morning he found Mrs. Brady had crept back into camp during the night. "Her Contrition & Intreaties, with the consideration of its being in a manner impossible for her to carry her Clothes & an Infant 120 Miles back again," induced Newman to let her stay, on condition she behaved herself. On August 15 Sergeant Williams was found to have been drunk all day while on guard duty, and Newman had him sent under arrest to Fort Pitt to stand trial. Two days later Sergeant Pierce was drunk, giving a prisoner being held for desertion the opportunity to escape. Finding that the other prisoners had been privy to his escape and were planning their own, Newman had them all flogged, with their hands chained behind their backs. "Heaven knows," Newman wrote, "my heart…bled upon the occasion." He also complained that many of the men were "scandalously negligent," and he threatened immediate punishment if they got their cartridges wet or let their guns get rusty.

The command marched into Pittsburgh on August 27. On the 29th Newman "pass'd an Agreable Evg. With some of the Belles of Pittsburgh & retir'd to Camp at Eleven." Low water had detained troops at Pittsburgh for weeks, but now it began to rain, the Ohio rose quickly, and Newman and his men were able to complete the six-hundred-mile journey to Fort Washington, traveling day and night by boat, in a week. Newman seems to have been suffering from pneumonia by this time, but on Sunday, September 11, he "waited upon Genl. St. Clair & encamp'd in front of ye. Battalion."[82]

The men in other units were no better. They lacked training and discipline. St. Clair called for a muster of volunteers for federal service, but volunteers from Kentucky were slow in coming. General Scott and Wilkinson were reluctant to put themselves under the command of St. Clair, in whom they had no great confidence and who had made known his opinion that Kentuckians who retaliated against Indian raids "without attending precisely to the nations from which the injuries are received" were as much to blame as the Indians for the spiraling violence on the frontiers. Scott, Wilkinson, and every other general officer in Kentucky pleaded illness or found other reasons not to lead the volunteers. Scott and the Kentucky Board of War finally had to draft one thousand "reluctant citizens" to serve under St. Clair, placing them under the command of Colonel William Oldham, the highest ranking Kentuckian they could find.[83] Winthrop Sargent was not impressed by Oldham's men. "Picked up from the offscourings of large towns and cities; enervated by idleness, debaucheries and every species of vice, it was impossible they could have been made competent to the arduous duties of Indian warfare," he declared. They displayed, in his view, an "extraordinary aversion to service" and were "badly clothed, badly paid and badly fed." Many of them deserted.[84] Although few other officers were as scathing as Sargent, at least before the congressional investigation into the disaster, Harmar and Denny agreed that the soldiers were hastily recruited, unprepared, and poorly led.[85]

Infantrymen, wrote the late military historian John Keegan, "however well trained and well armed, however resolute, remain erratic agents of death." Without proper direction they might choose the wrong targets, open fire or cease firing at the wrong time, shoot high or wide, be distracted by the wounding of comrades, and give in to fear or excitement. Eighteenth-century armies spent hours training, marching in rank and file, and practicing volley fire in an effort to overcome such behavior, reduce the danger of self-inflicted casualties, and maximize their capacity for effective collective action. Training, instilling order and discipline, was also essential in preparing men for the shock of violent combat and the experience of being fired upon. "A handful of men, inured to war, proceed to certain victory," wrote Publius Flavius Vegetius Renatus in the late Roman Empire, "while on the contrary numerous armies of raw and undisciplined troops are but multitudes of men dragged to slaughter."[86] St. Clair acknowledged to Knox in August that he wished his troops could have been better trained and more accustomed to discipline. The First Regiment comprised almost entirely raw recruits, and many of them had been employed at other duties. No pains would be spared instructing them, St. Clair added, but the season was already far advanced and it was time for the campaign to be under way.[87] Describing the battalions of British volunteers dispatched with minimal military training to the Western Front on the eve of the Battle of the Somme, Keegan saw "the promise of tragedy which loomed about these bands of uniformed innocents."[88] He could have been referring to the soldiers in St. Clair's army.

At Fort Washington Denny found the preparations for the campaign "very backward" and secretly wished to accompany Harmar when he left for Pittsburgh and retired to civilian life. Harmar predicted that St. Clair would be defeated. Nevertheless when Harmar sensed that Denny might resign, he discouraged the idea. "'You must,' said he, 'go on the campaign; some will escape, and you may be among the number.'"[89] No doubt bolstered by such optimism, Denny joined his regiment and was appointed aide-de-camp to St. Clair.

Problems, frustrations, and plodding progress led St. Clair to doubt whether the campaign should go ahead so late in the season. But he knew that Washington and Knox needed a successful campaign after Harmar's debacle. Washington had been frustrated when failures in the supply system delayed the start of Sullivan's campaign against the Iroquois for two months in 1779.[90] Now, said St. Clair, the secretary of war wrote repeatedly "in the name of the president, in the most positive terms, to press forward the operations." On September 1, for example, Knox wrote, "The president enjoins you, by every principle that is sacred, to stimulate your exertions in the highest degree, and to move as rapidly as the lateness of the season, and the nature of the case will possibly admit." Pressured from the top, St. Clair had little choice but to push ahead.[91] General Butler, the quartermaster, and three companies of the Second Regiment finally arrived on September 10.[92] A week later St. Clair assured Knox that "every possible exertion shall be made to bring the campaign to a speedy and happy issue."[93]

THE ARMY HEADED NORTH from Fort Washington along a route the Indians knew well, a trade path that ran between the Ohio and the Glaize. As Braddock had found in 1755, weather and terrain took a heavy toll on morale and schedule, and the strength of the army diminished as it advanced, its resources depleted by the need to defend lines of supply and communication, and its numbers reduced by disease and desertion. The journals kept by Ebenezer Denny, Winthrop Sargent, Samuel Newman (until October 23), St. Clair (from October 21), and more briefly by Lieutenant Daniel Bradley describe the process, although they sometimes differ slightly with regard to the details of date and distances covered.[94] Hacking its way through the woods, the artillery and many of the wagons pulled by oxen, the army made painfully slow progress, sometimes advancing only a few miles each day. The "going rate" for an army of that era in Europe was six to eight miles a day when it "was in no particular hurry," and the leisurely pace allowed the baggage and guns to keep up; during more urgent phases of a campaign that rate might be increased to a dozen miles a day. Sullivan's army in 1779 had managed twelve to sixteen miles a day except when it halted to burn Iroquois villages and destroy crops.[95] St. Clair's army, under pressure to forge ahead, never came close.

September 15: The roads were so muddy the baggage train could not keep up; the men had to sleep in the woods on wet ground without blankets or greatcoats.

September 19: There was heavy thunder, lightning, and rain the previous night. An unidentified officer, writing to "a gentleman" that

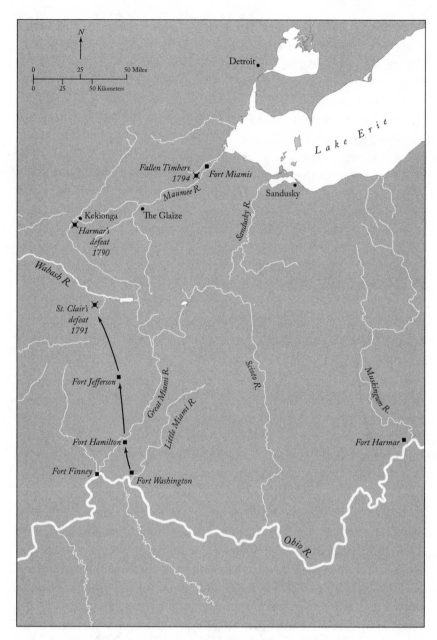

Map of St. Clair's invasion. (Map drawn by Meg Calloway.)

day, said they knew a large force of Indians was gathered at the Miami towns, supplied and encouraged by the British at Detroit. "That the enemy are numerous I doubt not," he warned, "but as we are, and shall continue to be, prepared for the expected interview, of course nothing will be left undone to keep up the spirits of the army." In the face of desertions those morale-boosting efforts included daily courts-martial "on the trials of officers arrested, and offenses of soldiers, many of the latter for crimes capital."[96]

September 23: Newman's son, who had been at the hospital at Fort Washington, caught up with the column. "Poor boy, ye. Scenes are so Novel, & as he conceives hard, that it affects his Spirits & makes him unhappy," wrote his father; "however, he little thinks that the fatigues & dangers are yet to come!" Newman expressed trepidation as he anticipated "a Winter's Campaign, in a Country inhabited only by wild beasts, or ye. Still more ferocious *biped* of ye. Forest, without baggage, & I very much fear in a manner without provisions" and without forage for the horses and cattle.[97] Major Jonathan Heart had brought his twelve-year-old son with him from Connecticut, and Captain Joseph Shaylor had brought his eleven-year-old boy.

September 24: It rained all day and "absolutely pour'd in sheets & torrents all night!" Tents, beds, and clothes were soaked. Hodgdon had contracted to buy lightweight tents that might have been suitable if the campaign had gone ahead as planned in the summer and fall, but the drenching rains the army experienced in late September and October rendered them virtually useless. "D—d the Economy of the Contractor for ye. Thinness of our Tents," fumed Newman, "thro which the rain beat, as if thro a Sieve! this is the Country cheated, and the Soldier imposed on."[98]

September 27: Indians stole horses. That day St. Clair gave Butler orders to march the army north from Fort Hamilton. He was to advance in two columns on two parallel roads, 250 yards apart, each forty feet wide, an order of march that would enable the men to form battle lines quickly in the event of attack. St. Clair returned to Fort Washington and then Lexington to oversee the raising of Kentucky militia units. He was absent from the army until October 8.

October 1: Indians killed a soldier, captured another, and stole six horses only two miles from camp.

October 3: A sergeant and twenty-five men deserted in the night. Newman had a violent cold, but he was the only captain in his regiment well enough for duty.

October 4: The troops forded the Great Miami River, with the water up to their waists. Then they marched only two miles farther as they had to cut the roads.

October 5: The army was making painfully slow progress. Butler changed the road building from two parallel broad roads to a single road twelve feet wide, but things did not speed up appreciably; hacking their way through dense woods, the men marched only three miles. The advance picket saw an Indian on horseback gallop away.

October 6 and 7: The army advanced five miles each day.

October 8: St. Clair rejoined the army from Fort Washington. That night he publicly criticized Butler for altering the order of march, an exchange that permanently alienated his second-in-command.

October 9: St. Clair assumed active command of the army, but its slow progress continued, advancing five miles.

October 10: The force covered seven and a half miles. It passed some old Indian camps and saw some fresh tracks.

October 11: The army was delayed because horses had gone missing. They marched no more than six miles and then encamped on a wet prairie. They saw many Indian tracks, and riflemen in advance of the army saw some Indians on horseback.

October 12: Four miles were covered. A scouting party came on a hastily vacated Indian cabin—a deer was being cooked—and another party surprised and fired at several Indians. Indians who had run off two of the artillery horses left a pair of moccasins as if in exchange. The weather turned cold during the night, and the soldiers woke to find ice on the water containers.

October 13: The day was spent locating a suitable site for constructing a fort, and the army moved only one mile. The weather had changed dramatically, becoming hot and humid, the last warm day many of the men would enjoy. Thunder and lightning storms moved in that night.

October 14: Two hundred men were employed under the command of Major Ferguson building the new fort. They lacked the tools for the job, having only eighty axes, one crosscut saw, and one frow (a cleaving tool with a wedge-shaped blade). The rest of the men sheltered in their small, leaky tents. It rained heavily before dawn, most of that day, all the next day, and all through the night of the 16th.

October 17: Construction of the new fort was going slowly. The militia were discontented, and the levies looked forward to the expiration of their tour of service. Four men of the First Regiment had deserted since the army arrived at the site. Today or the next day an Indian sniper wounded a member of the militia hunting a few miles from camp. Newman said two riflemen were killed while hunting six miles from camp. It rained and hailed all night.

October 18: The wet, disagreeable weather continued, turning the road into a muddy morass. Clothes shrank, shoes fell apart, and many men were sick from exposure and inadequate rations. The horses were weak from lack of forage "& die daily."[99] The army would have been without bread after today, had not a small supply of forty-eight horse loads arrived.

October 19: All the horses of the army, quartermaster's as well as contractors', were sent back for a supply of flour. St. Clair put the troops on a half allowance of flour. "Unpardonable mismanagement in the provision department," noted Denny. "Failure on the part of the contractor," said Lieutenant Daniel Bradley. "It is feared the expedition will fail on account of provisions."[100] In addition St. Clair put all officers and others entitled to extra rations on a single ration. Officers used their "extra rations" to provide for wives, children, or guests, and each company was allowed extra rations for up to four women employed as washerwomen. By cutting the extra rations, St. Clair ordered "all but one woman per company to be expelled from the army. Within days, once the order was implemented, only thirty or so women and a very small number of children (one of whom was Major Heart's son) remained in St. Clair's column."[101] In tightening the army's belt St. Clair may have saved the lives of more than one hundred noncombatants, although his orders would not have affected prostitutes and other camp followers who were not on army rations, so the exact number of women who remained with the army at the time of the battle is difficult to determine.

October 20: "Discontent and murmuring prevails in the militia camp."[102] Officers were at odds with one another; regulars insulted the militia; everyone seems to have disliked Winthrop Sargent, and everyone was furious at the contractor. The levies' enlistment terms were starting to expire, and the levies from Virginia wanted their discharges. Ten were discharged this morning, several a few days ago. Captain Newman received a letter from home, making him think of the "peaceful scenes of domestic life."[103] That night was the coldest yet.

October 21: There was a severe frost during the night, and the men woke to ice on the water almost half an inch thick. Frosts had been damaging the forage for the horses and cattle for more than two weeks now. "A strong guard escorted the cattle and horses to the best pasture, and every afternoon one-half the army off duty turn out and bring grass from the prairie to serve them over night." This, noted St. Clair, in "a country which, had we arrived a month sooner in it, and with three times the number of animals, they would have been all fat now." The campaign was way behind schedule, and desertion and sickness had thinned the ranks. Conscious of the fact that the levies' terms were winding down and they would start leaving, St. Clair was anxious to get them into battle before their terms expired, or at least, as he wrote to Knox that day, get them so far into Indian country that they would see it was safer to go forward with the army than to head for home and be picked off by Indians.[104]

October 22: Twenty men deserted during the night, and more followed this morning. St. Clair, however, was feeling better: "The indisposition that had hung about me for some time, sometimes appearing as a bilious colic, and sometimes as a rheumatic asthma, to my great satisfaction, changed to a gout in the left arm and hand, leaving the breast and stomach perfectly relieved, and the cough, which had been excessive, entirely gone." The relief proved to be temporary. Although often associated with heavy drinking, the term *gout* was often used for rheumatism, neuritis, arthritis, or some other ailment accompanied by pain, swelling, and stiffness. In St. Clair's case it was likely "inflammatory arthritis brought on by the standard army rations and exposure to dampness and cold."[105]

October 23: Two artillery men who had attempted to desert to the enemy were sentenced to death, together with one of the levies for shooting another soldier and threatening an officer. The whole army was drawn up to watch the hangings. Notice of the execution was the last entry in Samuel Newman's journal. When the army marched on the next day, he left his journal at the fort with all his baggage except what he could carry in his knapsack, presumably intending to update it later. He never did.

October 24: The army marched on, leaving about 120 men who were unable to march at the new fort, called Fort Jefferson. St. Clair was so ill he had to be carried in a wagon. The soldiers saw many old and recent Indian campsites, some with ashes still warm.

October 25: It rained hard most of the night, and the army was obliged to remain in camp waiting for provisions.

October 26: The army remained encamped; St. Clair was very ill, and the Virginia battalion was "melting down very fast." A scouting party of militia surprised a camp of five Indians but let them "slip through their fingers."[106] The rain turned to snow.

October 27: The army still waited for supplies. The last pound of flour was served out. Dissatisfaction increased among the militia and levies. "Forage almost entirely destroyed; horses failing and cannot be kept up," wrote Denny; "provisions from hand to mouth." The Chickasaw chief Piomingo and nineteen warriors arrived in camp to serve as scouts for the army. Piomongo had led the Chickasaw in making peace with the United States at the Treaty of Hopewell in 1786, and the Chickasaw had old scores to settle against the northern tribes. According to Winthrop Sargent, they had "the most inveterate animosity to all the Indian tribes northwest of the Ohio, but most particularly to the Kickapoos, and have been at war with the whole of them from time immemorial."[107] St. Clair was so unwell he could manage only to bid Piomingo welcome, "but entered on no business."[108] Sargent thought their "prospects [were] gloomy" as transportation difficulties were getting worse every day as the season wore on and threatened to prove fatal as the army got farther from its supply base. But with desertions and levies insisting on their discharges, St. Clair had no choice but to keep going and march the army so far into Indian country that the men would be afraid to risk heading back in small groups.[109]

October 28: Seventy-four horses loaded with flour finally arrived; they brought about twelve thousand pounds, which would feed the army for four days. "Some few Indians about us."[110] A soldier was killed and scalped three miles from camp. Hail and snow.

October 29: A sentry alarmed the camp last night, firing three times at what he imagined was an Indian. Piomingo and his warriors, accompanied by Captain Richard Sparks and "four good riflemen,"[111] set out on a scout. They planned to be gone at least ten days.

October 30: The army made seven miles but it was hard going. The horses were weak, and the men abandoned many of the tents along the way, as they were useless in these conditions. A violent thunderstorm with strong winds brought tree limbs crashing down, causing the men a sleepless and frightening night.

October 31: "A very unpleasant camp in the woods."[112] The army remained encamped, waiting for packhorses. About sixty of the militia deserted. Concerned that they would plunder the oncoming packhorses, St. Clair sent Major Hamtramck and the First Regiment after them, depriving the army of three hundred of its best soldiers.

November 1: The army remained encamped. Sargent assumed the reason was to give St. Clair time to catch up on dispatches to the war office, "as no other cause is obvious."[113] St. Clair did indeed write to Knox that day. "Nothing material has happened," he said, "and, indeed, I am at present so unwell, and have been so for some time past, that I could ill detail it if it had happened." But now he could bring Knox up to date on the events of the past week, including his worry that the Virginia battalion was melting away, "notwithstanding the promises of the men to the officers."[114] William Darke also wrote several letters that night, complaining about the bad management and incompetent leadership of "our Glorious Campaign," which had managed to march only eighty-three miles in two months. In his letter to his wife he predicted that their "scandalous expedition" was about to peter out and he would soon be on his way home: "I expect we shall march tomorrow early on towards the Indian Towns, where we, I believe, shall not find an Indian."[115]

November 2: The army marched eight miles and encamped. It snowed lightly all day.

November 3: After marching nine miles, the tired, cold, and hungry soldiers encamped on an area of high dry ground barely sufficient to contain them; "lines rather contracted." Except for the militia who had to bivouac three hundred yards away across the creek (the Upper Wabash), the men were cramped together. Instead of making any defensive fortifications that night, a plan was "agreed on intended to be commenced early tomorrow."[116]

WHEN THE ARMY ADVANCED from Fort Jefferson, wrote Denny, "it did not exceed two thousand men; discharges, desertions and the absence of the first regiment, reduced the effective strength on the day of action to about fourteen hundred."[117] Nevertheless St. Clair still felt he had a strong enough force to get the job done. He had no accurate information about Indian numbers but had no doubt they would field as many men as possible. He dismissed talk of thousands of warriors; it might be possible to assemble 1,200 to 1,500 Indians, but it was "certainly impossible to subsist them long in that country which is very far from being plentifully stored with game."[118]

As his army struggled on, St. Clair saw nothing to change his assessment of the Indians' capacity for organized resistance or to change his assumption that his army could march on to the Miami villages without having to fight a pitched battle. "It seems somewhat extraordinary that they should have allowed us to be here so long in the interior of the country and never looked at us, nor stolen a horse," he wrote to Knox after the army had advanced almost sixty-nine miles into Indian country. A few horses had gone missing, but St. Clair saw "no reason to think they were taken away by the Enemy. The few Indians that have been seen were hunters only, who we fell upon by accident, and most probably of the Ouabash tribes."[119]

The warning signs were there, but St. Clair could not see them. Nor did Piomingo and his Chickasaw warriors; they found some Indians, but they missed the Indian army that was coming to fight St. Clair. The soldiers saw few traces of Indians and assumed that those they did see were out hunting. Even when Indians began to kill and capture the occasional soldier, St. Clair did not seem to consider that his army was being watched, monitored, and even stalked by scouts from a formidable Indian force. "There is not a people on earth who watch the motions of their enemies, when in open war, with closer or more eager attention," St. Clair wrote later, and the Indians must have known of his movements. It seemed "most probable," he wrote, "that as they did not attempt to molest us in our advances, which they might have done with great effect, they had been disappointed in collecting a sufficient force; that they either would desert their towns on the approach of the army, or sue for peace... and it was this last event that I most expected."[120] As Denny observed, St. Clair and his army were "perfectly ignorant... of the collected force and situation of the enemy."[121]

When the army halted on November 3, Thomas Irwin recalled, he and the other wagon drivers kindled a large fire to keep warm. St. Clair and some of his officers gathered around it to warm their hands and "chatted on several subjects." They did not know exactly where they were, but the general opinion was "that we had passed over the dividing ridge between the waters of the Miamis and St. Mary's" and were on the St. Mary's River. The talk then turned to the movements of the Indians, as more of them had been seen that day than on any previous day. St. Clair "observed that he did not think the Indians was watching the movements of the army with a view to attack them," only to steal horses or take a captive if they had the chance. The officers present agreed with him.[122] Tracks near the stream indicated that about fifteen Indians had left just before the army arrived. "Colonel Oldham, who has long been conversant with Indian affairs, supposes it a party of observation, and the first that has been about us since he joined the army; imagining all the others that have been noticed mere hunters."[123]

During the night nervous sentries disturbed the camp, firing at fleeting shadows, and "reported the Indians to lie skulking about in considerable numbers." Some of the officers became concerned, and Butler dispatched a scouting party of about twenty men under Captain Jacob Slough. Slough "discovered the Indians in such numbers that he thought it necessary to draw in his party." Back in camp, Slough testified later, he found Butler warming himself near a fire and reported what he had seen. He asked if he should go and report to General St. Clair. Butler "paused a little" and told him to get some sleep. Slough "did not wake until the attack commenced," and St. Clair claimed that Slough's "very material intelligence…was never imparted to me."[124]

St. Clair knew he was encamped at a place Indians frequented. He knew he was nearing their villages, estimating that he was about fifteen miles away from the Miami towns. He knew as well that Indian scouts had been watching the encampment. But still he did not expect an attack. As soon as the First Regiment came up, he intended to advance as early as possible the next day and attack the Miami town.[125] "To the last moment, I had the most sanguine hopes of accomplishing the objects of the campaign, by taking post at the Miami villages, and restoring peace and harmony between the savages and the United States."[126] In fact St. Clair was at the Wabash River, not the St. Mary's. Kekionga was still some forty-four miles away. The Indian army, however, was only two and a half miles away.[127]

CHAPTER 4

The Indian Resistance Movement

S T. CLAIR COULD NOT IMAGINE that multiple tribes would unite and strike as one. "You may be assured," he had told Henry Knox three years earlier, "that their general confederacy, if it exists at all, has not that efficiency which would enable the heads of it to direct its force to a point, in the security of which many of the Members would not feel themselves much interested, when each had to fear for themselves separately."[1]

True, the Indian army that was poised to strike St. Clair had not been assembled easily or quickly. The Indians had to make preparations that were as much diplomatic as military. Opposing the invasion required building and maintaining a united resistance movement of many nations committed to the principle that they all held land in common and faced a common threat. Why else should Ojibwa from the shores of the Great Lakes join Shawnee who were fighting to defend the Ohio River? The Indian nations that formed the confederacy were scattered over immense distances, spoke many different and often mutually unintelligible languages, and had separate experiences, agendas, and rivalries. But after multiple tribes resettled in Ohio and then retreated toward the northwestern reaches of the region, people of several tribal affiliations often lived alongside each other in the same village. Such mixing and mingling aggravated what many non-Indians regarded as inherent political weaknesses in Native American society but also facilitated allegiances that transcended tribal barriers.

Tribal social structures were fluid and flexible and political systems decentralized. They operated at the band and village level, functioning horizontally and according to kin relations and consensus rather than in response to authority and orders. Samuel Parsons said Indians had "no government but that of Influence from advice of their Chiefs." David Jones, a Baptist minister who went as a missionary to the Shawnee in the early 1770s, maintained that they were "strangers to civil power and authority." They believed that God made them free and "that one man has no natural right to rule over another."[2] In eastern woodland societies the term *chief* embraced a variety of people in a variety of roles. Put simply, village chiefs tended to be mature men who had earned a reputation for good sense, who guided the people during times of peace and in everyday affairs, and who debated and decided important matters in council. Councils of warriors, older men, and women might exercise different kinds of authority at different times and in different circumstances. In times of war younger men who had attained a following because of their military prowess led war parties out from the villages. Women might exert their influence as mothers who gave life to stop warriors from going to war and taking or losing life. Although some chiefs occupied their role by heredity, they led by reputation and example, not by rank or office, and often exercised their leadership through family networks. Successful leaders demonstrated a strong connection to the spiritual forces whose guidance and assistance was essential in making consistently good decisions for the well-being of the community. They had no means of enforcing their will, and they rarely made decisions without consulting their people.[3]

Whether in war or peace, chiefs exercised only limited authority. The Moravian missionary David Zeisberger explained that a war chief had "no more right to conclude peace than a [civil] chief to begin war" and that no chief dared presume to rule over the people, "as in that case he would immediately be forsaken by the whole tribe, and his counselors would refuse to assist him." The British superintendent of Indian affairs, Sir William Johnson, said that a chief's authority depended on his wisdom and abilities, the number and status of his relatives, and the strength of his particular tribe, and that the chiefs' authority over their warriors had diminished after the introduction of firearms.[4] In short, chiefs' influence depended on their individual character, their continued effectiveness, and the willingness of people to listen to their counsel or follow them into battle. Leaders led because followers followed.

Nevertheless tribal leaders could act decisively to bring Native power to bear, and the fluidity of Native political systems could be a source of resilience and flexible strength. When the need arose leaders could mobilize warriors over an impressive geographical area. However, it took time and effort. They had to persuade individuals and groups among their own people of the need to stand and fight; they had to reach out along networks of kinship and alliance to leaders of other tribal groups, and together they had to assemble an alliance of warriors from different regions and villages, who sometimes had been enemies or who might simply choose to opt out. The confederacy they built was a loose and fragile coalition of villages, and, it has been argued, the participants were actually fighting a coordinated set of national wars rather than a single "Indian war." Given the potential and often real fractures between individuals, clans, villages, and regional confederations and divisions of opinion that arose over issues of war and peace, over relations with the United States and relations with the British, and over what tactics were best pursued and when and where, the Indian force that came together and cooperated to defeat St. Clair represented a triumph of collaborative coalition leadership, collective vision, and intertribal consensus politics.[5]

Americans commonly blamed the British for fomenting and supporting multitribal resistance by spreading lies, but even Rufus Putnam recognized that something more than British influence was at work. The Indians rallied to the cause in greater numbers "than the British Government, with all their arts and money were able to persuade," he said. Clearly their motive was "the fear of losing their lands, or, in other words, that the Americans intend to take their lands from them without their consent, whenever they think proper, agreeably to the doctrine of the treaties at Fort McIntosh and the Big Miami."[6] John Graves Simcoe, lieutenant governor of Upper Canada and no friend to the United States, of course blamed American aggression, not British meddling. The U.S. government seemed "to have thrown off all appearance of moderation and justice in respect to the Indian Nations, the division of the Country into Provinces was among their first public Acts, the extirpation of the Indians was their Philosophical language: and the sale of their lands was held forth as the avowed foundation of their National Wealth." Indian leaders clearly saw what was coming, and, according to Simcoe, "a general War has been the consequence of the claims of the Congress, and of the self defense of the Indian Confederacy."[7]

The American invasion generated a flurry of diplomatic activity across Indian country. Indian messengers hurried along forest trails, carrying wampum belts, tobacco painted red, and calumet pipes decorated with paint and feathers. According to one Jesuit missionary, Indians used calumet pipes "to put an end to Their disputes, to strengthen Their alliances, and to speak to Strangers."[8] Ritually smoking a pipe was a sacred act that established good relations, opened the way for productive negotiation, and bound the participants in a collective commitment to speak the truth. Indians revered the calumet as "the symbol of peace," said one trader; "a violation of any treaty where it has been introduced would, in their opinion, be attended with the greatest misfortunes."[9] While St. Clair's army stalled at Fort Washington and then lumbered northward, Indian messengers carried wampum belts and tribal delegates offered calumet pipes, inviting other nations to join them; and more warriors accepted the belts and smoked the pipes, binding themselves to the cause.

By 1790 the tribes represented in the Northwestern Confederacy fell into three broad camps: the Iroquois; the Miami, Shawnee, and Kickapoo; and the Three Fires of the Ojibwa, Ottawa, and Potawatomi. According to John Norton, an adopted Mohawk of Scots Cherokee descent, "Col. Brant and the other Chiefs of the Five Nations advised moderate measures to obtain the Establishment of an Equitable boundary between the United States, and the various tribes whose territories were comprised within the Limits surrendered by Great Britain." Joseph Brant had been a forceful voice in organizing an Indian confederacy and articulating the need for a united Indian stand on land sales after the Revolution, but he and his followers had migrated to Upper Canada (now Ontario) after the war and were living on lands granted by the British government on the Grand River, so the stakes were not as high for him to hold American expansion at the Ohio. He wanted to use Indian unity as a source of strength in negotiating peace rather than in continuing war, and he was willing to compromise on the boundary issue. Brant had traveled to England in 1786 (his second visit; he had been there in 1776 as well) to ascertain just how much British support the Indians could expect in their struggle against the United States. Well connected in British government circles and in direct contact with many high-placed ministers, he may have had fewer illusions about the depth of British commitment than did the Shawnee and others whose information on British policy was filtered through Indian agents living among them. Leaning toward winning concessions rather than holding the line, Brant recommended accepting the Muskingum River rather than the Ohio as the boundary and proposed giving the United States all lands east of the

Joseph Brant (1742–1807), 1786, by Gilbert Stuart (1755–1828). Oil on canvas. Gift of Stephen C. Clark. The terror of the American frontier during the Revolution, by 1790 Joseph Brant represented the moderate wing of the Indian confederacy, advocating unity to strengthen the Indians' negotiating position. Courtesy of Fenimore Art Museum, Cooperstown, New York (N0199.1961). Photograph by Richard Walker.

Muskingum rather than go to war. He continued to work for compromise, but Iroquois influence, which had never recovered from their betrayal of the western tribes at Fort Stanwix in 1768, was in decline. Norton said the Five Nations sent no assistance in the war of 1790–91 "except from straggling parties, that went to the Shawanons."[10]

Many Wyandot in the Sandusky Valley and some Delaware who had already ceded land favored Brant's position, but the Shawnee, Miami, and Kickapoo rejected talk of compromise and insisted on the Ohio boundary. In the war to defend that boundary, said Norton, the Shawnee "were sometimes the leaders, and always the most active agitators in every enterprize."[11] The Miami had earlier pursued calculated diplomacy in their dealings with rival French and British colonial powers, but now that their Wabash and Maumee Valley lands were under immediate threat they joined with the Shawnee and Kickapoo in determined resistance to hold the Ohio River as the boundary between Indian and white land and took a leading role in the confederacy. At a council on the Miami River in October 1788 the Wyandot urged the Miami to attend peace talks and offered them a large wampum belt, asking them to take hold of one end of it as a gesture of unity. When the Miami refused, the Wyandot delegation placed the belt over the shoulder of the Miami war chief, Little Turtle, "recommending to them to be at peace with the Americans, and to do as the Six Nations and the others did." Little Turtle said nothing, tipped his shoulder, and the wampum belt fell to the ground. The insulted Wyandot stalked out of the council house.[12]

By 1790 Indian resistance centered at the cluster of towns around the principal Miami village of Kekionga. American reports stated that the other tribes of the Wabash, primarily the Wea and Piankeshaw bands of Miami, resolved "to be guided entirely by those of the Miami Village." But the Wea and Piankeshaw were not governed by Kekionga. Exaggerating the warrior strength of the tribe, Americans often mistakenly labeled the entire coalition the Miami Confederacy. The name was not entirely inaccurate since the confederacy centered on the Miami-Maumee River frontier.[13] Hundreds of refugees from the Ohio country and beyond gathered there, close to one another, distant from the threat of American assault and near to the source of British supplies and support.

What the Americans called the seven "Miami towns" in fact comprised a multitribal cluster of Miami, Shawnee, and Delaware villages, totaling hundreds of wigwams and log cabins. Kekionga itself had long been the town of the Miami chief Pacanne, described by the U.S. Indian agent John Johnston as a "remarkable steady sedate and substantial man, devoted to the interests of his people." Seeing his people caught between the British at Detroit and American forces arriving at Vincennes, Pacanne gravitated toward the latter and favored peace with the Americans. He moved his village to within thirty miles of Vincennes and operated for a time as an intermediary between the Americans and the Wabash tribes. Jean Baptiste Richardville (Peshewa), the son of Pacanne's sister and a Quebec trader, was emerging as the principal figure in the community now.[14]

Little Turtle's town was located a few miles northwest of Kekionga, near the headwaters of the Eel River; Le Gris's town near the junction of the St. Joseph and Maumee rivers. French and British traders occupied a stockaded village near Le Gris's town. Other villages—Wea, Kickapoo, Potawatomi—lay within a few days' travel to the southwest on the Wabash River.[15] The Delaware had long fought alongside the Shawnee and like them had moved time and again. The Delaware had made a treaty with the United States in 1778, but the peace did not hold, and four years later American militia bludgeoned to death ninety-six Delaware men, women, and children at the Moravian mission village of Gnadenhütten. Few Delaware harbored any illusions about the possibility of peaceful coexistence with the Americans. Displaced Delaware now had villages on the White River in Indiana as well as in northwestern Ohio, from where they sent warriors to the fight.

Warriors from the Three Fires, primarily from the Michigan peninsula, also joined the fight, but, farther removed from the immediate threat of American expansion, they sometimes wavered in their commitment to the cause of defending the Ohio River. The Ojibwa were by far the largest and most populous of the three tribes, but they were geographically scattered around the Great Lakes, occupying more than fifty villages in what is today Michigan, Wisconsin, Minnesota, and southern Ontario; only Ojibwa villages in Michigan could realistically and regularly contribute to the resistance movement.[16] Segments of the Ojibwa, Ottawa, and Potawatomi had signed the Treaty of Fort Harmar, and the Potawatomi themselves were not united or bound to a single course of action: in 1789 a band from the St. Joseph River first offered to place themselves under U.S. protection and then sent a war party across the Ohio River to raid American settlements in Kentucky. But St. Clair's refusal to compromise at the treaty negotiations only pushed the Three Fires tribes closer to the militant position of the Miami, Shawnee, and Kickapoo.[17] Even so, the Ottawa chief Egushaway, who had warned the Indians not to attend the Fort Harmar treaty negotiations, remained ambivalent in 1790; that summer he advised his people "to sit still" and not trouble themselves "about the Shawnees, who are alone out in war."[18]

Building and sustaining the confederacy depended on the character and charisma of leaders whose reputation, war record, spiritual power, oratory, and sound counsel could attract warriors and keep them committed to the cause. Those individuals sometimes differed in their positions, advocated different strategies, or altered their stance as Brant had done.

According to William Wells, who was living with the Miami at the time and in a position to know, when Harmar marched against the Miami towns, Little Turtle led the Miami warriors against Colonel John Hardin; the Shawnee were commanded by their own chief; Buckongahelas led the Delaware, and Egushaway led the Ottawa and Ojibwa.[19]

Little Turtle, or Mishikinaakwa, was in his forties, having been born sometime between 1747 and 1752.[20] The Indian agent Antoine Gamelin described him as "the great chief of the Miamis," but he was head warrior, not principal chief.[21] Colonel Richard England, the British officer commanding at Detroit in 1794, described Little Turtle as "the most decent, modest, sensible Indian I ever conversed with." President John Adams, who met Little Turtle in 1798, described

Little Turtle. Lithograph reputedly based on a portrait by Gilbert Stuart that was destroyed when the British burned Washington, D.C., in 1814. Courtesy of the Ohio Historical Society (OHS-AL02985).

him as "certainly a remarkable man."[22] Years after the victory over St. Clair, Wells said that Little Turtle commanded the entire Indian army. But Little Turtle's role in leading the Indian army and masterminding the victory was almost certainly exaggerated. A former captive said that the Shawnee war chief Blue Jacket commanded the Indian army, which General Anthony Wayne and James Wilkinson also understood to be the case.[23]

In 1791 Blue Jacket, or Waweyapiersenwaw, was nearing fifty. A nineteenth-century story (perpetuated by some twentieth-century writers) that Blue Jacket was actually an adopted white captive named Marmaduke van Sweringen obscured his accomplishments as an Indian leader. He had fought during the Revolution, and his town near the headwaters of the Mad River was a bastion of Shawnee resistance. Nevertheless he was not culturally inflexible. He sent his son to Detroit to be educated. Two American women who had been taken captive during the Revolution recalled that he and his French Shawnee wife slept in a four-poster curtained bed and ate with silver cutlery. Both women said he was kind to them; one considered herself fortunate to have been taken into his family; the other liked to visit his home, where they always offered her tea.[24]

By 1790 decades of constant warfare had elevated the war chiefs over the civil chiefs in the affairs of the Shawnee nation, and Blue Jacket had built his reputation as the premier war chief. Oliver Spencer, a captive in the Indian villages at the time, called him "the celebrated Blue Jacket" and said he was considered "one of the most brave and most accomplished of the Indian chiefs." He described him as a muscular six-footer with an open and intelligent countenance, "the most noble in appearance of any Indian I ever saw." In spite of his name, Blue Jacket often "was dressed in a scarlet frock coat, richly laced with gold and confined around his waist with a party-colored sash, and in red leggings and moccasins ornamented in the highest style of Indian fashion. On his shoulders he wore a pair of gold epaulets, and on his arms broad silver bracelets; while from his neck hung a massive silver gorget and a large medallion of His Majesty, George III."[25] Blue Jacket's role in leading the Indian confederacy seems to have equaled if not surpassed that of Little Turtle, but his historical reputation has tended to be overshadowed both by Little Turtle, who became renowned after the war was over, and by the great Shawnee war chief Tecumseh, who built a more famous confederacy in the first decade of the nineteenth century.[26]

William Wells said that when the Indians gathered to resist St. Clair's invasion, as when they repulsed Harmar's attack, "each nation was commanded by its own Chief, and the Chiefs appeared to be all governed by Little Turtle, who made the arrangements for the action, and commenced the attack with the Miamies under his immediate command."[27] In reality it is unlikely that anyone functioned as commander in chief of the Indian coalition. Oliver Spencer said the Indians "were led by several brave and experienced leaders." Another captive said that Indians thought that no one man should command an army and that a council of leaders determined "when, and how an attack is to be made."[28]

The Delaware chief Buckongahelas had also established a village on the Maumee River. Normally "mild and affable in his manners; friendly and humane," Buckongahelas was nonetheless committed to the welfare of his people and to the confederacy, and the Delaware said he was "such a man among them as General Washington was among the white people."[29] According to Wells, there was heated disagreement among the Indians about whether Little Turtle or Buckongahelas should lead. "At length Buckongahelas himself decided the controversy by yielding to the Little Turtle, saying that he was the youngest and most active man, and that he preferred him to himself. This reconciled the parties, and the Little Turtle took the command."[30]

Sustaining the confederacy also depended on British support. The British in Canada and the Indians between the Ohio River and the Great Lakes shared a common interest in holding back American expansion, and the Indian confederacy looked to Detroit for assistance. The British encouraged and supplied Indian resistance and prepared for the possibility of renewed war with the United States. Nevertheless they also avoided taking any overt actions that might precipitate war. Preoccupied with events in Europe and the actions of revolutionary France, the last thing Britain needed was another war against the United States. How firmly British officials and agents adhered to that policy, and how clearly they articulated it to their Indian allies, varied according to whether they were in London or Montreal or on the banks of the Maumee River.[31] Ministers wearing powdered wigs and poring over maps in London might frame Britain's policy on the North American frontier, but practical implementation devolved upon the Indian department, whose employees often lived in Indian country, wore Indian clothes, spoke Indian languages, and lived with Indian women. They included English, Scots, Welsh, Irish,

French Canadians, American ex-patriots, Métis, Indians, and men whose Indian wives gave them Indian families and tied them into the fabric of Indian societies. Indian department personnel frequently exercised considerable freedom of action and interpreted government instructions liberally. Many of them were determined to defend the world they shared with the Indians.

The Indian resistance movement consequently was not exclusively Indian. Some of the traders and agents who lived in and around the Indian villages actively supported the Indians, whether or not the crown sanctioned their actions, and many shared in the suffering that American invasion brought to Indian communities. Alexander McKee, son of a Pennsylvania trader and a Shawnee mother, had a Shawnee wife. He had remained loyal to the crown during the Revolution and was now a pivotal member of the British Indian department at Detroit. He operated a depot at the foot of the Maumee rapids, just downriver from the Glaize, from where he supplied the Indian war effort. Born in County Donegal, Ireland, Matthew Elliott had traded into the Ohio country from Pennsylvania, joined the British cause in the Revolution, and had a Shawnee wife. In 1790 he was appointed assistant agent of Indian affairs at Detroit, under his friend and colleague McKee.[32] George Ironside, a trader and agent who had a master's degree from King's College, Aberdeen, lived most of his life in Indian country with his Indian wife. Another trader living at Kekionga, John Kinzie, married Margaret McKenzie from West Virginia, who had been captured with her sister by a Shawnee raiding party and grown up among the Shawnee. Kinzie and Margaret made their life around Kekionga and had three children between 1788 and 1793. Their home went up in flames when Harmar's troops burned Kekionga, but the family escaped and built a house about thirty miles away at the Glaize.[33]

There were also captives and former captives living with the Indians. Captured as a boy with his brothers, George and James, Simon Girty was adopted by the Seneca and lived with them for several years before returning to Pennsylvania. During the Revolution, along with McKee and Elliott, he went over to the British and sided with the Indians during that war and the conflicts that followed.[34] Having grown to manhood among the Miami, William Wells accompanied the Indians on raids against American settlements, helped lure travelers on the Ohio River into ambush, and fought against Harmar. He had a Miami wife and child, who were captured in Wilkinson's campaign in 1791, and subsequently married Little Turtle's daughter, Manwangopath (Sweet Breeze).[35] Girty, Wells, and other captives made common cause with the Indians when the Americans invaded.

Like Anthony Shane (Antoine Chene), the son of a French or Métis father and an Indian mother, who was raised as a Shawnee and fought with them against Harmar and St. Clair, many of the warriors who gathered to resist the American invasion would have had some degree of European ancestry. French traders and Indian women in the Great Lakes region had been intermarrying for generations.[36]

The Indian confederacy centered at the Miami towns grew in numbers and confidence. "All those Scoundrels now Sir profess to hold the Americans in the most Supreme Degree of Contempt," Winthrop Sargent wrote St. Clair in August 1790. "They will they say send their Women to fight us & with Sticks instead of Guns."[37] Nevertheless when Harmar's forces invaded in October, the Indians still lacked the assembled manpower to make a stand or launch a direct attack. They were unable to gather enough warriors or bring enough allies from distant locations in time to stop the invaders. They ordered the French and British traders to remove as much merchandise as possible but commandeered all their powder and ball; they slaughtered the local cattle, and they hid more than one thousand bushels of corn in trenches dug beneath the log cabins. Then they set fire to Kekionga, evacuated their towns, and removed their women and children. Ebenezer Denny described the site after the Indians had left: "Several little towns on both branches, but the principal one is below the confluence on the north side. Several tolerable good log houses, said to have been occupied by British traders; a few pretty good gardens with some fruit trees and vast fields of corn in almost every direction."[38] The Miami evacuated their women and children northwest to the Elkhart River; the Shawnee moved down the Maumee to the Auglaize River; and many Delaware withdrew south to their villages on the White River in Indiana.[39]

Nevertheless, according to a private letter from Detroit, the Indians were "very inveterate against the Americans and have exerted themselves to make an effectual stand." Matthew Elliott reported that the Indians were a thousand strong but that the Sauk and Fox who were on their way from the upper Mississippi had "forbid them to attack the Americans until their arrival." They reached the Miami towns on October 20. The Indians were all, Elliott noted, in "the highest spirits, and very confident of success." Demanding ammunition from the resident traders in their villages, they set off to resist the invaders. Indians from Detroit hurried to assist them with "spirit and alacrity," reported Major John Smith, the British commander at Detroit.[40] They harried Harmar's forces and inflicted heavy casualties but were unable to mount a major attack. At one point, when the confederacy leaders thought the moment was right to deliver a crippling blow on the retreating American army, the Ottawa refused to fight and left for home, following a lunar eclipse which they interpreted as a bad omen.[41]

After the American attacks the Indians regrouped downriver, and the Glaize now became the core of the Indian resistance and a meeting ground for intertribal councils. There were Shawnee towns under Captain Johnny and Snake, whom the captive Oliver Spencer described as "a plain, grave chief, of sage appearance,"[42] a Delaware town under the civil chief Big Cat (Buckongahelas was war chief), Little Turtle's Miami village, and a traders' village. Interspersed among the main villages were small settlements of Nanticoke and Conoy who had been displaced from Maryland, and Chickamauga Cherokee, and within the villages were also some families of Iroquois. A Mohawk medicine woman named Coocoochee, whose husband was killed fighting against Harmar, lived in a cabin between Blue Jacket's and Little Turtle's towns. Her daughter was married to the British trader and agent George Ironside.[43]

Soon after the Indians repulsed Harmar, Blue Jacket went to Detroit to ask the British for help. The Indians had defeated the Americans on their own, but they needed British support and supplies to keep their forces assembled in one place. He asked the British to send traders to the Indians' villages, provide food and clothing for families that had lost their homes, and dispatch soldiers to encourage the war effort. The young warriors who raided the American frontiers had "done it without our nation's sanction," he said; "we as a People have made no war." Nevertheless, "as a People we are determined to meet the approaches of an Enemy, who came not to check the Insolence of individuals, but with a premeditated design to root us out of our Land, which we and our forefathers and children, were and are bound as men and Indians to defend, and which we are determined to do." Major Smith promised to do what he could but cautioned that he had no authority to commit troops, saying, "I am only a Small Finger on the hand of your Father at Quebec."[44] The Indians needed British support to sustain a war against the United States, but Blue Jacket had not forgotten that Britain had abandoned its Indian allies at the end of the Revolutionary War. He understood that the redcoat garrisons on the frontier were there to protect imperial, not Indian, interests. McKee distributed supplies to the Indians, but that was as far as Britain was willing to go. When St. Clair invaded Indian country in the fall of 1791, Blue Jacket would fight without redcoats, with the exception of those who volunteered as individuals.

Yet British assistance or lack of it was also a secondary consideration in the Indian preparations for the campaign. Successful resistance depended on bringing disparate tribes into line in support of a common cause, and then bringing that united force to bear at the right time and the right place.

Harmar's incursion confirmed Indian fears of American aggression, and the mauling the Indians dealt him encouraged others to join the ranks of resistance. In early January 1791 Captain David Zeigler wrote St. Clair from Fort Harmar, with its garrison of little more than twenty men, that the Indians were staying away from the fort. A Wyandot woman he called Polly had told him on New Year's Day, "in a crying manner, that she apprehended all the savages were hostile inclined; when being in their town, numbers of the Chippewas and Ottawas have passed to join those *banditti*, with their usual mode of singing, by giving farewell to their nation for some time."[45] That spring at the Glaize other parties of Indians came and went, with rumors of American intentions and reports of American movements. Indians from the Wabash Valley left their wintering grounds six weeks earlier than usual in anticipation of an American attack, and the Wea, Kickapoo, and Piankeshaw were all determined to defend their villages. Ottawa arrived from Michilimackinac and "danced the war dance," joining other parties going to war. In late April Saginaw Indians who had killed four Americans came in with letters and papers they had taken that reported that St. Clair was appointed commander in chief, General Butler had command of two thousand men, and Major Doughty was appointed lieutenant colonel of the Second Regiment. Two days later a Shawnee and a man named Contepas arrived at the Miami village "from Capt. Johnny, Chief of the River Glaize with a pipe and a piece of red tobacco." According to an observer, the men told those gathered that they had "reason to fear the Americans would make a second attack on them, that they sent this tobacco to pass the word for all the warriors to assemble & to take courage & not to be surprised in their villages by the appearance of the Indians who will go before the army." The observer noted that they appeared "very determined."[46] Charles Scott's raid on Indian villages in May 1791 highlighted the need for a united front.

When news came that St. Clair's army was on the march, the Indians decided to advance to the Miami towns "and there wait the event." Even Joseph Brant said he felt "obliged by every tie of friendship to join them in defense of their country." The Shawnee and Miami sent war belts and painted tobacco, summoning warriors of other nations to join them.[47] Thomas Rhea, who was captured by Indians in early May 1791, saw Brant, Alexander McKee, his son Thomas, and other British officers camped on the south side of the Maumee River. "The Indians came to this place in parties of one, two, three, four, and five hundred at a time, from different quarters, and received from Mr. McKee and the Indian officers, clothing, arms, ammunition, provision, &c and set out immediately for the Upper Miami towns, where they understood the forces of the United States were bending their course [which explains why Scott and Wilkinson encountered few warriors in their raids on the Wabash region], and in order to supply the Indians from other quarters collected there." Those "Indians from other quarters" sometimes came from far away. In the first week of June on the Detroit River, Rhea

met from sixty to one hundred canoes, in three parties, containing a large body of Indians, who appeared to be very wild and uncivilized; they were dressed chiefly in buffalo and other skin blankets, with otter skin and other fur breech cloths, armed with bows, and arrows; they had no guns, and seemed to set no store by them, or know little of their use, nor had they any inclination to receive them, though offered to them. They said they were three moons on their way. The other Indians called them Mannitoos.

Rhea also reported that about 150 Canadians and others from Detroit set off for the Miami villages to join the Indians as volunteers. He understood that McKee, Elliott, and the other officers intended to stay there only until they had supplied the Indians for war, and then return to Detroit, but Simon Girty, for one, declared that he would go and join the Indians. Another captive who was at Detroit maintained that he had seen a hundred canoes down the river come to join the force; there were eight to ten men in each canoe. He confirmed McKee's report that the British were supplying the warriors.[48]

Throughout the summer and fall of 1791 many nations sent delegates to what appears to have been a huge council or, more accurately,
a series of councils. The raids by Scott and then Wilkinson in August
seemed to confirm Shawnee and Miami (and no doubt British) warnings that the Americans intended to invade tribal homelands beyond
Ohio. The Indians denounced St. Clair's message to the Wyandot and
Delaware as an attempt to divide their confederation and reaffirmed
their determination to defend their country. The Miami and Shawnee
were the hardliners, reported Brant, but the other tribes too were
committed to the confederation. Assembling warriors to meet the
invasion was only the first step, however; the concentration of population placed enormous pressure on the food resources of the area, and
warriors frequently dispersed to go hunting. The Indian army needed
British supplies to help keep it together.[49]

When St. Clair's army began to advance from Fort Washington
and headed up the Great Miami, the Indians had no doubt about its
destination. Warriors representing the Delaware, Shawnee, Kickapoo,
Miami, Wyandot, Ottawa, Ojibwa, and Potawatomi, together with
some Conoy and Nanticoke, some Mohawk from Canada, and a
few Creek and Cherokee, gathered at the Miami towns to resist.
Blue Jacket, Little Turtle, and Buckongahelas led the alliance; Simon
Girty, Alexander McKee, and Matthew Elliott of the British Indian
department, together with various French and British traders living
in the vicinity, supported and supplied the coalition.[50] Henry Knox
estimated later that the combined Indian force opposing St. Clair's
army amounted to about three thousand: "The hostile Indians were
before estimated at twelve hundred, and to them it was possible
might be added the Wyandots, Delawares, and Pottiwatimies, in all
amounting to about one thousand more. The excess of these two
numbers probably came from the waters of lakes Superior, Michigan, and Huron, and are denominated Ottawas and Chippewas."
(These were likely the warriors Rhea saw paddling up the Detroit
River.)[51]

Americans at the time, including Knox, and military historians
since asserted that the individualistic Indians lacked discipline and
did not have the social organization necessary to plan and execute
military operations and coordinate group maneuvers.[52] St. Clair
shared and indeed fueled the secretary of war's low opinion of the
Indians' military capabilities. Even after Harmar's defeat and acknowl-
edging that the Indians might be able to bring 1,100 warriors into the

field at one time, St. Clair assured Knox in November 1790, "It is not in their power to keep them long together." They were "totally unacquainted with economy in the use of their provisions" and could not feed so many men for long. When they did fight they would do so "by detachment." They "could not be brought to a general action."[53] If anything, St. Clair worried that the Indians would scatter and run before he could bring them into a fight.

Colonel James Smith, who had spent four years with the Indians after being captured as an eighteen-year-old in 1755 and who fought with Colonel Henry Bouquet against the Indians in 1763–64, knew differently. In the narrative of his captivity that he published in 1799, Smith included a section on the Indians' "discipline and method of war." Calling Indians undisciplined, he said, was "a capital mistake"; they had "all the essentials of discipline."

> They are under good command, and punctual in obeying orders: they can act in concert, and when their officers lay a plan and give orders, they will cheerfully unite in putting all their directions into immediate execution; and by each man observing the motion or movement of his right hand companion, they can communicate the motion from right to left, and march a-breast in concert, and in scattered order, though the line may be more than a mile long, and continue, if occasion requires, for a considerable distance, without disorder or confusion. They can perform various necessary manoeuvres, either slowly, or as fast as they can run: they can form a circle, or semi-circle: the circle they make use of, in order to surround their enemy, and the semi-circle, if the enemy has a river on one side of them.

Well-equipped and adept in the use of their weapons, Indian warriors fought as individuals once the action began, but their chiefs made plans and commanded operations, and they advanced or retreated in concert.[54] In other words, Indians might lack the rigid discipline of British or American regular armies, but they had their own kind of discipline and fought with greater flexibility and fluidity than soldiers trained to respond to drill and command.

Indians had no doubt that when their war medicine was strong they could defeat any force that came against them. Shawnee said that "on the eve of a battle which is expected to be severely contested they address their prayers to Mōtshee Mōnitoo, and when they can muster faith to rely on him, they say that fear is entirely banished from them and that no man could be induced to fly, but would sell his life dearly, dealing death & destruction to all whom he met."[55] "The white people are, in their eyes, nothing at all," wrote one missionary to the Ohio tribes. What the missionary called "their conjuring craft" made the warriors feel invincible. "In their way of fighting they have this method, to see that they first shoot the officers and commanders; and then, they say, we shall be sure to have them. They also say, that if their conjurers run through the middle of our people no bullet can harm them. They say too, that when they have shot the commanders, the soldiers will all be confused, and will not know what to do."[56] It was the strategy they had employed in defeating Braddock; they would use it again to defeat St. Clair.

In his account of Henry Bouquet's campaign against the Ohio Indians in 1764, William Smith had explained how fighting Indians "in woods without end" differed from fighting on the battlefields of Europe:

> Let us suppose a person, who is entirely unacquainted with the nature of this service, to be put at the head of an expedition in America. We will further suppose that he had made the dispositions usual in Europe for a march, or to receive the enemy; and that he is then attacked by the savages. He cannot discover them, tho' from every tree, log or bush, he receives an incessant fire, and observes that few of their shot are lost. He will not hesitate to charge those invisible enemies, but he will charge in vain. For they are as cautious to avoid a close engagement, as indefatigable in harassing his troops; and notwithstanding all his endeavours, he will find himself surrounded by a circle of fire, which, like an artificial horizon, follows him everywhere.

In such circumstances, against such an enemy, the outcome was inevitable. Indian warriors fled whenever the troops attacked, only to return with equal agility and vigor, wearing the soldiers down, until their morale drooped and their strength finally failed them. This, Smith stressed, was not "an imaginary supposition" but the actual experience of troops who had fought against Indians. Published twenty-five years before St. Clair's defeat, Smith's account is almost an exact description of the tactics the Indians employed that day and their effects on the American soldiers.[57]

While St. Clair's intelligence efforts, such as they were, failed, leaving his army to lurch blindly toward the Miami villages, the Indians monitored the American advance.[58] St. Clair's ponderous, noisy, tree-felling army, with its camp followers, bellowing oxen, and lumbering wagons, would have been hard to miss. Scouting parties, the young Shawnee warrior Tecumseh apparently among them, reported the invading army's strength, daily progress, marching formation, supply problems, desertions, and disposition in encampment. The lack of American sightings indicates the effectiveness of the Indian scouting parties, not their absence. In addition to watching, the Indians interrogated those soldiers they captured about the strength and condition of the army.[59] Indian leaders gathered the information, planned their battle strategy, and timed their attack.

St. Clair was convinced that the Indians' inability to provision a large force would always prevent them from keeping an army in the field, but in these circumstances the Indians had the logistical advantage. While St. Clair's army hacked its way through the forest, its progress further retarded by dependence on slow-moving supply wagon trains, mobile Indian warriors sustained by pouches of cornmeal easily covered the distance between their villages—their supply base—and the approaching American force. As James Smith noted, they went into battle naked except for breechcloths, leggings, and moccasins, and so they fought unencumbered. And while many of the men in St. Clair's army were green troops, out of their element deep in Indian country, the Indians, in the words of one officer, were "the veterans of the forest."[60]

Estimates—often conjectures—of the number of Indians at the battle varied. Matthew Bunn, a soldier being held prisoner in the Miami town, said that about 1,500 Indians gathered for a week and then marched out to meet St. Clair's army.[61] Another prisoner, Ensign Samuel Turner from Maryland, who was thought to have been killed in the battle, turned up in Philadelphia in the spring. His story was that, being hotly pursued during the retreat, he had given himself up and the Indians took him to Detroit, "where a private gentleman ransomed him for an inconsiderable sum of money." While he was a prisoner he learned that the Indian force amounted to 1,500 men "under the command of Blue Jacket," with another nine hundred not far away.[62] William Wells said Little Turtle "reviewed his men" and gave them their final orders before marching against St. Clair's army. According to Wells, Little Turtle had 1,400 warriors and divided them into "bands or messes" of about twenty men. Each day four of these "messes" were to hunt for provisions. Wells said there were 1,133 Indians in the army that defeated St. Clair.[63] John Norton heard that 1,050 warriors were already assembled at the Miami towns when they heard the Americans had stopped to build Fort Jefferson and that "the Chiefs, from many reasons, finding it most expedient, determined to go to meet them."[64] Joseph Brant said that about a thousand Indians marched against the American encampment.[65] A witness interviewed by the congressional committee of inquiry into the defeat heard from "a chief at Niagara, who was in the action," that 1,040 Indians fought in the action and that six hundred more who had gathered were off hunting at the time of the battle.[66]

On October 28 the Indian force left the Miami towns and advanced toward the American army.[67] Simon Girty counted 1,040 warriors as they set out to do battle. "The Indians were never in greater Heart to meet their Enemy, nor more sure of Success," he wrote to Alexander McKee; "they are determined to drive them to the Ohio, and starve their little Posts by taking all their Horses & Cattle." Any thoughts of a negotiated settlement were "now laid aside," said McKee; he anticipated that "a few days will determine the affairs" of the American army and the western Indians for the season.[68] Before they set out, Indian warriors prepared themselves for battle by fasting, abstaining from sexual intercourse, and strictly observing rituals that gave them access to spiritual power, and they sang prayers "at every stage of a war expedition." John Norton said the woods echoed with their war songs as they marched.[69] The Indian warriors were not only better prepared physically and militarily than the Americans; they were better prepared spiritually for the violence of combat.[70]

William May, a deserter who was captured by the Indians the following year and was saved from death by Girty, said that Girty commanded the Wyandot in the battle. He also heard that a Captain Brumley of the Fifth British Regiment was in the battle "but did not learn that he took any command," and that another captain named Sylvly of the same regiment was on his way with three hundred Indians but did not reach the battlefield in time to participate. Girty told him that there were 1,200 Indians at the battle, but three hundred were taking care of the horses and did not take part. In other words, nine hundred fought out of a total force of 1,500.[71] Another count, attributed to Indian sources, had 1,200 Indians in the battle, mainly Miami and Lake Indians; that another six hundred arrived the day after the battle, and three hundred more were out hunting to supply the rest.[72] James Wilkinson heard that six hundred of the 1,200 Indians in the battle were Lake Indians, "by which I suppose they mean the Chipeways and Hurons."[73] Another Indian, known as Billy, said no more than six hundred warriors were engaged.[74]

Covering about fifty miles in four days, the Indians reached the upper Wabash River and waited for St. Clair's army. Scouts reported that the Americans were encamped on the evening of November 3 within a few miles of the Indians' position. The Indians had held back and harried Harmar's army; they decided to launch a full-scale assault on St. Clair's army. They advanced until they were about two and a half miles from the American camp and then stopped, about two hours before sunset. George Ash, who had been captured in 1780 when he was about ten years old and was raised as a Shawnee, was with the Indian army. Later in life he recalled what happened next: "'It was too late,' they said, 'to begin the play.' They would defer the sport till next morning." After dark Blue Jacket called the chiefs around him and invoked spiritual assistance in the battle to come. "Our power and our numbers bear no comparison to those of our enemy, and we can do nothing unless assisted by our Great Father above," he said. As the snow fell around him, Blue Jacket prayed "that tomorrow he will cause the sun to shine out clear upon us, and we will take it as a token of good, and we shall conquer."[75]

Judging by the number of sightings and shootings during the night, Blue Jacket and Little Turtle had a hard time keeping all the warriors in line. About fifty Potawatomi deserted but the rest of the Indians were up and ready to march an hour before sunrise. It had stopped snowing. The Indian army advanced until they could see St. Clair's campfires. "The General Blue Jacket began to talk, and to sing a hymn, as Indians sing hymns," said Ash. John Norton heard that "before the dawn the War Chiefs began to exhort the Warriors to prepare for battle."[76]

At the Battle of Point Pleasant in 1774, the Shawnees had attacked at dawn in a crescent formation; Blue Jacket employed the same tactics now. According to Norton, the lead in the battle "was given to the Shawanons." Brant and Norton both said that the Shawnee, Delaware, and Miami under Blue Jacket, Buckongahelas, and Little Turtle occupied the center of the crescent; the Ottawa, Ojibwa, and Potawatomi formed the left flank; and the Wyandot and Iroquois took the right flank.[77] (The Iroquois were mainly Mingo. Brant himself was not there; according to McKee, a chief named Du Quania and ten warriors "were the only Six Nations Indians who came to the assistance of their friends.")[78] Deployed in half-moon formation on the edges of St. Clair's encampment, the warriors waited for daylight.

CHAPTER 5

The Battle with No Name

A COUPLE OF MONTHS AFTER HIS VICTORY over Napoleon at the Battle of Waterloo, the Duke of Wellington wrote, famously, "The history of a battle is not unlike the history of a ball. Some individuals may recollect all the little events of which the great result is the battle won or lost, but no individual can recollect the order in which, or the exact moment at which, they occurred, which makes all the difference as to their value or importance."[1] St. Clair's defeat was no Waterloo, where some 140,000 soldiers clashed in a sea of carnage, and it was certainly no ball, yet Wellington's comment applies well to the struggle that occurred on the banks of the Wabash on November 4, 1791. Even so, the action that day was so congested that most of the survivors' accounts are in substantial agreement, and their individual, piecemeal experiences provide a composite picture of how the battle unfolded.

"The violence of combat," Karl Marlantes recalls from Vietnam in his book *What It Is Like to Go to War*, "assaults psyches, confuses ethics, and tests souls."[2] For the ordinary soldier, John Keegan writes, battle "takes place in a wildly unstable physical and emotional environment." Battles involve leadership, courage, duty, and trying to maintain order in a context of extreme violence, but they also always involve fear and disintegration, "for it is towards the disintegration of human groups that battle is directed." How a soldier behaves in the heat of battle depends on a contest between his discipline, courage, and sense of duty or loyalty and his natural instinct for self-preservation. Military training tries to ensure that the former keep the latter in check. When order breaks down and soldiers seek safety in flight, they often, ironically, expose themselves to the greatest immediate danger until they put distance between themselves and their enemies. Panic spreads, other soldiers are swept up in the scramble for safety, and in their flight they act more like a crowd than a military unit. Men with little or no military training are more likely to run than are regulars, but—as at Waterloo, where the battle-hardened veterans of Napoleon's elite Imperial Guard faltered in the teeth of devastating British musket fire and then fled in disarray—none is immune to the possibility.[3] In the end, observes the historian James Wright, "combat is about simply staying alive."[4]

Poorly trained, badly provisioned and equipped, dispirited by a month of frustrating delays, tedious marches, cold wet weather, desertions, and dissension, St. Clair's troops confronted an enemy Ebenezer Denny described as "brought up from infancy to war, and perhaps superior to an equal number of the best men that could be taken against them."[5] Discounting the militia, officers' servants, and guards who immediately dispersed, Winthrop Sargent reckoned that once the battle got under way the effective American fighting force was reduced to 1,080 "raw and undisciplined troops, ignorant totally of the Indian and indeed all other mode of fighting." With the exception of the Second Regiment, the army consisted of new recruits who had signed up for only six months. Even the Second was "but of the moment, just brought into the field, without time for instruction and never having fired even a blank cartridge." In the circumstances, said Sargent, "we entertained an unequal war and long maintained the contest, too soon rendered doubtful by the Indian mode of fighting."[6]

The 1,100 or so regulars and levies of the main army were camped in two parallel lines, about seventy yards apart, on elevated open ground overlooking the river and surrounded by woods. The right wing of the army, commanded by Richard Butler and comprising the battalions of Major Thomas Butler, Major John Clark, and Major Thomas Patterson, formed the first line, closest to the river. The left wing, commanded by Lieutenant Colonel William Darke and consisting of Major George Bedinger's Virginia Battalion, Major Henry Gaither's Maryland Battalion, and the Second Regiment under Major Jonathan Heart, formed the second line. Captain William Faulkner's company of Pennsylvania riflemen were on the right flank, together with a troop of horse under Captain Alexander Truman. Captain Jonathan Snowden's dragoons were on the left flank. The Kentucky militia were camped across the creek, about three hundred yards ahead of the main army.[7] Among them was Captain Samuel Wells, the elder brother of William Wells, who was in the Indian army. During the night the militia were aware of Indians in the woods but, like St. Clair, assumed they were scouts looking for the chance to steal a horse or lift a scalp. "Certain it is," recalled one Kentucky ranger, Robert Bradshaw, "we were not prepared for what took place."[8]

Most of the soldiers heard the Indians before they saw them. On November 4 the troops paraded at the usual time, before daybreak. Lieutenant Colonel Darke ordered the officer of the day to dismiss the troops "as the men suffered from the cold."[9] They had been dismissed from the lines "but a few minutes, the sun not yet up, when the woods in front rung with the yells and fire of the savages." Sargent said that the firing was preceded for about five minutes by "the Indian yell, the first I ever heard; not terrible, as has been represented, but more resembling an infinitude of horse-bells suddenly opening up to you than any other sound I could compare it to." "A Gentleman in the Quarter Master's department," writing to his friend afterward, said it was "a confused kind of noise." Some thought it was the howling of wolves; others packhorse bells; and only a few "deemed it to be the war-yell of Indians." The militia scarcely had time to return a shot before they turned and fled for their lives with the Indians hot on their heels. Dashing "helter skelter" into the main camp, they threw Butler's battalion and part of Clark's into disorder and confusion.[10] Lieutenant Colonel William Oldham, who had been commander of the Kentucky militia a little more than a month, was killed trying to stop the flight. (Oldham had moved to Kentucky with his friend Hayden Wells, who had been killed by Indians, and would have known Hayden's son, William, who was now in the Indian army.)[11] Butler's line steadied, and the Indian charge checked for a moment, "but they were soon rallied by their leader on horseback, dressed in a red coat."[12] This may have been a Mississauga Ojibwa chief from Canada named Wapacomegat, who, according to Henry Rowe Schoolcraft, led the Indians in the rout of the militia.[13]

"That battle always reminded me of one of those thunder storms that comes up quickly and rapidly," the wagoner Thomas Irwin recalled in later life. Firing from the front line checked the Indians' advance, but when the Indians reached within about sixty yards of the creek, Irwin estimated, the wings of their crescent "wheeled to the right and left with a view to surround the army, which they done in a very short time."[14] The Indians executed the move so rapidly that

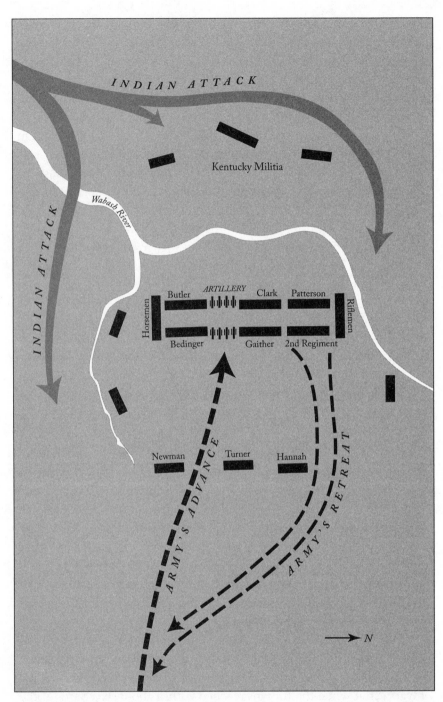

Map of the battle based on sketches by Arthur St. Clair, Ebenezer Denny, and Winthrop Sargent. (Map drawn by Meg Calloway.)

Sargent thought the Americans "were completely surrounded at the time of the first onset upon the militia."[15] Captain John Buell was not in the action himself but heard from other officers who were that "in an instant, the Indians were like a swarm of bees round the whole camp, and the action became general."[16] St. Clair said they enveloped the camp on the right and left flanks, and in "a few minutes, our whole camp, which extended above three hundred and fifty yards in length, was entirely surrounded and attacked on all quarters." He thought his army was overpowered by numbers but on reflection acknowledged that he based his judgment only on the impact of the Indians' firepower.[17] Moving from tree to tree, Indian marksmen made deadly work among the soldiers, who found themselves compressed into a small area. "The Indians seemed to brave everything," recalled Denny, "and when fairly fixed around us they made no noise other than their fire, which they kept up very constant and which seldom failed to tell. . . . It appeared as if the officers had been singled out." Firing from "behind every tree, stump and log," the Indians "cut our men down at a shocking rate," recalled Lieutenant Daniel Bradley.[18] The site became literally a killing field.

Once a battle plan was implemented, Indian warriors tended to fight individually and independently rather than rely on orders from their chiefs. Since the introduction of firearms, "they no longer fight in close bodies, but every man is his own general," said Sir William Johnson. "They say of themselves that every one of them is like a king and captain, and fights for himself," said one missionary.[19] But they understood that European and American soldiers depended on constant orders from their officers, so their immediate strategy was to take out the officers and the artillery, and they did both with deadly efficiency. The rate of casualties among the men and the loss of officers shattered morale as well as the soldiers' ability to fight as a cohesive unit.[20] In the chaos and confusion of the battle the "discipline" that St. Clair assumed would prevail over "undisciplined savages" proved lethal for his troops. The artillery made a lot of noise but had little impact. Located at a higher elevation than their attackers, the gunners fired high, crashing canon shot through tree branches. William Wells was reputedly given the task of silencing the guns, and his Indian sharpshooters, "creep[ing] up on their Bellys," systematically eliminated their crews. Darke said the Indians grew so bold that they came "to the very Mouths of our Cannon." Major Ferguson was one of the first to fall, and thereafter the artillery fire lacked any coordination. Before long all the artillery officers were dead, except Captain Mahlon Ford, who was badly wounded, and the crews cut off, although not before they spiked the guns by breaking off the tips of bayonets in the firing touch holes. Less than ninety minutes after the start of the action, the artillery fell silent.[21]

The hollow square where the noncombatants were collected between the army units was a scene of confusion. Women and children were in a state of shock. "Some were running to and fro, wringing their hands and shrieking out their terrors," wrote Robert Bradshaw; others stood speechless, like "statues of horror," with their hands clasped and their eyes fixed on the battle raging around them. Some women knelt in prayer, "calling on Heaven for protection"; others clung to each other "sobbing and groaning," and some "lay upon the ground as if dead."[22]

St. Clair had stumbled out of bed when the attack began. With no time to dress in his uniform, he pulled on an old hooded cloak and a three-cornered hat, drab attire that concealed his rank from the Indian marksmen and may have saved his life. Even so, two horses were killed, preventing him from mounting.[23] Instead he set off on foot to the battle, adrenaline presumably giving some temporary relief from the pain of his illness.

"Finding no great effect from our fire, and confusion beginning to spread from the great number of men who were falling in all quarters," wrote St. Clair after the battle, "it became necessary to try what could be done with the bayonet."[24] The American forces launched a series of bayonet charges—St. Clair, on foot, led a countercharge that gained ground on the left flank, and Darke led two charges—but each time the Indians melted before the advancing soldiers and then, as the bayonet charge lost momentum, resumed their fire. "They seemed not to fear anything we could do," wrote Denny. "They could skip out of the reach of the bayonet and return, as they pleased."[25] Captive Oliver Spencer, who was not at the battle but heard about it from prisoners afterward, said "the Indians fled at first before their charge as if to draw them out some distance from their lines, then suddenly turning upon them, compel[led] them to retreat, leaving their wounded to certain destruction."[26] Butler's and Clark's battalions made several bayonet charges, but always with the same result and sustaining heavy losses, especially among the officers, which, noted St. Clair, "with some raw troops, was a loss altogether irredeemable." Major Heart and every officer in the Second Regiment fell except for three, and Butler himself was wounded.[27] Captain Samuel Newman was also severely wounded during one of the charges, as was Captain Joseph Darke, William Darke's son.

After their bayonet charges, only about thirty men remained standing in Lieutenant Colonel Darke's command. One of them, Jacob Fowler, found that even when he shot an Indian, his bullets lacked sufficient force to bring the man down. The cock of his rifle lock wore loose, and he had to pick up another gun. His fingers were so numb with cold that "at times I had to take the bullets in my mouth and load from it." He shot an Indian through the hips, and as the wounded man tried to crawl away on all fours, Darke "made at him with his sword and struck off his head."[28] Winthrop Sargent later described Darke as a brave man but no general: "In action, he is most passionately intent on Indian-killing himself, but inadequate to performing it by battalion, or even by platoons."[29]

Elsewhere resistance and discipline broke down. Many wounded were taken into the center for safety. With their officers falling around them, many of the men also sought momentary refuge in the center of the field, "and no exertions could put them in any order even for defense."[30] According to Sargent, the women "drove out the skulking militia and fugitives of other corps from under wagons and other hiding places by firebrands and the usual weapons of their sex."[31] Avoiding the American bayonet charges, the Indians twice during the battle got into the American encampment, plundering the tents and wagons and scalping the dead and dying.[32] Among their victims was Samuel Newman's son, who had joined his father after being hospitalized at Fort Washington and had viewed the upcoming campaign with trepidation.

As the American lines crumbled and fell back, the Indians squeezed them closer together, subjecting the huddled soldiers to a vicious crossfire. "At length our men got into universal confusion," reported an account reprinted in the *Columbian Centinel*. "The Indians in the meantime were contracting their circle, and keeping up a constant fire both with rifle and smooth bored muskets."[33] Soldiers gathered in knots, "having nothing to do but to present mere marks for the enemy. They appeared stupefied and bewildered by the danger." Some broke into the officers' tents and devoured the breakfasts the officers had left when they were called to the battle; some of these men were "shot down in the very act of eating." The ground was covered with the dead. Recalling the scene fifty-five years later, eighty-two-year-old

Jacob Fowler remembered, "The freshly-scalped heads were reeking with smoke, and in the heavy morning frost looked like so many pumpkins through a cornfield in December."[34]

Richard Butler was wounded again in the side, this time severely. Captain Slough saw him being carried in a blanket. Four soldiers moved him to the center of camp, placed him in a reclining position supported by knapsacks, and gave him a loaded pistol. Butler was killed and scalped after the army retreated. The Shawnee knew Butler well. He had traded with them, married a Shawnee woman, and bullied the Shawnee delegation into accepting the American terms at the Treaty of Fort Finney five years before. John Norton said a Shawnee warrior tomahawked Butler. Other sources said the Indians cut his heart out and divided it into as many pieces as there were tribes. Another source said Butler's scalp was dried and preserved so that it could be sent to Joseph Brant to chide him and the Six Nations for their absence at the battle.[35]

Facing imminent annihilation, St. Clair ordered a desperate retreat. "Delay was death," recalled Denny; "no preparation could be made; numbers of brave men must be left a sacrifice, there was no alternative." Even then men acted dazed and confused, "incapable of doing anything."[36] Darke said that had it not been for the exertions of the surviving officers, the soldiers would have stood rooted to the spot until they were all killed. A few of the officers put themselves in front, including Captain Alexander Truman, commander of the dragoons. He gathered his surviving horsemen and the men followed, managing to effect a feint and retreat. Charging the Indians as if attempting to turn their right flank, the desperate throng instead made for the road by which the army had arrived the day before. Once the escape route opened up they began a headlong flight. The Indians appeared to have been taken by surprise, but perhaps they saw that it played to their advantage. Darke remembered that "the whole Army Ran to Gether like a mob at a fair." Benjamin Van Cleve, who was caught up in the flight, said the soldiers pressed "like a drove of bullocks." Major Clark and what was left of the West Pennsylvania Battalion did their best to cover the retreat for a time, but as the Indians threatened to engulf the rearguard it became every man for himself. The confusion of the retreat, according to Darke, was "beyond description."[37] Sargent believed that the Indians could have killed them all but must have turned their attention to plunder and to the wounded who had to be left behind. The road for miles was covered with firelocks, cartridge boxes, and regimental accouterments, cast aside by soldiers in flight.[38]

The rout yielded stories of heroism, desperation, and tragedy. As the retreat got under way, some of Samuel Newman's soldiers tried to get their wounded captain on to a horse, but another bullet struck him, killing him instantly.[39] Farther along, a soldier named McDowell, seeing a woman carrying a year-old infant and about to fall by the wayside, picked up the child and carried it. "Afterwards, to save her own life, the woman threw away the child in the snow." The Indians were said to have taken the child to the Sandusky towns and raised it.[40] Benjamin Van Cleve completed the final leg of the flight to Fort Jefferson in company with a Corporal Mott and a woman called Redheaded Nancy. Her real name was Catherine Miller; she was the wife of a soldier in Heart's Second Regiment and had carried her child with her on the campaign and in camp. She and Mott both were in tears when Van Cleve took up with them; "Mott was lamenting the loss of his wife & Nance of an infant child."[41]

Eighteen-year-old William Kennan, who had been in the ranger corps camped ahead of the main army beyond the creek, survived the initial assault by outrunning his pursuers. In flight again, he stopped to pick up a comrade who had a broken thigh. Horsemen galloping past refused to relieve him of his burden, but Kennan managed to carry the wounded soldier several hundred yards. Falling behind, and with the Indians gaining rapidly, Kennan saw they would both be killed unless he dropped his companion, but the man refused to let go and "clung convulsively to his back." Pulling his knife from its sheath, Kennan slashed his companion's fingers and cut him loose. Rolling helplessly to the ground, the man was tomahawked before Kennan had gone thirty yards.[42]

Robert Bradshaw likely embellished his account of his own role in the battle—he maintained that he had coolly picked off nine Indians from behind a tree—but, wounded in the right wrist (he later lost his arm), he joined the flight, hurrying past wounded men calling for help and water. He reached the place where the women and children had collected: "I beheld a large body of Indians busy at their work of slaughter, and I turned off in another direction and ran down to the road."[43] The Indians stuffed dirt into the mouths of some of the dead, a gesture of contempt for land-hungry Americans.

Colonial and American sources regularly condemned torture and indiscriminate killing as a trait of Indian warfare. "Civilized nations" supposedly took prisoners and treated them mercifully. Fear of scalping and torture certainly added to the terror of the fleeing Americans, and their fear was justified, but killing those who cannot fight or have given up fighting has always been commonplace in warfare. French knights at Agincourt slaughtered English boys when they attacked the supply train, and Henry V in turn slaughtered French prisoners. The Duke of Cumberland's troops gave no quarter to Highland Scots after the Battle of Culloden in 1746. European armies regularly sustained heavier casualties fleeing a battle than they had fighting it; the "true horror of battle began" when ranks crumbled and men ran for their lives in "panic fear." The "mood of collective savagery" that overtook soldiers, especially cavalry, once they had the enemy on the run, produced massacre and atrocity on the battlefields of "enlightened" Europe as well as in the forests of North America. Even after the Hague Convention prohibited the killing of enemies who had surrendered, twentieth-century soldiers frequently killed people rather than take the risk or inconvenience of keeping them as prisoners.[44] Indians were known for torturing prisoners, but often they treated them well and adopted them. Colonial and American forces rarely took Indian prisoners.

The retreat started at around 9:30 in the morning, St. Clair later reported, and "continued quite to Fort Jefferson, twenty-nine miles, which was reached a little after sun-setting."[45] Hearing the gunfire of the battle, Major Hamtramck and the First Regiment advanced out of Fort Jefferson. About nine miles up the trail he met the first refugees. They told him that "the army was cut up" and very few had escaped. With the Indians likely coming on, Hamtramck decided against risking either the regiment or the fort, "which at that time had invalids and convalescents only for a garrison." He turned his force around and returned to protect Fort Jefferson rather than advancing to assist what was left of St. Clair's army. St. Clair doubted that the outcome would have been any different had the First Regiment been present at the battle; if it had been, he feared, "the triumph of the enemy would have been more complete, and the country would have been destitute of every means of defense."[46]

According to an Indian account, only two hundred to three hundred of the Indians pursued the fleeing soldiers. After four or five miles they gave up the chase and returned to join their comrades plundering the encampment.[47] "Such a horid scene, I believe, never was acted before in this Country," wrote Daniel Bradley. "Braddock's defeat & Harmar's expedition is not to be compared to this."[48] Some later writers credited Little Turtle with calling a halt to the slaughter, testimony to the then-famous chief's humanity, but, given the chaos of the rout and the limits of his leadership, the explanation is implausible; the story that he stood up on a rock and gave a single cry that commanded his men to cease pursuit is ludicrous.[49]

Sargent, the adjutant-general, tabulated the material losses: six canons, two pieces of iron ordinance, two traveling forges, four ox teams; two baggage wagons with horses, 316 packhorses fully harnessed, as well as horses from the contractor's department, the artillery, and private horses; 384 common tents and eleven marquees; 1,200 muskets and bayonets, with belts, cartridge boxes, and other accouterments; horsemen's swords and pistols; all the army's drums; 163 felling axes, eighty-nine spades, eighty-eight mattocks; armorer's, blacksmith's, carpenters, and tinsmith's tools; two medicine chests, quartermaster's stores, and the provisions of beef and bread—worth in total, he estimated, $32,810 (roughly $840,000 in current dollars).[50] In addition the Indians captured official papers, copies of which made their way to the British Indian department.[51]

The Indians came away from the battlefield carrying scalps and plunder and leading packhorses, some loaded with kegs of wine. A captive, John Brickell, said that the Indians returned to their villages "loaded with the spoils of the army." The Delaware chief Big Cat's share of the spoils included two fine horses, lots of clothing, axes, guns, and four tents, one of which was an officer's marquee, "which made us a fine house in which we lived the remainder of my captivity." Brickell got a soldier's coat to wear. Another captive, Oliver Spencer, saw Indians strutting around wearing the uniforms of dead officers. One Shawnee wore the dress coat of an artillery officer "with silver epaulets on his shoulders and a watch suspended from each ear." John Norton said that most of the Indians returned to their camp after the battle "to divide the plunder and regale themselves with the whisky. Then was the tragic followed by a comic scene. The Warriors, painted red and black, dressed themselves in the Officers' Cloathes, and some in those of the soldiers, putting on their heads the fierce cocked hat, they looked like an American Army in Masquerade."[52]

William May, the American deserter who was captured by the Indians and taken to Detroit the following June, told the British that one of the doctors in St. Clair's army had orders to poison the stores of liquor in case of defeat, but, busy attending to the mortally wounded

Major Ferguson, he had forgotten to do so until it was too late. May said the packhorse masters were all supplied with poison to spike the liquor "on any appearance of being surprised by the Indians."[53] May could have been feeding his captors a line; there seemed to be few other precautions or preparations to indicate that St. Clair feared a surprise attack. At any rate the Indians appear to have consumed the captured liquor with no more than the usual side effects. Military historians sometimes attribute the missed opportunity to destroy the rest of St. Clair's army to the Indians' lack of discipline and propensity for drinking and plundering, but even famously disciplined soldiers indulged in such behavior in the euphoria and exhaustion of victory. Late in the afternoon at the Battle of Prague in 1757 General Zieten found his Prussian hussars "lying gorged and bloated" in the captured Austrian camp and could not rally enough sober men to mount a pursuit of the retreating Austrian army.[54]

The Indians rolled three pieces of artillery into the creek and buried others.[55] May said the Wyandot gave Simon Girty three cannons.[56] The division of the plunder evidently caused some dispute, and the Indians from the Great Lakes "went off very dissatisfied," feeling that they should have received the things that were smallest in bulk and easiest to carry as they had a long way to go. Even so "they had so much plunder as would amply supply them all winter."[57]

The American wounded and stragglers trickled into Fort Jefferson early on November 5. What was left of the U.S. Army reached Fort Washington on the afternoon of November 8. "The officers appear to have lost almost the shadow of command," wrote Sargent, and the soldiers "seemed to have lost all consideration for military propriety and service." By the next day every house in Cincinnati was "filled with drunken soldiers and there seems one continued scene of confusion." The levies "were lost forever" as their terms of service wound down. Ill with gout, St. Clair could do little to restore discipline or stop the further disintegration of his army.[58] An eighteen-year-old ensign named William Henry Harrison, who had arrived at Fort Washington too late to participate in the campaign, got his first image of Indian warfare. It would not be his last.[59]

A couple of days later Piomingo and the other Chickasaw allies returned from their scouting expedition with five scalps. They had missed finding the Indian army and had gone about twenty miles beyond the Miami towns toward Detroit. "Here they fell in with an Indian," Winthrop Sargent wrote in his diary, who, mistaking them for friends, bragged about the recent Indian victory. He said there were only seven hundred warriors engaged in the battle and that his "own arm was quite weary with tomahawking." The Chickasaw shot him dead before he could finish his account.[60]

The losses were staggering. Lieutenant Colonel Darke dismissed the loss of the levies as of no great consequence, although he was full of praise for the courage and sacrifices of his fellow officers.[61] Denny reported thirty-seven officers, 593 enlisted men killed; thirty-two officers and 252 enlisted men wounded. Sargent's papers contain a return of 593 killed and missing out of a total of 1,669 effectives in action and a separate list of the killed and wounded officers. Oliver Spencer gave the same total of killed—630, including thirty-seven officers—with 244, including thirty officers, wounded. There were also packhorsemen, wagon drivers, and others, and he said only three of about two hundred women escaped, about fifty of them killed and the rest taken captive, although his estimates of the female casualties were high. According to Sargent, "We lost about thirty of them, many of whom were inhumanly butchered, with every indecent and aggravated circumstance of cruelty that can be imagined, three only making their escape."[62] One of the captives, Mary McKnight, escaped from the Indians the following summer; by the time she made it to Fort Jefferson fifteen days later she "was reduced to a Skeleton & withal was very ill."[63] Another, Margaret Pendrick, saw her child "tomahawked on the spot" and was taken to the Indian villages at the Glaize, where she "suffered much hardship." She escaped the following October, made it to Detroit after a three-week trek in company with another woman, and returned home by June 1793.[64] Soldier Henry Ball and his wife, Polly Meadows, were captured and taken to the Shawnee village on the Auglaize River. When Oliver Spencer met them there in the summer of 1792, Ball was operating a boat between the village and the Maumee River, perhaps hauling British supplies, and Polly was working as a laundress and seamstress. The Shawnee were letting them work to earn their ransom money.[65]

Indian losses seem to have been relatively light. Billy, "an Indian lad of the Owatanon tribe" whom St. Clair had taken with him from Fort Washington to act as a messenger to the enemy if need arose, apparently said he was in the council house when the war chiefs gathered after the battle to report their respective losses. Each chief lay down "a number of small sticks equal to the number of men they had lost," and "they made a great heap." In the version reported by St. Clair,

Billy thought the number "could not be less than three or four hundred."[66] In another account "Billy the Indian who was with the Army" said the Shawnee lost twenty men, the Miami fifteen, "and all the other nations more in proportion." He was sure from the heap of sticks that more than 160 men were killed.[67]

If Billy's story was true, his numbers were inflated. Alexander McKee said the Indian loss was "trifling"—twenty or twenty-one killed and forty wounded.[68] William Wells said they "had thirty killed, and, it is believed, fifty wounded."[69] John Norton was told the Shawnee lost six men in the battle, the Wyandot four, the Mingo two, Delaware five or six, and the Ottawa a smaller number.[70] Sargent acknowledged that, whatever others might claim, "it is not probable that many of the Indians fell this day." The Indians acknowledged "only thirty killed," although Hamtramck told Sargent that an Indian said he had heard they lost only seventeen. Hamtramck maintained that the Indians' loss was "very inconsiderable."[71] Indians told a Frenchman after the battle that they lost only twelve killed but many wounded.[72] Another Indian report said they lost sixteen killed and about fifteen wounded.[73] Yet another Indian account said they lost fifty-six.[74] George Ash, who sustained a bullet wound in the back of the neck in the battle fighting alongside the Shawnee, said the Indians lost thirty-five dead. Many years later he discovered that he'd had a brother in St. Clair's army, who died.[75] William Wells's brother, Samuel, escaped the battle unhurt.[76]

Sargent returned to the battlefield, "this melancholy theater of our recent misfortunes," on February 1, 1792, to bury the dead, look for the artillery, and recover any remaining ironwork. What he saw forced him to relive the battle in his mind. Looking again at the thick cover afforded by trees and bushes and seeing the deadly effects of the Indians' fire, he realized that, for an army caught by surprise, the site of the encampment had been a death trap. "Although the whole field was covered with twenty inches of snow, yet, at every tread of the horse's feet, dead bodies were exposed to view, mutilated, mangled and butchered with the most savage barbarity; and, indeed, there seems to have been left no act of indecent cruelty or torture which was not practiced on this occasion, to the women as well as men." Sargent and his men buried many of the dead, but not all, "the bodies being frozen down to the ground, quite covered with snow, and breaking to pieces in tearing them up."[77]

CHAPTER 6

Recriminations and Reversal

O N NOVEMBER 9, with the remains of his army back at Fort Washington, St. Clair picked up his pen and resumed writing for the first time since the battle. The handwriting in his journal was cramped and barely legible.[1] He sat down to the "painful task" of sending Henry Knox his report of the disaster, a "melancholy tale" that would be reprinted many times in many newspapers in the months that followed.[2] Eight days later he wrote a second, barely legible account and a private letter defending his actions.[3] He sent the first report "by way of Lexington," the second "by Mr. Denny, by way of the Ohio."[4]

Leaving the "remains of our wretched army" at Fort Washington on November 19, Ebenezer Denny took the dispatches and embarked on the four-hundred-mile journey up the Ohio River to Wheeling. He had made that trip in fifteen days more than once, but winter came early that year, and, with the crew of the fourteen-oar barge rowing against heavy rains and snow, high water, and finally ice, the first leg of the journey took twenty days. Hiring a boy and horses on December 10, he reached Pittsburgh the night of the 11th. He left on the morning on the 13th and, riding night and day, reached Philadelphia late on the 19th, a full month since he had left Fort Washington and forty-five days after the battle. It had been a trip of eight hundred miles. During that time Denny "endeavored to banish from [his] mind, as much as possible, every idea of the slaughter and defeat of the enemy."[5]

The next morning Henry Knox called at his quarters and took him to the president's house, "where we breakfasted with the family, and afterward had much talk on the subject of the campaign and defeat."[6]

Another account, given by or attributed to Washington's private secretary, Tobias Lear, has a weary and mud-spattered messenger interrupting a dinner party at the president's mansion. Leaving the room to receive the dispatch, Washington composed himself and returned to his dinner guests. Only after they had left did he fly into a rage against St. Clair: "BEWARE OF A SURPRISE! You know how the Indians fight us. He went off with that, as my last solemn warning, thrown into his ears." St. Clair had allowed the army to be surprised and cut to pieces. He was "worse than a murderer," and the blood of the dead was on his hands. But then, as the storm passed, Washington supposedly told Lear, "This must not go beyond this room," and, after a long pause, "General St. Clair shall have justice."[7] Washington may have recalled his own words thirty-six years earlier in the wake of Braddock's defeat: "How little does the World consider the Circumstances, and how apt are mankind to level their vindictive Censures against the unfortunate Chief, who perhaps merited least of the blame."[8]

News of the disaster had reached the East before Denny did. A Frenchman who had "fallen in" with some Indians after the battle brought word of the defeat to Vincennes "a few days before" November 27.[9] On November 26 a gentleman who heard about the defeat on his way from "Spanish America" through Kentucky sent Governor Henry Lee a copy of General Scott's circular letter to the county lieutenants of Kentucky together with an extract from the Kentucky *Gazette* and a list of the officers said to be killed and wounded.[10] Thomas Jefferson said the news of the defeat reached Philadelphia the night of December 8.[11] Washington communicated the news to Congress on December 12, providing copies of St. Clair's reports to Knox and a list of the officers who had been killed and wounded.[12]

A week later Washington's message, the reports, and the list were reprinted in broadside form in Boston, and most newspapers reprinted them in full.[13] Accounts of the defeat appeared in many eastern newspapers in December: in the *New York Journal & Patriotic Register* on December 14; in Boston's *Columbian Centinel* on December 17 and 19; in the *Connecticut Courant* on December 19; in the Baltimore *Maryland Gazette* on December 19; the Annapolis *Maryland Gazette* and the *Connecticut Gazette* on December 22.[14] *The Connecticut Courant* got its account from the *Virginia Gazette* in Richmond, which got it from the *Lexington Gazette* in Kentucky. The *Columbian Centinel* also obtained its first news of the event, together with names of the officers thought to have been killed and wounded, from the *Lexington Gazette*. The

Centinel thought it "rather extraordinary the melancholy account of the defeat" would first make its way to Washington by means of a Kentucky paper before St. Clair's official accounts. Two days later the *Centinel* published Washington's message to Congress of December 12; the *Connecticut Gazette* printed it on December 22.[15] News of the battle appeared in the London press the following February.[16]

The reactions began coming in as well. For one resident in northwestern Pennsylvania, St. Clair's defeat constituted retribution. Recalling how American militia in 1782 had murdered Moravian Indians at Gnadenhütten as they knelt praying and singing hymns, he told the missionary John Heckewelder that Harmar's and St. Clair's expeditions had failed "because great blood-guilt lay upon the land and must be atoned for."[17] Few shared his perspective. More typical was the person who wrote from Providence, Rhode Island, that the thoughts of those who had died filled him "with a Thirst for reveng[e]."[18]

As happened in other times and places, the victory of supposedly undisciplined savages over the armed forces of a supposedly civilized nation demanded explanation and rapid reversal.[19] The United States in 1791 lacked the military and industrial power—in fact after November 4, 1791, it lacked an army—to reverse a defeat of this magnitude as quickly and efficiently as it did in 1876 after the Little Bighorn. Before the nation recommitted itself to subjugating the Indians who blocked its path to empire, there was much debate about how and even if it should continue the war, while newspaper editors, politicians, and army officers conducted postmortems and pointed fingers to assign blame for the disaster.

At Fort Washington three weeks after the battle St. Clair reported some progress on the personal front. "Yesterday, for the first time, I have been able to leave my room, but can neither eat, drink, nor sleep," he wrote Knox; "it is exactly a month since I made the last meal…nevertheless, I am recovering."[20] Others were not: Joseph Darke died of his wounds, and this may have prompted his father to place Major Hamtramck under arrest for his conduct in turning back to Fort Jefferson instead of carrying on to protect and assist what was left of the army. Lieutenant Colonel Darke charged him with "cowardice and shamefully retreating for fear of the enemy." Hamtramck was later honorably acquitted.[21]

John Cleves Symmes had had his differences with St. Clair, accusing him of dictatorial conduct as governor, but he had sent him his best wishes and "most devout prayers" for success and followed the progress of the campaign closely. Frustrated by reports of delay, he nevertheless hoped and prayed for victory over the Indians, who were holding back his plans for settlement and colonization in the Miami Purchase. For the second time in little more than a year he was disappointed. The news was "dreadful," he complained; the defeat was "shameful." Settlers were in great consternation; some had fled across the river to Kentucky, and others were preparing to follow.[22] Symmes redoubled his attacks on the now discredited governor. Other people criticized the government for waging a war to promote the interests of the land speculators, some of whom were members of the government.

St. Clair knew he would be blamed for the disaster and immediately prepared to defend his actions. Pride cometh before a fall, and he had certainly had a fall, he wrote to Knox, but it was not preceded by pride. "I cannot, upon a cool reflection, accuse myself with having neglected any thing which depended on me." Although sick and in pain, he had been in virtually every part of the action. "How I escaped God only knows."[23] St. Clair did not attempt to deflect blame onto his officers and men. He maintained he had no complaints about his troops, except their lack of discipline, "which, from the short time they have been in service, it was impossible they should have acquired." Once they were thrown into confusion, it was very difficult to restore them to order.[24] In St. Clair's view responsibility for the outcome of the battle did not lie with the officers and men who fought it.

General John Armstrong, recognized as something of an authority on Indian warfare since his attack on the Delaware town of Kittanning in 1756, also credited the officers and men with great bravery. He stressed that "the loss of a battle is not always the loss of the cause." But things would have to change. To defeat the Indians they would have to fight like them.[25] Gilbert Imlay, a former Kentucky land speculator now living in England, said much the same. "You will, no doubt, have heard of the defeat of our army," he wrote to a friend. "It is surprising, that the experience of upwards of thirty years warfare with the Indians, should not have taught us before now, that our success or loss in these rencontres was to be expected alone from the abilities or talents of the Commanding Officer." St. Clair was a gallant officer and a gentleman, but he had trusted too much in the comparative strength and discipline of his army and was taken by surprise. What was needed was men who had been accustomed to such perils from infancy and were "practiced in the necessary vigilance, to ward off the effects of that singular prowess of those heroic people."[26] Some survivors of the battle blamed St. Clair for not dispatching scouts or making the troop dispositions that could have prevented the disaster, and there were rumors that the general had been drunk.[27]

As news of the disaster and the magnitude of the losses sank in, the press and Congress debated the defeat, what led to it, and who was responsible. The papers printed rumors of expanding Indian war and accounts of the western settlers' peril at being left exposed to Indian attack. A vocal opposition emerged, as correspondents, often writing under pseudonyms, denounced the Indian war and the government's Indian and land policy. Who stood to profit from the war? asked "ANTI-PIZARO" in the *Boston Gazette*. The Indian war was cruel and unjust. The nation already had more land than it could settle for at least a century, and the government had no more right to march an army into the Indians' country "than Great Britain would have to march a body of troops through the centre of the United States." Was the war being fought to conquer more land "or to serve as a pretence for augmenting the standing army?" Was it to punish the Indians for murdering our settlers, or was it "to promote the interests of jobbers and speculators in the western lands?"[28] Hearing of the Indian victory, and shuddering at the prospect of Indian raids on frontier settlers that winter, Robert Hamilton, a prominent Canadian merchant and an accomplished land speculator north of the border, blamed American land hunger: "The Americans seem possessed with a species of mania for getting lands, which have no bounds. Their Congress, prudent, reasonable, and wise in other matters, in this seems as much infected as the people."[29] There were some in the United States who agreed with him.

In February 1792 readers of the weekly *Carlisle* (Pennsylvania) *Gazette* followed the congressional debate on the bill for frontier defense, with competing views on the merits of militia and regular troops for fighting Indians, the justice and injustice of the Indian war, and the cost and necessity of increasing the size of the army. They read additional accounts of the battle, and they learned that Eli Lewis's poem "St. Clair's Defeat" was available for purchase, "price one eighth of a dollar."[30] Lewis's poem, "A tale, which strongly claims the pitying tear, / And ev'ry feeling heart, must bleed to hear," was one of several renditions in verse memorializing the defeat and the men who fell, including a song, "General St. Clair did command as may remember'd be, / And he has lost nine hundred men in the Western Country."[31]

The *Gazette* that month also published a letter written by Ensign John Morgan to Henry Knox and sent to Mary Butler "as justice due to

General Butler's memory." The issue was St. Clair's disputed claim that Butler had failed to alert him to Captain Slough's report of impending Indian attack on the night before the battle. Major Edward Butler took exception to St. Clair's assertion as a stain on the reputation of his deceased brother and denied that Slough made such a report, a charge that St. Clair refuted.[32] The parties took the controversy and its related correspondence into the newspapers. In an open letter "General Butler's friends" accused St. Clair of impugning a dead hero's reputation and publishing the imputation "to the world." They requested that all printers who had published St. Clair's charge also give a place in their papers for their rebuttal. They demanded that St. Clair make public "every circumstance relating thereto" so they could fully investigate the charge, which they regarded as an attempt to divert blame for his own failures. St. Clair had recommended the Indian war and made the arrangements for the campaign; he lost it by not understanding his enemy, dividing his forces, and making a careless choice for his encampment. "Exculpate yourself from these," they wrote, "and no imputation against General Butler will be necessary."[33]

The defeat and the crisis it produced opened the way for widespread criticism of the Washington administration. Washington had spent most of his adult life speculating in western lands, which was what the war was about, said some critics, and now his military leadership was questioned. In February 1792 William Darke published an anonymous diatribe against Washington for having sent an infirm and bedridden general who had to be carried into battle against "the most active enemy in the world."[34] Henry Knox as secretary of war also came in for scathing criticism. But the opposition increasingly targeted Alexander Hamilton. It was Hamilton who had authorized his crony William Duer to supply the army, and it was Hamilton who wanted the war in order to maintain the national debt and promote his financial policies. As their opposition spread to the administration's Indian policy, some contributors went so far as to defend the Indians' rights and title to the land and questioned the legality and morality of the government's attempts to take it. The government claimed to offer the Indians peace and a fair price for their land, these critics pointed out, but American policy was predicated on the certainty that Indians would and must sell their land; if they refused, they were treated as hostile. Supporters of the administration were quick to respond, and Knox stepped up to defend his policies.[35]

The press became a battleground in which emerging political parties began to take shape over issues thrown into the limelight by the disaster on the banks of the Wabash.[36]

Debates in Congress closely paralleled those in the press. Critics questioned the war as well as the creation and funding of the army, and an emerging Republican faction squared off against Hamilton and the Federalists.[37] In fact Congress was charged with conducting the official postmortem on St. Clair's campaign. St. Clair himself requested an inquiry into his conduct. Washington replied that there were not enough officers of sufficient rank in service to form a court of inquiry. St. Clair intended to clear his name and then resign his command, but Washington asked for his immediate resignation so a successor could be appointed and dispatched to the frontier. St. Clair would have an opportunity "of explaining your conduct in a manner satisfactory to the public and yourself" in the inquiry that Congress initiated. The exchanges between the president and his unfortunate commander were reprinted in the press.[38]

William Branch Giles of Virginia introduced a resolution in the House of Representatives calling on the president to institute an inquiry into the causes of the failure of the campaign "and into such other causes as may, in any manner have been productive of said defeat." This generated "an animated debate, during which party spirit was displayed." Finally Thomas Fitzsimmons of Pennsylvania suggested, and the House agreed, that it was improper to ask the president to institute such an inquiry and that the House should do so itself. Giles's resolution was defeated by a vote of twenty-one to thirty-five, and a second resolution establishing a House select committee to do the same thing passed forty-four to ten. The committee consisted of Fitzsimmons, Giles, John Steele of North Carolina, John Mercer of Maryland, John Vining of Delaware, Abraham Clark of New Jersey, and Theodore Sedgwick of Massachusetts and was authorized to "call for such persons, papers, and records as may be necessary to assist their inquiries."[39] It was the first congressional investigation under the new Constitution.[40]

The Special Committee investigated much more than St. Clair's conduct. The inquiry and report, said Winthrop Sargent, "created great political commotion at the time, and led to animated debates and much newspaper and pamphlet writing of an ardent partisan cast."[41] Many saw it as an opportunity to expose corruption at the highest level, to follow the money and mismanagement to Secretary of War Knox and Secretary of the Treasury Hamilton. When Knox first received St. Clair's report of the battle, he had consoled his general that the misfortune was "one of those incidents, which sometimes happen in human affairs, which could not, under existing circumstances, have been prevented." He assured him that his reputation was "unimpeached." Initial reports indicated the Indian army numbered 2,500; St. Clair had simply been "beaten by superior numbers." The reports proved untrue, and Knox became much less forgiving once accusatory fingers began to point in his direction. A month after Knox wrote his reassuring letter, St. Clair complained to Fitzsimmons that the communications made to the committee by Knox and Quartermaster General Samuel Hodgdon seemed "intended to give a new turn to the inquiry" and to attack him personally.[42]

The committee also raised questions about the authority of the new federal government, the accountability of elected officials, and executive privilege. Concerned about the congressional request for papers and conscious of establishing precedents, Washington consulted his cabinet: Secretary of State Thomas Jefferson, Secretary of the Treasury Hamilton, Secretary of War Knox, and Attorney General Edmund Randolph. They concluded that Congress had every right to conduct an inquiry and request papers from the president, and they recommended that Washington release those papers that "the public good would permit and ought to refuse those the disclosure of which would harm the public good." The notion that the president had the right to withhold documents that might be deemed harmful to the public good was thus established and with it the foundation for executive privilege. Washington ordered Knox to provide the House with the relevant documents and had copies made for the committee.[43] A clerk from the House was allowed to observe as the transcripts were being made to ensure the copies were complete and accurate.

The committee's sessions were public, and the witnesses received $1 per day compensation. St. Clair attended most of the sessions; Knox testified before the committee, and Hamilton presented his papers to the Senate. After "a very minute and laborious investigation extending throughout the session," the committee reached unanimous agreement and communicated its report to the House of Representatives in May 1792. The committee absolved St. Clair of any responsibility for the defeat. It blamed congressional delay in apportioning funds for the campaign, the "want of discipline and experience in the troops," the lateness of the season, and, most of all, "the delays consequent upon the gross and various mismanagements and neglects in the quarter master's and the contractor's departments." Although Washington and Knox were not identified by name, the committee made it clear that, despite delays and deficiencies, St. Clair was under orders from the top to forge ahead with the campaign, orders that were so "express and unequivocal" as to "preclude the commander in chief from exercising any discretion relatively to that object."[44]

Knox and Hodgdon, who had been removed from his position as quartermaster general, tried to shift the blame to St. Clair and submitted a long memorial and additional evidence (as did Duer, in the form of a letter sent from debtor's prison, where he had been since March 1792). St. Clair submitted his own memorial and a point-by-point rebuttal of Knox's statements. The committee tweaked its findings and softened some of its statements but stuck to its conclusions.[45] By this time Hodgdon had taken off for Europe. The committee did not recommend that the House take action against any government official.

Although the committee blamed the defeat on contractor fraud rather than St. Clair, he felt his reputation remained tarnished. "Bye the by, it was a sad Committee," St. Clair complained to Sargent in June 1792. Sedgwick, Fitzsimmons, and Vining were the only fair men on it, and Sedgwick attended only one day, Vining very seldom. "The rest were under the strongest prejudices against me for which I believe I am indebted to the good office of our friend, the J...e [Judge Symmes?], who was very intimate with some of them."[46] He continued to try to restore his reputation. In 1812, by which time he was an old man, he published by subscription his own 275-page *Narrative of the Manner in which the Campaign against the Indians, in the Year One Thousand Seven Hundred and Ninety-one, was Conducted, under the Command of Major General Arthur St. Clair*. It contained his own accounts and defense of his actions, the committee's reports, Knox's memorial, copies of correspondence, and claims for reimbursement for personal monies he expended during the Revolution.[47] The government never reimbursed him.

Others preferred to place the blame for St. Clair's defeat squarely on the shoulders of the nonsoldierly elements in St. Clair's army. Doing so provided the government with the impetus to create a permanent and professional army. It also explained an Indian victory that was otherwise inexplicable. The battle on the Wabash was not the last time discipline broke down and courage failed American soldiers

facing Indian assault. Archaeological evidence from the Little Bighorn battlefield and Native American testimony reveal that Custer's
command disintegrated and that many of his men died singly or in
knots of two or three, hunted down and killed as they ran for their lives.
But none survived to tell the tale (and Indian testimony was ignored
or dismissed until the twentieth century), which left writers, artists, and
filmmakers free to fabricate the myth of Custer's Last Stand, in which
an embattled band of American soldiers fought courageously to the
end atop a hill surrounded by hundreds of savage warriors. It is an
image that has endured, despite compelling evidence to the contrary
and multiple attempts to debunk it. Unlike Custer's men, some of
St. Clair's men survived—their desperate flight succeeded. No heroic
deaths or martyrdom for them. They indulged in conduct unbe-
coming American soldiers because they were *not* American soldiers;
they were the dregs of society called into service by a nation that had
not yet established a professional military. That explained their behavior, and that explained the defeat; both were an aberration.

Knox warned that the Indian victory would cause the Indian alliance to grow, spreading to some of the Six Nations and to the Cherokee and Creek. The prospect of an alliance between the Northwestern
Confederacy and the powerful nations of the South was especially
alarming: "The emissaries of the hostile Indians will be disseminated
among all the Southern tribes. Councils will be held, and the passions
of the young men will be inflamed with the tales of prowess and glory
acquired by the hostile Indians."[48] An account by "a gentleman from
Lake Erie" that made its way into the press reported that about six
hundred Indians from Lower Canada had joined the general confederacy at the Miami towns and that Blue Jacket and Egushaway now
commanded somewhere between four thousand and five thousand
men, "about four times the number which defeated Gen. St. Clair."
Amply supplied by the British at Detroit, they were "waiting for the
Americans to pay them another visit."[49]

Frontier inhabitants were alarmed—"exceedingly and justly alarmed,"
Knox told St. Clair.[50] The destruction of the army, following on the
heels of Harmar's ineffectual campaign, reaffirmed westerners' concerns that the federal government lacked the resolve to bring order in
the West.[51] Residents of Pittsburgh warned the secretary of war that
after the Indian victory "there can be no doubt but the enemy will
now come forward, and with more spirit, and greater numbers, than
they ever did before, for success will give confidence, and secure allies."

Pittsburgh was defenseless, without garrison, arms, or ammunition, and if it was lost "the whole country is open to them, and must be abandoned." Inhabitants of Westmoreland, Washington, Fayetteville, and Allegheny counties wrote to the governor of Pennsylvania expressing similar concerns about their own defenseless situation in the face of impending Indian attacks. Representatives from Ohio and Harrison counties expressed their fears to the governor of Virginia. Washington ordered troops to Fort Pitt to be posted along the Upper Ohio, and county lieutenants were authorized to pay experienced woodsmen to serve as scouts and patrols.[52]

Washington consistently maintained that the only irreparable loss of St. Clair's defeat was the men who died there. Everything else, he told Congress, could be recovered. The government must stay the course in its policies toward the Indians and its efforts to take control of the West and its lands.[53] He was proved right, but for the moment the United States was in a precarious position. The British government now hoped to push for turning the Northwest Territory into a neutral Indian barrier state. Such a state would be independent of Britain and the United States and closed to further settlement but open to trade; it would protect Indian lands from American expansion, protect Canada from both American aggression and Indian resentment, and help maintain British trade among the Indian nations.[54] At Detroit, Alexander McKee was elated by the Indian victory. "The astonishing success of a few Indians, not more than 1040, who have opposed and destroyed, the whole American force, will most probably cause a more Numerous collection of Indians at that time than was Ever before known in this part of the Country." The Indians now needed supplies to keep them together in one place, and Britain should supply them. McKee hoped that "the Americans, now convinced of the difficulty of Subduing a Brave & warlike race of People, may listen to the Voice of Equity and Reason and Establish a firm and lasting Peace on the Principles of natural Justice & Humanity."[55]

IT WAS NOT TO BE. The concentration of Indian population put a strain on food sources, and river flooding destroyed many crops. By the winter following their great victory the Shawnee, Delaware, and Miami were short of corn and their families were starving. Warriors dispersed to go hunting, but deep snow hampered their efforts. The Indians turned to the British to help feed and provision them. "We are of ourselves a thousand Warriors exclusive of our Wives, Children and Old men," the Indians at the Maumee River told Matthew Elliott in May. The Indians had come to Britain's assistance in the Revolutionary War; it was now time for the British to assist the Indians and alleviate their distress.[56] The Indians left their towns on the Maumee, now deemed unsafe, and moved closer to Detroit, but escaped captives reported that "they live very poor—can scarcely get provision to keep them alive."[57]

At the same time, cracks began to appear in the Indian confederacy. The loose and fragile coalition of many nations that had united to resist the American invasion had less unity or unanimity of purpose once that assault was repulsed. The U.S. government set to work to exploit the divisions and undermine the confederacy. Messages were sent to the Six Nations and the southern Indians, assuring them that the United States would now redouble its efforts and crush the hostile tribes; the Iroquois would do well to remain "fast friends." The government tried to enlist the Six Nations as mediators between it and the western tribes. In March it brought a delegation of almost fifty chiefs to Philadelphia, where they received a dignitaries' welcome. Washington and Knox sent Joseph Brant a flattering invitation, which brought him to the nation's capital a month later. Lacking an army, the commander-in-chief and the secretary of war worked to preserve the alliance with the Six Nations and urged Brant and the Iroquois to use their influence to broker a peace.[58]

Knox also dispatched Captain Peter Pond and William Steedman to Niagara. The United States wanted peace, but that peace "must not be inconsistent with the national reputation. We cannot ask the Indians to make peace with us, considering them as the aggressors: but they must ask peace of us. To persuade them to this effect," Knox told Pond and Steedman, "is the object of your mission." When they reached Detroit, Knox instructed, they were to

assume the characters of traders with the Indians—a business Mr. Pond is well acquainted with. Mix with the Miami and Wabash Indians. Find their views and intentions, through such channels as your discretion shall direct. Learn the opinions of the more distant Indians. Insinuate, upon all favorable occasions, the humane disposition of the United States; and, if you can by any means ripen their judgment, so as to break forth openly, and declare the readiness of the United States to receive, with open arms, the Indians, notwithstanding all that is past, do it.

The agents were also to try to find out what numbers and tribes had fought in the battle; what losses they sustained; how many prisoners they took and what became of them; what they did with the canons and other plunder; what their intentions were for the next year; the numbers in the alliance; and how they were provisioned and armed.[59] In April Colonel John Hardin and Major Alexander Truman set off to the western tribes with a message from Knox to disabuse them of the idea that the United States wanted to take their lands and drive them out of the country. Quite the contrary: it wanted to impart to them the blessings of civilized life, teach them to cultivate the earth, raise domesticated animals, live in comfortable homes, and educate their children. Transforming Indian men from hunters to farmers became part of the American strategy of separating Indians from lands they would then no longer need in such quantity, but in Knox's message the stated purpose was to enable the Indians "ever to dwell upon the land." The Indians should not be fooled by their victory into thinking they could escape ruin if the war continued. They should send chiefs to Philadelphia, where chiefs of the Six Nations were currently having talks, and make peace.[60] In May, Washington appointed Rufus Putnam to the rank of brigadier general, and in company with the Stockbridge Mahican chief, Hendrick Aupaumut, Putnam set out with a similar message for the tribes that were going to meet in council at the Miami River and "to convince them that the United States require none of their lands."[61]

Truman and Hardin never made it to the western tribes. Hardin had survived Harmar's campaign, and Truman had escaped St. Clair's defeat with only a leg wound, but now Indians killed and scalped them both. Apparently Hardin had had a premonition of his death when he was selected for the mission because he said the Indians "had long hated and feared him."[62] Putnam concluded that there was little prospect of making peace with the northwestern Indians and headed instead to Vincennes to try to detach the lower Wabash tribes from the confederacy. In September he met in council at Vincennes with Jean Baptiste DuCoigne, chief of the Kaskaskia, and thirty chiefs and several hundred Piankeshaw, Kickapoo, Wea, and other Wabash tribes. Putnam employed William Wells as an interpreter. It was less than a year since Wells had fought St. Clair's army, and he gave "good, thorough, & reliable accounts of all that has happened there."[63] Putnam returned the women and children captured by Scott the previous year, made peace offerings, and accepted the chiefs' position that they opposed any future settlements north of the Ohio but would tolerate the existing ones. But the chiefs who signed the treaty were not committed members of the Indian confederacy. A delegation of sixteen chiefs accompanied by the missionary John Heckewelder traveled to Philadelphia to meet with Washington. The Senate rejected the treaty the following year.[64]

In the meantime the United States was rebuilding its armed forces, which had been reduced to a shambles. The administration's proposal to increase the army to five regiments revived anxieties about a standing army, sparked a heated debate in Congress, and generated disagreement about the relative strengths of regular troops and militia for Indian fighting. When Jefferson first heard of St. Clair's defeat, he hoped it would "have the effect of preventing the enlarging of our army of regulars and inducing us to confide more in Militia operations," but George Hammond, Britain's first envoy to the United States, observed that the militia's conduct "must render any future confidence in them absolutely impossible."[65]

Knox drew up a plan for an army of more than five thousand to be enlisted for three years. Militia, especially mounted militia, might be called up "for sudden enterprises, of short duration," but in general they were "utterly unsuitable to carry on and terminate the war in which we are engaged, with honor and success." Man for man, regular troops were the equal of militia, but when one took into account "the obedience, the patience, the promptness, the economy of discipline, and the inestimable value of good officers, possessing a proper pride of reputation, the comparison no longer holds." On March 5, 1792, Congress passed an "Act for making farther and more effectual Provision for the Protection of the Frontiers of the United States." The two infantry regiments and the artillery battalion then in existence were to be completed to full strength. Three additional regiments of 960 men each were authorized, to be enlisted for a term not exceeding three years and to be discharged "as soon as the United States shall be at peace with the Indian tribes."[66]

Washington and Knox also reorganized the army: instead of a regimental structure with the infantry, cavalry, and artillery in distinct units, they divided the 5,120 men into four sublegions, each of 1,280 men, commanded by brigadier generals. Each sublegion was organized into two battalions (eight companies) of infantry, one battalion (four companies) of riflemen, one company of artillery, and one troop of dragoons. Like the French adoption of divisions at about the same time, the reorganization into sublegions enhanced tactical flexibility and represented a departure from the eighteenth-century practice of regarding the entire army as a single tactical unit. The act also outlined the size and composition of the general staff, the regimental staff, the artillery battalion staff, and the dragoon squadron staff. The title of the act suggested that it did little more than augment American forces on the frontier, but "in fact it completely overhauled and reorganized the startlingly inadequate United States Army." Washington was not willing to abandon combined regular-militia operations, and the act also authorized the president to call into service militia cavalry and to employ Indian scouts as he saw fit. Nevertheless the burden of fighting the war shifted from irregular soldiers to a new and more professional military. The government appropriated $1 million to fund the new army, which received more supplies and better training than either Harmar's or St. Clair's armies.[67]

In May 1792, despite misgivings about the value of militia, Congress responded to St. Clair's defeat and the threat of Indian attacks on the frontiers by passing two militia acts. The first gave the president the power to draft state militias into a federal force on his own authority "whenever the United States shall be invaded, or be in imminent danger of invasion from any foreign nation or Indian tribe" and when necessary to ensure that the laws of the United States were "faithfully executed," as prescribed in the Constitution. The second provided for the organization of state militias, requiring every able-bodied free white male citizen of the states between eighteen and forty-five to enroll and arm himself with "a good musket or firelock, a sufficient bayonet and belt, two spare flints, and a knapsack, a pouch, with a box therein, to contain not less than twenty four cartridges." Although the Militia Act initially required consent of a federal judge, Congress later removed that restriction, giving the president "all-but-unfettered powers" to raise troops and send them into combat without a declaration of war by Congress.[68]

After considering the options available, including General Charles Scott and James Wilkinson, Washington appointed General Anthony Wayne to build the new army and to finally get the job done in Indian country. Wayne made it clear that he would accept the command only if the army was his to command as he saw fit, subject to supervision only by the secretary of war and the president.[69] Despite his nickname, "Mad Anthony," which he had earned during the Revolution, he set about the task of translating a paper army into an actual army with methodical determination. He recruited and trained his soldiers to be an effective fighting force in Indian country, a process that involved, among other things, staging war games and sham Indian attacks.[70] Expected "to efface the Stain, which the late defeat has cast upon the American Arms," Wayne was determined not to repeat St. Clair's mistakes.[71] Having seen what happened when St. Clair was ordered "to advance prematurely," Wayne accepted his appointment with "an express stipulation" that he should not be required to march until his army was fully prepared.[72] Unlike St. Clair, he would not be caught off-guard. "Our Indian guides, scouts, spies & Cavalry, who shall always patrol & hover widely round me will not suffer the savages to advance undiscovered, nor will I wait their attack," he assured Knox.[73] Wayne would follow the route taken by St. Clair's troops,

Engraved copper portrait of General Anthony Wayne from the original painting by Charles Willson Peale. Courtesy of the Ohio Historical Society (OHS-AL00709).

from Pittsburgh down the Ohio to Fort Washington, and then up the Miami Valley. But the United States had opted to negotiate, and whether the army's preparations were intended to induce the Indians to make peace, or the peace overtures were merely a pretense, Wayne was ordered to await their outcome. Knox kept his general regularly apprised of developments on the diplomatic front, but Wayne fretted at being held in check.

While Wayne fretted, Blue Jacket and other Indian emissaries traveled to the Great Lakes and the Mississippi, calling on the western nations to join the confederacy and gather at the Glaize.[74] In the late summer of 1792 Indian delegates assembled there for a great council at which the noted Seneca orator Red Jacket and an Iroquois delegation presented an American peace offer. The captive William May said there were 3,600 warriors. Cornplanter said "there were so many nations that we can not tell the names of them."[75] In addition to Shawnee, Miami, Delaware, Wyandot, Ottawa, Ojibwa, and Potawatomi, there were Sauk and Fox from the upper Mississippi; some Creek and Cherokee from the South; Conoy, Nanticoke, and Mahican from the East; and Iroquois deputies from the Six Nations in New York and the Seven Nations in Canada.[76] Alexander McKee and other British Indian agents attended, ostensibly as observers. Hendrick Aupaumut, who like Red Jacket was there as an emissary for the United States, accused McKee of working behind the scenes to influence the outcome of the talks, although, according to Henry Knox, the Indians allowed no white men into their councils except Simon Girty, "whom they considered as one of themselves."[77]

"You were very fortunate that the great Spirit above was so kind as to assist you to throw the Americans twice on their back when they came against your villages, your women & children," Red Jacket told the confederated nations. But now the Americans were holding out the offer of peace; they were willing to compromise and might accept the Muskingum River as the boundary line. "Don't be too proud Spirited and reject it, the great Spirit should be angry with you," Red Jacket advised.[78]

But the assembled Indians saw no need to compromise. "All of us are animated by one Mind, one Head and one Heart," said Buckongahelas, "and we are resolved to stick close by each other & defend ourselves to the last." A Shawnee chief named Messquakenoe, or Painted Pole, spoke for the confederacy. They knew from papers captured at St. Clair's defeat that the Americans intended to build a fort at the Miami towns, then build more forts and "drive all the Indians entirely out of the Country." The allied nations had twice defeated American armies while the Iroquois had sat by doing nothing, and the confederacy could accept no peace unless the Americans agreed to the Ohio River boundary. The Seneca were tools of the Americans. They had come from visiting Washington in Philadelphia and were trying to divide the confederacy. "Speak from your heart and not from your mouth," sneered Painted Pole. He picked up the strings of wampum on which Red Jacket had spoken and threw them at the feet of the Seneca delegation.[79]

Despite his public rebuff, Red Jacket managed to persuade the confederacy to hear American offers at the Rapids of the Maumee the following spring. The western Indians called on Joseph Brant and the Six Nations to be ready to join them at that council. Brant agreed but warned the Shawnee and Delaware to be on their guard: "General Washington is very cunning, he will try to fool us if he can—He speaks very smooth, will tell you fair stories, and at the same time want to ruin us."[80]

After the council at the Glaize, the Shawnee sent red-painted tobacco summoning warriors to prepare for the next American invasion.[81] In the South their emissaries called on the Creek and Cherokee to join the fight and told the Spanish governor at Pensacola "they would be at war with America as long as any of them should live."[82] But while the Shawnee, Miami, and Delaware remained constant in their resolve to fight to halt American expansion at the Ohio River, the Lake nations—the Ojibwa, Ottawa, and Potawatomi— like the Six Nations, were willing to consider a compromise boundary at the Muskingum River if it would help bring peace.[83] And the Chickasaw, as they had during St. Clair's campaign, supplied the United States with scouts to serve against the northern nations; so did the Choctaw.

In April 1793 Anthony Wayne moved his troops down the Ohio from Pittsburgh. His army was at Fort Washington by the first week of May. But even as Wayne was preparing for another invasion, the American peace commissioners Benjamin Lincoln, Timothy Pickering, and Beverly Randolph headed north to meet the Indian nations in council at Lower Sandusky.[84] Wayne suspected that any

peace overtures on the part of the Indians were merely procrastina-
tion. "The Indians are an artful enemy," he wrote Knox.[85] John Graves
Simcoe, lieutenant governor of Upper Canada, felt the same way
about the American peace efforts. "It appears to me that there is little
probability of effecting a Peace," he wrote. "I am inclined to believe
that the Commissioners do not expect it; that General Wayne does
not expect it." In Simcoe's view the peace commission was no more
than a formality before "pre-determined extirpation of the Indian
Americans."[86]

Delegates from sixteen nations assembled at the foot of the
Maumee rapids, where Alexander McKee kept his storehouse, and
held their own discussions before meeting with the American
commissioners. McKee and Elliott attended the councils, and, like
Hendrick Aupaumut at the Glaize council, Joseph Brant accused
McKee of trying to undermine the peace talks. Brant suggested
ceding land east of the Muskingum River but his arguments carried little weight with warriors who felt they were winning the war
for the Ohio country.[87] They suspected that the American commissioners were simply trying to divide the confederacy ahead of the
coming campaign: why was Wayne was advancing if the United
States was serious about making peace? The Indians and the commissioners sent messages back and forth for two weeks, but neither
side was willing to compromise and the talks got nowhere. The
Indians wanted the Ohio River boundary restored and American
settlements north of the river removed. The commissioners replied
that that was out of the question: the Indians had ceded the lands
north of the Ohio by treaty and American settlers were already living there. There could be no peace as long as white settlers were
living on their lands, said the Indians, and they offered a solution:
"We know these settlers are poor, or they would never have ven-
tured to live in a country which has been in continued trouble ever
since they crossed the Ohio; divide, therefore, this large sum of
money, which you have offered to us, among these people ... and
we are persuaded, they would most readily accept of it, in lieu of
the lands you sold them." Factor in the vast sums the government
would save by not having to raise and pay armies to fight the
Indians, and there would be plenty of money to compensate the
settlers for their labor and improvements. The Indians denied the
Americans' claim that the king of England had given the United

States the exclusive right to purchase Indian lands at the Peace of Paris: they had never given the king any such power and they would sell their lands to whomever they wished. All they asked for was "the peaceable possession of a small part of our once great Country. Look back and view the lands from whence we have been driven to this spot," they told the commissioners; "we can retreat no further, because the country behind hardly affords food for its present inhabitants. And we have therefore resolved, to leave our bones in this small space, to which we are now confined." All the tribal delegates except Brant and the Iroquois affixed their marks to the message. The Indians held a war feast, with "the Chiefs of the Shawanoes singing the War Song encouraging the Warriors of all the Nations to be active in defending their Country." They said their English father would assist them and pointed at Alexander McKee.[88]

The American commissioners headed for home, telling Knox that the Indians refused to make peace.[89] The Moravian missionary John Heckewelder, who was present, described the Indians' speech as "both Impertinent and Insolent, & intended to put an end to Treaty Bussiness." He saw British hands at work.[90] "Our negociations with the NorthWestern Indians have completely failed, so that war must settle our difference," said Jefferson. "We expected nothing else, and had gone into the negociations only to prove to all our citizens that peace was unattainable on terms which any one of them would admit."[91] British lieutenant governor Simcoe was vindicated in his cynical assessment of the U.S. strategy. The breakdown of the talks ensured that, in accordance with the pledges made in the Northwest Ordnance, Wayne's invasion would be "just and lawful."

Wayne sent a detachment forward to the site of St. Clair's defeat. They arrived on the ground on Christmas Day 1793, pitched their tents on the battlefield, and slept amid the bones. The next day they buried the remains. "After this melancholy duty was performed," they built a fort and named it Recovery, to mark their repossession of the site from the Indians. A company of artillery and a company of riflemen occupied it for the winter.[92] The British rebuilt Fort Miamis on the banks of the Maumee River and in February the governor of Canada, Sir Guy Carleton, Lord Dorchester, told an Indian delegation in Quebec that Britain and the United States were likely to be at war within the year.[93]

The confederacy chiefs called their warriors back to the fight in the spring. In mid-June, according to an English officer who was in the Indian villages, a council decided "that every white man, either English or French, residing among, or getting their livelihood by the Indian trade, or otherwise, now within the limits of their country shall immediately join the Indian army to defend the territory in which their mutual interest is so greatly concerned." The English had always told them to defend their country, and now the Indians needed their assistance. Food was scarce, and the difficulties of assembling a multinational force resurfaced: Indians from Mackinac and Saginaw who joined the army reportedly "committed depredations and ravished the women in the villages where they had to pass."[94]

On June 30 the Indians ambushed a party of dragoons from Fort Recovery, but when they attacked the fort itself, the American artillery drove them off. After this setback most of the Ottawa and many Ojibwa and Potawatomi returned to their homes in the north. Weakened by the departure of the Three Fires warriors, the Indian confederacy was no longer the force that had destroyed St. Clair's army, and it now faced a different kind of army.

Unlike St. Clair, Wayne led an army that was trained for combat in the Ohio country and organized to win control of the Northwest. The four sublegions, each one comprising a troop of dragoons, a company of artillery, two battalions of infantry, and a battalion of riflemen, combined multiple arms and provided flexibility. Wayne had built "the first United States regular army that could operate without fear of defeat in Indian country."[95] With a disciplined army of 2,200 regular infantry augmented by 1,500 mounted Kentucky militia as rangers under General Scott, he advanced methodically into Indian country. (Meanwhile his second in command, General James Wilkinson, true to character, was waging a campaign of his own, vilifying Wayne in hopes of destroying his reputation and getting the command himself, but Wayne was apparently unaware of his intrigues.) Wayne targeted villages and food supplies, and, as his army marched along the Auglaize River, Indian people abandoned their villages, loading canoes and ponies and hurrying away with their children.[96] In August Wayne built Fort Defiance at the junction of the Maumee and Auglaize rivers and prepared for battle.

As Wayne occupied the area that had been the heart of the confederacy, the confederacy itself was unraveling. American diplomacy had aggravated tribal divisions; disheartened warriors had gone home, and Little Turtle began to talk of peace and may have relinquished his leadership. According to Jonathan Alder, who was living with the Shawnee, Blue Jacket was now "commander in chief."[97] The Indian resistance movement was further weakened on the eve of battle. Blue Jacket drew up his warriors ready for combat on August 19 at a place called Fallen Timbers, after a tornado had left the area strewn with uprooted trees. But Wayne's army halted, and the expected battle did not take place until the next morning, by which time many warriors who had fasted in ritual purification prior to combat had dispersed in search of food.

The Indian army was drawn up in the crescent formation that had overpowered St. Clair's army, with the Shawnee on the left wing. As at St. Clair's defeat, the mounted American volunteers turned and ran under the initial impact of the Indian attack, causing momentary confusion in the ranks behind. But this time the lines steadied and held. Outnumbered and outgunned, the Indians could not withstand the disciplined advance of the American bayonets. Driven from the battlefield, they sought refuge at Fort Miamis, but the British garrison refused to open the gates or to assist them. Britain by now was at war with revolutionary France and could ill afford to get embroiled in a conflict with the United States. The fort's commander and Wayne exchanged angry words but no gunfire.[98] "The conduct of the British Fort dispirited the Confederates much more than the issue of the battle," John Norton reported. They had fought with inferior numbers, in a disadvantageous position, and had not suffered great casualties. They could have fought another day and reversed the outcome of the battle, but the British betrayal "they did not know how to remedy."[99]

The American army burned the villages and cornfields that stretched along the banks of the Auglaize and Maumee rivers. Wayne said he had never "beheld such immense fields of corn in any part of America from Canada to Florida." By putting these fields to the torch, he destroyed "the grand emporium of the hostile Indians of the West."[100] McKee claimed the Americans scalped and mutilated the Indians who were killed in the battle, and then dug up graves, exposed the rotting corpses, and drove stakes through them—"Evident marks," he said, "of their boasted Humanity."[101]

In September Wayne marched his army back up the Maumee River and began building a fort—Fort Wayne—on the site of Kekionga. Colonel Hamtramck was placed in command. Along with other British traders, John Kinzie had his home destroyed by American troops for the second time in four years.[102]

Many younger warriors wanted to keep fighting, and some moved farther west with Tecumseh to continue their resistance. But the older chiefs now made peace. Wearing his scarlet coat with gold epaulettes, Blue Jacket went to meet Wayne. "You see me now present myself as a war chief, to lay down that commission, and place myself in the rear of my village chiefs, who, for the future, will command me," he announced. "We must think of war no more."[103]

At the Treaty of Greenville in the summer of 1795, chiefs from the confederacy that had twice defeated American invasions of Ohio signed away the southern and eastern two-thirds of Ohio, smaller tracts of land in Indiana, and an area that became the site of the future city of Chicago. Little Turtle, Blue Jacket, Painted Pole, and Black Hoof for the Shawnee, Tarhe of the Wyandot, Egushaway of the Ottawa, Buckongahelas of the Delaware, and other band chiefs all made their marks on the treaty. William Wells and Isaac Zane were there as interpreters. "The famous Blue Jacket has pledged himself as a man of honor and as a war chief that he will now make a permanent peace and be as faithful a friend to the United States in future as he has lately been their inveterate enemy," Wayne announced. "The Shawanese, Miamies, and Delawares, who lived at the gate, and who caused all our misfortunes, have wisely buried the hatchet forever," said one of the Potawatomi chiefs.[104] Some of the chiefs who had signed the treaty died in its aftermath. The Potawatomi accused the Americans of poisoning their leaders, but if foul play was involved it was as likely to have been by Indian hands, as the confederacy that had crushed St. Clair finally unraveled in bitter disappointment and recrimination.[105]

Although the war was over, the federal government maintained a military presence in the Ohio country, with forts and garrisons that protected commerce and that needed to be provisioned. Just seventeen days after the Treaty of Greenville ended, Arthur St. Clair, James Wilkinson, Jonathan Dayton, and Israel Ludlow together purchased lands along the Miami River, the supply route to the American forts. Dayton, Ohio, grew into the most important settlement there.[106]

IN 1791 FEDERALISM AND THE ARMY WERE both weak. The destruction of St. Clair's army reaffirmed westerners' concerns that the federal government lacked the resolve to bring order, and they increased the pressure on the government to establish its authority in the West. Three years later the federal government and its new army answered the pleas and prayers of westerners by defeating the Indians and taking title to most of Ohio. But it also asserted its authority in ways westerners had not bargained for. In the fall of 1794, just months after Fallen Timbers, in order to enforce compliance with the tax on whiskey, Washington used the authority granted him by the Militia Act and personally led an army of thirteen thousand militia to quash the Whiskey Rebellion in western Pennsylvania, which rapidly evaporated.[107] "The displays of military power in western Pennsylvania and northern Ohio essentially made the same point," notes the historian Andrew Cayton. "They were tangible demonstrations of the seriousness with which the Washington administration approached the business of securing the West." Whether Indian or white, "lawless banditti" must respect the authority of the United States. At the same time, southerners took note that the federal government had deployed its power regionally, to protect settlers, secure lands, and stimulate national growth in the Northwest Territory rather than the Southwest Territory.[108]

In November 1794 Britain and the United States reached a conciliatory settlement in the Jay Treaty: Britain finally gave up the frontier posts, although Indians were allowed uninterrupted access to British trade north of the border. In the summer of 1795 Thomas Pinckney's treaty with Spain secured for Americans free navigation of the Mississippi, right of deposit at New Orleans, and a border with Spanish Florida at the thirty-first parallel. Coupled with these diplomatic advances, Wayne's victory and treaty confirmed the U.S. hold on the West. As Americans rushed to secure the fruits of their victories, the disaster on the Wabash could be forgotten.

Epilogue

THE TREATY OF GREENVILLE OPENED THE FLOODGATES to emigration and settlement in Ohio. The land rush that the government and land companies had tried to control and channel became a tsunami. The missionary John Heckewelder estimated that some 3,220 settlers, besides troops, lived north of the Ohio in 1793.[1] Jonathan Alder, who was living with the Shawnee, recalled that "white people began to make their appearance amongst us" soon after the treaty was signed. Five thousand Americans lived in Ohio in 1796. Five years later there were forty-five thousand, and in 1803 Ohio became the seventeenth state. By 1810 its population had passed 230,000; by 1820 more than 580,000. In 1830 Ohio had almost 938,000 citizens.[2] Forty years after American Indians had destroyed the American army there, Ohio was the fourth most populous state in the Union; only New York, Pennsylvania, and Virginia had more people.

The fortunes of those who had worked, fought, and connived to produce such a transformation were mixed.

Anthony Wayne did not have long to savor his victory; sixteen months after the Treaty of Greenville he died unexpectedly from complications of gout—St. Clair's disease. Henry Knox retired from government in 1795 and settled in Thomaston, now in Maine, where he continued to speculate in land. He died in 1806, apparently after swallowing a chicken bone that lodged in his throat and became infected.

Many other land speculators, who had bought land at 10 or 12 cents an acre and eagerly awaited the victory over the Indians, were unable to reap the rewards they had longed for. A financial panic in 1792, "the first of its kind in American history," notes Gordon Wood,[3] ruined many prominent speculators. William Duer went bankrupt and went to debtor's prison in New York, where he died in 1799. The Ohio Company and the Scioto group both foundered. Eastern speculators no longer monopolized Ohio country lands. Federal land sales made more public lands available to more people, permanently changing the nature of land speculation in Ohio.[4]

John Cleves Symmes had hoped that a favorable outcome at the Treaty of Greenville would allow him to develop new settlements, but the land rush swept past him. "All Kentucky and the back parts of Virginia and Pennsylvania are running mad with expectations of the land office opening in this country," he informed John Dayton just three days after the treaty was signed; "hundreds are running into the wilderness west of the Great Miami, locating and making elections of land. They almost laugh [at] me full in the face when I ask them one dollar per acre for first-rate land, and tell me they will soon have as good for thirty cents."[5]

In May 1796 Congress passed a law "for the Sale of the Lands of the United States, in the territory northwest of the river Ohio, and above the mouth of the Kentucky river." The law provided for the sale of half the townships in sections of 640 acres at a price of $2 an acre, confirmed the system of rectangular survey established by the 1785 Ordinance, and set up an administrative system to supervise the sale of public lands. Smaller tracts of lands were to be sold at auction at Cincinnati and Pittsburgh. The law made the secretary of the treasury responsible for keeping orderly records of sales of public lands.[6] It reaffirmed that the government would survey the land before it was sold and that there would be no variations in the procedure: "The public survey's definitive pattern of 6-mile-square townships, divided into 1-mile-square sections was established for good."[7] The expanding nation would impose regular and identifiable boundaries and property lines on the patchwork of tribal homelands that was Native America.

Rufus Putnam, who had done so much to initiate the transition, now supervised its completion: in November 1796 he was appointed surveyor general of the United States, with responsibility for surveying the rest of the Northwest Territory. Now that the fighting was over, the fort he had built at Marietta was torn down and replaced by elegant houses, the finest being the Putnam family home. Putnam was removed from office in 1803, but by the time he died in 1824 "the land survey had been pushed westward across Indiana and Illinois and stretched from Lake Michigan south to the Gulf of Mexico."[8]

With land at $2 an acre, the government was still more interested in using public lands to raise revenue than in making those lands available to settlers. But in 1800 Congress passed the Public Land Act, reducing the amount that could be purchased directly from the federal government to 320 acres, with a down payment of only $160, and permitting payment over four years. In 1800 federal land offices opened in Marietta, Cincinnati, Cleveland, and Steubenville. Four years later the minimum purchase was lowered even further, to 160 acres. Even so, buying land on such terms was a risky proposition: farmers who cleared their land and managed to turn a quick profit could pay for their land; those who failed to do so lost it. By 1810 only about 45 percent of Ohio adult males owned land, while 1 percent of its taxpayers held almost 25 percent of its real estate.[9] In 1820 Congress abolished the credit provision but lowered the price to $1.25 an acre and cut the minimum purchase to eighty acres; a settler with $100 could own eighty acres of land.

Arthur St. Clair was permanently discredited and, surely, permanently scarred. "In military affairs," he wrote in 1812, "blame is almost always attached to misfortune: for the greatest part of those who judge, and all will judge, have no rule to guide them but the event, and misconduct is ever inferred from want of success; and the greatest share of praise or blame, according as the event may be, will ever fall upon the principal officer."[10] He continued as governor, but his Federalist vision of an orderly settlement of the territory, and his many measures to ensure it, put him out of step with the times and with the rapidly growing population of the territory. "A multitude of indigent and ignorant people are but ill qualified to form a constitution and government for themselves," he wrote in 1799.[11] His administration was plagued with political squabbles, and he was often an absentee governor; territorial secretary Winthrop Sargent served as acting governor during his absences. Jefferson removed St. Clair from office in 1802, and the government, as we've seen, refused to reimburse him for money he had expended organizing and equipping troops in its service. His later years were marked by poverty. He lived for a few years in Cincinnati, then returned to Pennsylvania to run an iron furnace. After his business failed in 1819 he "eked out a living running a tavern and horse relay station." His name forever linked with the destruction of his army, St. Clair died in 1818.[12]

In 1798 Winthrop Sargent was appointed governor of Mississippi Territory, where his domineering personality and policies continued to alienate people. After the Federalist defeat in the election of 1800, President Jefferson replaced Sargent with William C. Claiborne, a Virginian by birth. Sargent died in New Orleans in 1820.

Ebenezer Denny married in July 1793 and lived with his family around Pittsburgh. In 1804 he was appointed a director of the newly established Pittsburgh branch of the Bank of Pennsylvania, which was subsequently merged into the Bank of the United States. His wife, Mary, died in 1806, leaving three sons—named Harmar, William, and St. Clair—and two daughters, the youngest of whom, an infant, died a few days after her mother. Ten years later Denny was elected the first mayor of Pittsburgh. Taken ill on a visit to Niagara Falls with his daughter in the summer of 1822, he returned home, where he died at age sixty-one.[13]

John Cleves Symmes's life of speculation produced not wealth but poverty. In 1811 his house burned to the ground, consuming all his personal belongings, together with his maps, deeds, mortgages, and account books. He did not know whether the cause was accident or arson. "I know that I came naked into this world and I can but go naked out of it," he consoled himself to his grandson.[14] Overextended, disappointed in his business ventures, and beset by creditors, he also suffered physically. "I am 71 years of age this 21st July, 1813," he wrote in his day book, "but am no longer healthy as usual, having as I believe a deadly cancer in my mouth & chin—my under lip being already gone by eight times cutting by the doctors—all to no purpose—my case is worse than when I began to practice on it 6 months ago."[15] He died seven months later in Cincinnati.

His son-in-law did rather better. William Henry Harrison had seen what was left of St. Clair's army straggle into Fort Washington, and he served at Fallen Timbers. At twenty-four he made captain and was put in command of Fort Washington. In 1797, having married Anna Symmes, he resigned from the army to accept an appointment as secretary of the Northwest Territory. The next year he resigned that position after he was elected as the Northwest's nonvoting territorial delegate to the House of Representatives, where he pushed for passage of the Public Land Act of 1800 and for splitting the territory in two, with the Illinois-Indiana region placed in the new Indiana Territory. Appointed governor of Indiana Territory and commissioner of Indian affairs in 1801, he built a career implementing Jefferson's policies of Indian dispossession, securing almost 30 million acres of Indian land. He also made a national reputation on the basis of his pyrrhic victory over the Shawnee Prophet at Tippecanoe in 1811 and his defeat of Tecumseh and the British at the Battle of the Thames in 1813. His success in acquiring Indian land and defeating Indian resistance carried him all the way to the White House in 1840, running with John Tyler on the now-famous slogan "Tippecanoe and Tyler too." He died of pneumonia a month later—the first president to die in office—and the nation got Tyler too.[16]

The fortunes of those who had fought to keep Ohio Indian country were also mixed.

The chiefs who had led the fight for the Ohio River boundary kept the peace they signed at Greenville. Many now tried to adapt to a world that was being transformed by American policies and population. Some found status and acceptance in the nation they had resisted for so long. In 1796 Anthony Wayne reported that Little Turtle and Blue Jacket were now vying for the honor of leading the Indians to their greatest victory. "The famous Shawanoe chief, Blue Jacket, who, it is said, had the chief command of the Indian army on the 4th of November 1791 against Genl. St. Clair," accompanied a delegation, but Little Turtle, "who also claims that honor, and who is his rival for fame and power...refuses or declines to proceed in company with Blue Jacket." Little Turtle, said Wayne, "possesses the spirit of litigation to a high degree."[17]

Little Turtle won the battle for fame and power, at least in American society. Credited with masterminding the great Indian victory and also with having the foresight to advocate peace and the wisdom to adopt policies of accommodation, his voice carried more weight with the United States than that of any other Miami, perhaps any other Indian. William Wells, who in 1796 made a written pledge in return "for what I may receive" to do to everything in his power to promote "the interest of the United States with the northwestern Indians," also promoted his father-in-law's standing with his new employers. But Little Turtle did not speak for all Miami. William Henry Harrison, who was always quick to identify and exploit any tribal divisions, pointed out that "when Wells speaks of the Miami Nation being of this or that opinion, he must be understood as meaning no more than the Turtle and himself. Nine tenths of that Tribe who acknowledge Richardville and Peccan [Pacanne] for their chiefs... utterly abhor both Wells and the Turtle."[18]

Nevertheless, in his role as a "famous Indian chief," Little Turtle became a regular visitor to the nation's capital, first Philadelphia and then Washington, and he met three presidents. In November 1796 he went with a delegation of chiefs. In one of his last public functions as president, George Washington invited him to his home and presented him with a ceremonial sword, a gun, and a medal displaying the likenesses of both men.[19] The celebrated physician Benjamin Rush inoculated him against smallpox by variolation, a process that involved infecting the patient with live smallpox matter, and he stayed at Rush's home for several weeks while he recovered. It was the first recorded federal inoculation of an American Indian.[20] Little Turtle was also treated for gout and rheumatism at the government's expense. On his second visit to Philadelphia, in 1798, he sat for Gilbert Stuart, the noted American portrait painter. (The portrait was destroyed when British troops burned the White House in the War of 1812.) The Revolutionary War hero Thaddeus Kosciusko presented him with a set of pistols.[21]

Little Turtle also met Constantin-François, Comte de Volney, a French scholar who had met Jefferson in Paris. Volney was interested in Indian languages and customs and had "nine or ten visits" with "the savage chief" and Wells in January and February 1798. On these occasions Little Turtle dressed "in the American fashion, a blue suit, with pantaloons, and a round hat." Wells interpreted and Volney wrote down his observations and speculations, as well as some of his conversations with Little Turtle, about the origins, skin color, population decline, customs, languages, and future prospects of the Indians. Like most scholars then and since, Volney believed that "the likeness of the Tartars to the savages of North America" indicated that the Indians had migrated to America from Asia, and to help make his point he laid out a map of eastern Asia and the northwest of America. Little Turtle "readily recognized the lakes of Canada, Michigan, Superiour, the rivers Ohio, Wabash, Missisippi, &c; the rest he examined with a curiosity, that convinced me it was new to him." Volney explained the hypothesis that Little Turtle's ancestors had crossed from Asia via the Bering Strait. Little Turtle considered the proposition and then asked "why... should not these Tartars, who resemble us, have come from America? Are here any proofs to the contrary? Or rather, why should we not both have been born in our own country?"[22]

Little Turtle was amazed by the bustling streets of Philadelphia and the booming population of the whites. "They spread like oil upon a blanket; we dissolve like the snow before the vernal Sun," he told Volney. He attributed the different demographic trajectories to

American agriculture and property owning and to the Indians' dependence on hunting; "If we do not change our course, it is impossible for the race of red men to subsist." His explanation convinced Volney "that this man has not without reason acquired in his own nation and in the United States the reputation of a person superior in understanding to most of the savages."[23]

Little Turtle returned east in 1801, with Wells and a delegation of chiefs. He met President Jefferson, who also had an interest in Indian languages. By then Edward Jenner had developed vaccination against smallpox using cowpox. Little Turtle was vaccinated, and Jefferson sent him additional vaccinations and instructions to administer to other Miami when he got home. Learning that Little Turtle was in Baltimore, retired secretary of war Dr. James McHenry, who had befriended Little Turtle when he was in office, invited the chiefs to his home for dinner at Christmas. While in Washington Little Turtle requested an agency and government trading post at Fort Wayne, which was granted. Part of the goal of both agency and trading post was to help curb the liquor trade by licensing traders. As Little Turtle lamented in a speech to the Baltimore Quakers, alcohol had left "more of us dead since the Treaty of Greenville, than we lost by the six years war before."[24]

The Miami Indian agency was located at Fort Wayne, built at Kekionga. William Wells was appointed agent for the Miami, but John Johnston, not Wells, was appointed government factor at the trading post. Indians and Americans alike often harbored doubts about Wells's loyalty and integrity. During his tenure as an Indian agent he continued to function as a culture broker between Indians and Americans and encouraged his father-in-law, Little Turtle, to follow the white man's path. In view of the life he lived, it is hardly surprising that he also played both ends and looked out for his own interests. Wells employed Anthony Shane as a messenger and interpreter in his dealings with the Shawnee war chief Tecumseh. Like Wells, Shane had fought in the Indian army against St. Clair. Angling to get control of the Shawnee annuities, Wells managed to get the Quaker William Kirk removed as Shawnee agent. But his intrigues did him little good. Wells himself was dismissed as Indian agent in 1808.[25] John Johnston took over as agent at Fort Wayne.

Little Turtle made his last visit to Washington in 1808–9. Johnston remembered him as "a man of great wit, humor, and vivacity, fond of the company of gentlemen, and delighted in good eating." At that time, Little Turtle "had two wives living with him under the same roof in the greatest harmony"; one was his own age, about fifty, and "performed the drudgery of the house." The other, a beautiful eighteen-year-old, "was his favorite." Little Turtle died, "of a confirmed case of the gout, brought on by high living," said Johnston, at Wells's house, near the site of Kekionga, on July 14, 1812, less than a month after the United States declared war on Great Britain. American settlers and army officers attended his funeral, and he was buried with military honors. The grave goods interred with him included corn and beans, red pigment, and a pipe tomahawk, as befitted a Miami chief, and also the sword, gun, and medal Washington had given him.[26]

His son-in-law died a few months later. Wells was at Fort Dearborn, site of the future city of Chicago, when the War of 1812 broke out. Fearing an Indian attack, the garrison and their families evacuated the fort, only to be ambushed by Potawatomi warriors. Wells escorted the column, dressed as an Indian and with his face painted black, as was the Miami custom when confronting certain death. The Potawatomi killed him, cut out his heart, and ate it, an act of respect for his courage. Also present at the evacuation of Fort Dearborn was John Kinzie, the trader who had been displaced from the Miami towns; he survived to become one of the founding fathers of Chicago.

Buckongahelas had fought in battle with Little Turtle in 1791 and signed the peace with him in 1795, but then he followed a rather different path. Although he signed another treaty with the United States in 1804, he remained distrustful of Americans. As chief of the largest Delaware town on the White River in Indiana, he continued to fight to preserve his people's religion and customs. Buckongahelas died of natural causes in 1805.[27]

The Shawnee, who had fought long and hard for Indian unity, divided. Black Hoof, who had battled the Americans since the Revolution, now attempted to ensure his people's survival and to hold on to what was left of their land by adopting and adapting to American ways of life. After signing the Treaty of Greenville, Blue Jacket tried to maintain his status by working for peace with the Americans he had previously fought against. His biographer comments, "Aging, a war chief without a war, Blue Jacket found it difficult to live with the peace he had helped to create."[28] In 1796 Blue Jacket and Painted Pole accompanied a delegation of chiefs to Philadelphia, where they spoke with George Washington. Painted Pole took ill and died on the way home at Pittsburgh and was buried in Trinity Church graveyard.

William Wells, who fought with Indians against Americans in 1791, died fighting with Americans against Indians in 1812. Courtesy of Chicago History Museum, ICHi-56110.

Around 1800 Blue Jacket established a new town on the American side of the Detroit River, where he raised livestock, owned black slaves, and traded alcohol and manufactured goods.

The vision of a united tribal defense of all Indian lands did not die, and a younger generation of Shawnee freedom fighters breathed new life into it. After experiencing a vision in 1805 in which he saw the Master of Life, a Shawnee prophet named Tenskwatawa began to preach a message of spiritual and cultural revitalization, calling on Indian people to rid themselves of the white man's contaminating evils and make themselves whole again by returning to traditional ways. Tenskwatawa's brother, the war chief Tecumseh, who as a young warrior had scouted the movement of St. Clair's army, preached a message of multitribal resistance, calling on all Indians to stop the piecemeal cessions of their homelands to the United States and, ultimately, to confederate in forming an indigenous state, supported by British allies, in the heartland of America. Tecumseh's vision and confederacy owed much to Blue Jacket's earlier confederacy, and the aging chief—he was now in his sixties and overweight—threw his support behind the younger war chief. But Blue Jacket died in his village on the Detroit River early in 1808. He did not live to see the final demise of the dream of a united Indian confederacy.

When the Indians and the British allied again in the War of 1812 and won some early victories, it looked for a moment as if Tecumseh's vision might become a reality. But Tecumseh was killed at the Battle of the Thames in October 1813—Anthony Shane identified the body[29]—and American expansion increasingly demanded that Indians living east of the Mississippi give up their lands and relocate to the West.

The defeat of the Indian confederacy and the loss of the Ohio country was a personal tragedy for men like Simon Girty, Alexander McKee, and Matthew Elliott, whose lives were intertwined with those of their Indian friends, relatives, and neighbors. They continued to aid and abet the Indian resistance movement but had to shift their locations and loyalties to Canada in the wake of American conquest of Ohio. McKee died near Fort Malden, present-day Amherstburg, Ontario, in 1799. White-haired Matthew Elliott watched in tears as the Indians were defeated at the Battle of the Thames in 1813 and died the next year. Girty was driven from his farm near Amherstburg during the War of 1812 but returned after the conflict and died there in 1818. By then the man who had led Indian warriors against St. Clair and had been given three canons in honor of his deeds was completely blind.

IN THE LONG VIEW OF AMERICA'S WARS, the Indians' destruction of the first U.S. Army was an anomaly. Not because Indians rarely won—the destruction of Braddock's army in 1755 and Custer's Seventh Cavalry in 1876 also demonstrated their capacity to inflict stunning defeats—but because over time the vast majority of American Indians who have fought in America's wars have done so as part of the U.S. Army, not against it.

Chickasaw served the U.S. Army as scouts in both St. Clair's and Wayne's campaigns. Indians fought on both sides in the American Revolution, the War of 1812, and the Civil War.[30] Indians from many tribes served alongside the U.S. Cavalry as scouts and allies in the so-called Indian wars of the West in the second half of the nineteenth century.[31] Indians served in the war against Spain in 1898. During the First World War more than twelve thousand Indians served in the U.S. armed forces, and many more contributed to the cause on the home front. Indian soldiers saw plenty of service on the front lines. Most served the infantry and field artillery, many acted as scouts, runners, and snipers. The casualty rate for Indian soldiers was more than twice the overall rate for American soldiers and sailors.

For many in American society, the fact that Indians were now fighting for the United States constituted evidence of assimilation, and many Indians pointed to their patriotism and sacrifice as evidence of their readiness for full citizenship. (Indians who served were eligible for citizenship; Congress made all American Indians U.S. citizens in 1924.) But many Indians served more out of devotion to their Native homeland and families than loyalty to the United States. Service in the U.S. armed forces also offered young men a chance to win war honors, as their fathers and grandfathers had done. They also believed that it demonstrated their capacity to take care of their own affairs and might help to bring more justice for Indian people.[32]

About twenty-five thousand Indians served in the armed forces during World War II. Some were drafted, others volunteered. Almost 100 percent of eligible Indians registered for the draft. The Iroquois challenged the right of the federal government to compel their men to fight, and a group of Iroquois issued their own formal declaration of war against the Axis powers in 1942, indicating that they were participating in the war as sovereign nations, not as subordinates of the United States. Several hundred Indian women served in the WACS, WAVES, and Army Nurse Corps. Another forty thousand Native women and older men worked in war-related industries. A contingent of Choctaw, using their own language, had helped ensure the security of battlefield communications during World War I; in World War II Navajo code talkers in the Pacific theater baffled the Japanese with a code based on Navajo words. (Their achievements were belatedly recognized by the U.S. government.) More than five hundred Indians gave their lives in the war.[33]

Indians continued to serve their country in the second half of the twentieth century, even as the United States continued to ignore treaty pledges and assault tribal sovereignty and cultures, and even though Indian veterans returned home to face racism, poverty, and stifled opportunities.[34] Between ten thousand and fifteen thousand

Indians served in the Korean War, and more than forty thousand in the Vietnam War, the vast majority of them volunteers in a conflict that Americans in increasing numbers tried to avoid. Many who came home went through traditional healing ceremonies to deal with postcombat stress.[35] Indians served in Operation Desert Storm in the First Gulf War. In the twenty-first century American Indians continued to serve in the U.S. Army in Iraq and Afghanistan. The first American woman to die in combat in the Iraq War was twenty-three-year-old Lori Piestewa, a Hopi who was raised on the Navajo reservation in Arizona. She was a single mother with two children.

In proportion to their population, more Native Americans serve in the U.S. Army than any other group. Soldiers are welcomed home with community dinners, dances, and honor songs. At powwows and other public events Native Americans regularly display the Stars and Stripes and honor their veterans who have served in America's wars, even as many remain deeply ambivalent about the country's past and present treatment of its original inhabitants. The locations and nature of the wars American Indians fight today have changed significantly, but the reasons for fighting have not. Socioeconomic factors obviously exert a powerful influence in determining who fills the ranks of America's army today, as was the case in 1791, but many Indian soldiers who fight in modern wars invoke the values of a traditional warrior ethos. And the commitment to defending families and homeland has remained constant, whether serving as American troops in Germany and Afghanistan or attacking American troops on the banks of the Wabash on a morning in November 1791.[36]

Notes

Introduction

1. Grenier, *The First Way of War*, 111–13; Crocker, *Braddock's March*.
2. Boyd et al., *The Papers of Thomas Jefferson*, 22: 389.
3. *Connecticut Courant*, Dec. 19, 1791, 3; *Massachusetts Spy*, Dec. 29, 1791, 3.
4. Lewis, *St. Clair's Defeat*; *St. Clair's Defeat: A New Song* (1791?), copy in the American Antiquarian Society, Worcester, Mass.; "Monody to the memory of the young heroes, who fell at the Miami, under general St. Clair," *American Museum, or Universal Magazine*, Dec. 2, 1792, 10–12.
5. *American State Papers. Class II.* 1: 53.
6. Cayton, "Radicals in the 'Western World'"; Cayton, "'Separate Interests' and the Nation-State"; Bergman, *The American National State and the Early West*.
7. Barnes, *Native American Power*, 151; Wooster, *The American Military Frontiers*, xii (agent of empire).
8. Millett et al., *For the Common Defense*, 85–86.
9. White, *The Middle Ground*, 420; Bergmann, *The American National State and the Early West*.
10. Quoted in Prucha, *The Sword of the Republic*, 26–27.
11. Denny, *Military Journal of Major Ebenezer Denny*, 170.
12. Darke to Washington, Nov. 9, 1791, Henry Knox Papers, 30: 12.
13. Coss, *All for the King's Shilling*.
14. Wright, *Those Who Have Borne the Battle*, 18–19.
15. Kelman, *A Misplaced Massacre*, 205.
16. Smith, *The St. Clair Papers*, 2: 48–49.
17. White, *Railroaded*.
18. "Forgetting…is a crucial factor in the creation of a nation." Ernest Renan, "What Is a Nation?" quoted in Bhabha, *Nation and Narration*, 11. Blight, *Beyond the Battlefield*, 1–5.

Chapter 1: Confederations: America in 1790

1. Rush quoted in Wood, *Empire of Liberty*, 36; Wood, *The Idea of America*, 233–37, quote on 234.

2. Ellis, *Founding Brothers*, 9.

3. Merrell, *The Lancaster Treaty*, 86.

4. Labaree et al., *Papers of Benjamin Franklin*, 4: 118–19.

5. Fixico, "The Alliance of the Three Fires"; Bellfy, *Three Fires Unity*; Sullivan et al., *The Papers of Sir William Johnson*, 10: 202 ("Allies to each other").

6. Dowd, *A Spirited Resistance*.

7. Fitzpatrick, *The Writings of George Washington*, 30: 491–94.

8. Ellis, *Founding Brothers*, 121, 124–25; Knox to Sargent, July 3, 1789, Sargent Papers, reel 3: 81; Boyd et al., *The Papers of Thomas Jefferson*, 16: 443–44; Fitzpatrick, *Writings of George Washington*, 31: 55.

9. Larkin, *The Reshaping of Everyday Life*, 68.

10. Griffin, *American Leviathan*, 187.

11. Barr, *A Colony Sprung from Hell*; Slaughter, *The Whiskey Rebellion*; Szatmary, *Shay's Rebellion*; Taylor, *Liberty Men and Great Proprietors*; Cayton, "'Separate Interests' and the Nation-State." Regional differences even undermined the unity of the Ohio Company's goals and operations described in chapter 2. See Shannon, "The Ohio Company."

12. Ellis, *American Creation*, ch. 4.

13. Fitzpatrick, *Writings of George Washington*, 27: 475; Cutler and Cutler, *Life, Journals and Correspondence*, 1: 134–35.

14. Nichols, *Red Gentlemen and White Savages*.

15. Griffin, *American Leviathan*, 185 (state), 191 (surveyor).

16. Jacobs, *The Beginning of the U.S. Army*, 14.

17. Weigley, *History of the United States Army*, 81–82; Jacobs, *The Beginning of the U.S. Army*, 18; Wooster, *The American Military Frontiers*, 4–5; Odom, "Destined for Defeat," 70; Lytle, *The Soldiers of America's First Army*, 15–17.

18. Carter, *The Territorial Papers of the United States*, 2: 31, 34.

19. Cutler and Cutler, *Life, Journals and Correspondence*, 1: 231.

20. Wooster, *American Military Frontiers*, xii.

21. Weigley, *History of the United States Army*, 15–16.

22. Quoted in Wood, *Empire of Liberty*, 111.

23. Guthman, *March to Massacre*, 174; Jacobs, *The Beginning of the U.S. Army*, 50; Weigley, *History of the United States Army*, 90. Knox's plan for organization of the militia is in *American State Papers, Class V*, 1: 6–13, quotes on 7.

24. Guthman, *March to Massacre*, 3.

25. Wood, *Empire of Liberty*, 95–103.

26. Wood, *Empire of Liberty*, 140–43; Ellis, *Founding Brothers*, ch. 2.

27. Wood, *Empire of liberty*, 143–45.

28. Ellis, *Founding Brothers*, ch. 3, quote on 118.

29. Fitzpatrick, *Writings of George Washington*, 27: 136, 140.

30. Bergman, *The American National State and the Early West*, 42–43.

31. Taylor, *Divided Ground*, 238.

32. McConnell, *A Country Between*, chs. 1–2.

33. Calloway, *The Shawnees*, chs. 2–3; Warren, *The Worlds the Shawnees Made*.

34. Schutt, *Peoples of the River Valleys*, 177.

35. Alford, *Civilization and the Story of the Absentee Shawnees*, 201.

36. Draper Mss. 2W: 345, 360.

37. Tanner, *Atlas of Great Lakes Indian History*, map. 18.

38. *American State Papers, Class II*, 2: 576.

39. Quaife, "Henry Hay's Journal," 228–29.

40. Schutt, *Peoples of the River Valleys*, 177–79.

41. Heckewelder, *History, Manners, and Customs*, 104.

42. Calloway, *Crown and Calumet*, 14–16. The proceedings of the Sandusky Council are in British Museum, Haldimand Papers, 21779: 132–39; National Archives (UK), C.O. 42/45:9–14.

43. The most complete biography of the Mohawk leader is Kelsay, *Joseph Brant*. Wallace, *Thirty Thousand Miles with John Heckewelder*, 228. Brant's speech at the Sandusky council is in Haldimand Papers, 21779: 136.

44. Wallace, *Thirty Thousand Miles with John Heckewelder*, 249.

45. "Narrative of John Brickell's Captivity."

46. Smith, *The St. Clair Papers*, 2: 82.

47. By 1790 Pennsylvanians had long since abandoned William Penn's legacy of fair dealings with Indians, and Indians lumped them together with Virginian "long knives" in their grasping after Native lands. Richter, *Trade, Land, Power*, ch. 10.

48. Brooks, *The Common Pot*, 124.

49. Fitzpatrick, *Writings of George Washington*, 31: 166.

Chapter 2: Building a Nation on Indian Land

1. Hinderaker, *Elusive Empires*, 268.

2. Fitzpatrick, *Writings of George Washington*, 27: 133, 136; Cayton, *The Frontier Republic*, 7.

3. Cayton, *The Frontier Republic*, ch. 1; Cayton, "Radicals in the 'Western World,'" 79–80; Onuf, *Statehood and Union*, chs. 1–2.

4. *Journals of the Continental Congress*, 25: 602.

5. Carter, *The Territorial Papers*, 2: 6–9; Hulbert, *The Records of the Original Proceedings of the Ohio Company*, 1: xvii–xviii.

6. Heart to Judd, January 8, 1786, quoted in Guthman, *March to Massacre*, 76.

7. Smith, *The Western Journals of John May*, 134.

8. Cutler and Cutler, *Life, Journals and Correspondence*, 2: 393–406, quotes on 397, 399–400. See also Cayton and Hobbs, *The Center of a Great Empire*, 1.

9. Bond, *The Correspondence of John Cleves Symmes*, 66.

10. Cutler and Cutler, *Life, Journals and Correspondence*, 1: 137–45; Fitzpatrick, *Writings of George Washington*, 27: 17.

11. Griffin, *American Leviathan*, ch. 7.

12. Onuf, *Statehood and Union*, xiii.

13. Fitzpatrick, *Writings of George Washington*, 27: 486; 28.

14. Cutler and Cutler, *Life, Journals and Correspondence*, 1: 131–32; Fitzpatrick, *Writings of George Washington*, 28: 108.

15. "Land Ordinance of 1785," in Carter, *The Territorial Papers*, 2: 12–18; Linklater, *Measuring America*; Onuf, *Statehood and Union*, ch. 2.

16. Shannon, "'This Unpleasant Business,'" 20.

17. Friedenberg, *Life, Liberty, and the Pursuit of Land*, 277.

18. Linklater, *Measuring America*, 149.

19. Quoted in Cayton, *Frontier Republic*, 8.

20. Hurt, *The Ohio Frontier*, 144–48; Smith, *The St. Clair Papers*, 2: 14.

21. Griffin, *American Leviathan*, 197–211.

22. Cutler and Cutler, *Life, Journals and Correspondence*, 1: 145.

23. Timothy Pickering Papers, reel 59: 122–23.

24. British Museum, Add. Mss., 24, 322: 112–13.

25. Vaughan, *Early American Indian Documents*, 18: 346–47, 593, n75; Denny, *Military Journal*, 73, 75; *Minutes of Debates in Council*, 10.

26. Denny, *Military Journal*, 83–84.

27. Smith, *The St. Clair Papers*, 2: 19; Denny, *Military Journal*, 94.

28. Denny, *Military Journal*, 55, 274–77.

29. The speech of the united Indians at Detroit in December 1786 is in *American State Papers, Class II*, 1: 8–9 Vaughan, *Early American Indian Documents*, 18: 356–58.

30. Carter, *Territorial Papers*, 2: 104.

31. *The New American State Papers*, 4: 17–18; National Archives (U.K.), C.O. 42/50: 66–68, 70–76; C.O. 42/87: 324–26.

32. Cutler and Cutler, *Life, Journals and Correspondence*, 1: 180–87; "Articles of Association by the Name of the Ohio Company," Winthrop Sargent Papers, reel 2: 652–58; Hulbert, *The Records of the Original Proceedings of the Ohio Company*, 1: 4–12; Hurt, *The Ohio Frontier*, 155–57.

33. Hulbert, *The Records of the Original Proceedings of the Ohio Company*, 1: 12; Cutler and Cutler, *Life, Journals and Correspondence*, 1: 191–92.

34. Linklater, *Measuring America*, 51–53; Buell, *The Memoirs of Rufus Putnam*, 217, 223; also in Cutler and Cutler, *Life, Journals and Correspondence*, 1: 168, 174.

35. Cutler and Cutler, *Life, Journals and Correspondence*, 1: 119.

36. Cutler and Cutler, *Life, Journals and Correspondence*, 1: 192–95.

37. Nichols, *Red Gentlemen and White Savages*, 89.

38. Cutler and Cutler, *Life, Journals and Correspondence*, 1: 306.

39. Wood, *Empire of Liberty*, 152.

40. Cutler and Cutler, *Life, Journals and Correspondence*, 1: 120–21, 293–305 (journal), 349 (forty letters), 2: 429–30 (forty letters).

41. *Journals of the Continental Congress*, 33: 399–401, 427–30: Carter, *Territorial Papers*, 2: 52–57.

42. Cutler and Cutler, *Life, Journals and Correspondence*, 1: 295.

43. Cutler and Cutler, *Life, Journals and Correspondence*, 1: 296.

44. Cutler and Cutler, *Life, Journals and Correspondence*, 1: 299–300 (Osgood and intrigue), 301 (machines).

45. Cutler and Cutler, *Life, Journals and Correspondence*, 1: 305; Sargent Papers, reel 2: 703–4.

46. Sword, *President Washington's Indian War*, 47–48.

47. Friedenberg, *Life, Liberty, and the Pursuit of Land*, 287.

48. Cayton, *Frontier Republic*, 24–25.

49. "Ordinance of 1787," in Carter, *Territorial Papers*, 2: 39–50; Onuf, *Statehood and Union*, ch. 3; Anderson and Cayton, *The Dominion of War*, 191 call it an instrument for "indefinite expansion."

50. "At a Meeting of the Directors and Agents of the OHIO COMPANY"; Cutler and Cutler, *Life, Journals and Correspondence*, 1: 319–22; Hulbert, *Records of the Original Proceedings of the Ohio Company*, 1: 13–17.

51. Hurt, *Ohio Frontier*, 157. Linklater, *Measuring America*, 80–81, estimates 12 cents an acre.

52. Cutler and Cutler, *Life, Journals and Correspondence*, 1: 322–23.

53. Cutler and Cutler, *Life, Journals and Correspondence*, 1: 333.

54. Cutler and Cutler, *Life, Journals and Correspondence*, 1: 326. The company's contract is in Hulbert, *Records of the Original Proceedings of the Ohio Company*, 1: 29–37.

55. Kohn, *Eagle and Sword*, 100.

56. Guthman, *March to Massacre*, 73–74.

57. Hulbert, *Records of the Original Proceedings of the Ohio Company*, 1: lxxxii; Knox Papers, 29: 76.

58. Carter, *Territorial Papers*, 2: 222–23; Cutler and Cutler, *Life, Journals and Correspondence* 1: 214n (death), 298, 301, 313.

59. Kohn, *Eagle and Sword*, 100.

60. St. Clair, *A Narrative*, 39.

61. Brown, "Arthur St. Clair," 26–40; Nichols, *Red Gentlemen and White Savages*, 88.

62. Wallace, *Jefferson and the Indians*, 136; Heart, "A Letter to Benjamin Smith Barton."

63. Hurt, *Ohio Frontier*, 179–86; McGlinchey, "'A Superior Civilization.'"

64. Cutler and Cutler, *Life, Journals and Correspondence*, 2: 443: Cayton, "Radicals of the 'Western World,'" 85 ("advance guard").

65. Carter, *Territorial Papers*, 2: 70–71; Bond, *Correspondence of John Cleves Symmes*, 8–9.

66. Bond, *Correspondence of John Cleves Symmes*, 219.

67. Bond, *Correspondence of John Cleves Symmes*, 9.

68. Linklater, *Measuring America*, 87; Friedenberg, *Life, Liberty, and the Pursuit of Land*, 294–95; Hurt, *Ohio Frontier*, 159–64; Hurt, "John Cleves Symmes and the Miami Purchase," 114–25.

69. Draper Mss., 3WW 3: 28–29; Bond, *Correspondence of John Cleves Symmes*, 47.

70. Draper Mss. 3WW: 36, 48; Bond, *Correspondence of John Cleves Symmes*, 80, 97–98, 105, 219–20, 228, 235, 241.

71. Hurt, *Ohio Frontier*, 186–87.

72. Friedenberg, *Life, Liberty, and the Pursuit of Land*, 294–95; Hurt, *Ohio Frontier*, 159–64; Hurt, "John Cleves Symmes and the Miami Purchase," 114–25; Carter, *Territorial Papers*, 2: 347 (St. Clair astonished).

73. Bond, *Correspondence of John Cleves Symmes*, 8–16, 29–32, 114 ("vexatious"), 224–25. (Dayton's reports of complaints). Symmes's correspondence regarding the Miami Purchase is in Draper Mss. 3WW, "vexatious" quote on 63.

74. Bond, *Correspondence of John Cleves Symmes*, 241–42.

75. Carter, *Territorial Papers*, 2: 78–79, 117; Smith, *St. Clair Papers*, 2: 37; *American State Papers, Class II*, 1: 9.

76. Carter, *Territorial Papers*, 2: 119; Smith, *St. Clair Papers*, 2: 49.

77. *Minutes of Debates in Council*, 8–11, 14.

78. Thornborough, *Outpost on the Wabash*, 119.

79. Bond, *Correspondence of John Cleves Symmes*, 208.

80. Horsman, *Expansion and American Indian Policy*, 30–49; *American State Papers, Class II*, 1: 9–10; Smith, *St. Clair Papers*, 2: 112–13; Carter, *Territorial Papers*, 2: 174–86, 192–93; Vaughan, *Early American Indian Documents*, 18: 438–39, 481–97; Denny, *Military Journal*, 127–30.

81. Smith, *St. Clair Papers*, 2: 113; Carter, *Territorial Papers*, 2: 193.

82. Thornborough, *Outpost on the Wabash*, 152.

83. National Archives (U.K.), C.O. 42/65: 60.

84. Bond, *The Correspondence of John Cleves Symmes*, 75. The Shawnee chief's observations were also printed in the *Universal Asylum, and Columbian Magazine*, Feb. 1, 1792: 108–9, and reported in Wallace, *Thirty Thousand Miles with John Heckewelder*, 275.

85. Griffin, *American Leviathan*, 197–211.

86. Wallace, *Thirty Thousand Miles with John Heckewelder*, 242.

87. Wooster, *The American Military Frontiers*, 7.

88. Thornborough, *Outpost on the Wabash*, 174. On the effects of earlier instances, see Silver, *Our Savage Neighbors*.

89. Buell, *Memoirs of Rufus Putnam*, 244.

Chapter 3: The United States Invades Ohio

1. Smith, *The St. Clair Papers*, 2: 126.

2. Calloway, *Crown and Calumet*, 5–13; National Archives (U.K.), C.O. 5/82: 446–47; Vaughan, *Early American Indian Documents*, 18: 278–79.

3. Malone, *The Skulking Way of War*, 98.

4. Rogers outlined his rules for fighting in *Journals*, 59–70. Carroll, "'Savages' in the Service of Empire."

5. Chet, *Conquering the American Wilderness*.

6. Grenier, *The First Way of War*, 10.

7. Smith, *St. Clair Papers*, 2: 146.

8. Wilson, *Arthur St. Clair*, 231–36.

9. Smith, *St. Clair Papers*, 2: 132.

10. Gamelin's Journal in Smith, *St. Clair Papers*, 2: 155–62; *American State Papers, Class II*, 1: 93–94; Burnet, *Notes on the Early Settlement*, 98–99.

11. Miami chief to Six Nations, transcribed by Alexander McKee, May 3, 1790, National Archives Canada, Claus Papers, 4: 213.

12. Smith, *St. Clair Papers*, 2: 145.

13. Knox to Washington, May 27, 1790, in Smith, *St. Clair Papers* 2: 147; Knox to Harmar, June 7, 1790, in *American State Papers, Class II*, 1: 97; Draper Mss. 2W: 268–69.

14. Smith, *St. Clair Papers*, 2: 162.

15. Smith, *St. Clair Papers*, 2: 181–82; *American State Papers, Class II*, 1: 100.

16. Nelson, "General Charles Scott."

17. Thornborough, *Outpost on the Wabash*, 51.

18. Draper Mss. 2W: 324–26.

19. *The Proceedings of a Court of Inquiry*, 2; Denny's report, Jan. 1, 1791, Ohio State Library, Arthur St. Clair Papers, 1788–1815 (hereafter OSL), card 22.

20. Sargent to St. Clair, Aug. 17, 1790, OSL; Carter, *The Territorial Papers*, 2: 301.

21. National Archives (U.K), C.O. 42/72: 77, 79, 81; *Collections of the Michigan Pioneer and Historical Society*, 24 (1895), 99–100, 102–3.

22. *Collections of the Michigan Pioneer and Historical Society*, 96–99, 100–102.

23. Denny, *Military Journal*, 145, 147; Denny's report, Jan. 1, 1791, OSL, card 22; "Journal of Harmar's Campaign," Draper Mss. 2W: 335–48, Kekionga and Chillicothe on 340–41; Harmar to St. Clair, Oct. 18, 1790 ("great stroke"),

Indiana Historical Society, Northwest Territory Collection, MO367, box 1, folder 32, no. 18.

24. Draper Mss. 2W: 340–42 (Harmar's quotes about the militia); Denny, *Military Journal,* 146–49; Denny's report, Jan. 1, 1791, OSL, card 22; Eid, "'The Slaughter Was Reciprocal.'"

25. St. Clair to Knox, Oct. 29 and Nov. 6, 1790, OSL, card 21 and in Smith, *St. Clair Papers.* 2: 188, 190; Carter, *Territorial Papers,* 2: 309–10, 313 ("sacrificed").

26. Thornborough, *Outpost on the Wabash,* 268; Draper Mss. 2W: 352.

27. Fitzpatrick, *The Writings of George Washington,* 31: 156; Carter, *Territorial Papers,* 2: 310.

28. Draper Ms. 2W: 395.

29. *The Proceedings of a Court of Inquiry,* in *American State Papers, Class V,* 20–30; Draper Mss. 2W: 402–6, 419–26, 4U: 19–64.

30. St. Clair to Knox, Nov. 26, 1790, OSL card 21 and in Smith, *St. Clair Papers,* 2: 194.

31. Nelson, *A Man of Distinction,* 159–60.

32. Hamtramck to St. Clair, Dec. 2, 1790, OSL cards 21–22 and in Smith, *St. Clair Papers* 2: 197–98.

33. Tanner, "The Glaize in 1792," 16.

34. Grenier, *First Way of War,* 109.

35. Symmes Papers, Draper Mss. 3WW 79–81; Bond, *The Correspondence of John Cleves Symmes,* 134, 136.

36. Griffin, "Reconsidering the Ideological Origins of Indian Removal."

37. Draper Mss. 2W: 385–90.

38. Bond, "Memoirs of Benjamin Van Cleve," 3–4, 19–20, 24.

39. Hulbert, *The Records of the Original Proceedings of the Ohio Company,* 2: 68. *American State Papers, Class II,* 1: 121 ("utmost danger").

40. Buell, *The Memoirs of Rufus Putnam,* 112–13, 247–49; "At a special meeting of the Agents & Proprietors of the Ohio Company," Jan. 7, 1791, OSL, card 22.

41. Carter, *Territorial Papers,* 2: 338–39. Also to Ames and Knox, in Buell, *Memoirs of Rufus Putnam,* 250–54.

42. *American State Papers, Class II,* 1: 112–13.

43. Smith, *St. Clair Papers,* 2:283.

44. Lytle, *The Soldiers of America's First Army,* 27–31, 35.

45. *American State Papers Class II,* 1: 104.

46. Denny, *Military Journal,* 257–58; Smith, *St. Clair Papers,* 2: 200–201.

47. Knox, report to the president, March 19, 1791, Indiana Historical Collection, Northwest Territory Collection, MO367, box 1, folder 36, no. 1; *American State Papers, Class II,* 1: 112, 171–74.

48. Wallace, *Jefferson and the Indians,* 172; Boyd et al., *The Papers of Thomas Jefferson,* 20: 145.

49. Sword, *President Washington's Indian War,* 145. Washington Irving in his *Life of Washington,* 88 (citing Rush, *Washington in Domestic Life,* 67) has the president recalling having said, "Beware of a surprise! You know how the Indians fight."

50. Hulbert, *The Records of the Original Proceedings of the Ohio Company,* 1: 82.

51. Knox to St. Clair, March 23, 1791, OSL, card 23; St. Clair to Knox, April 19, 1791, "Indian Goods for Col. Timothy Pickering for Treaty to be held with the Six Nations, May 16, 1791, OSL, card 24.

52. Fitzpatrick, *The Writings of George Washington*, 31: 179–84, 197–99.

53. *American State Papers, Class II,* 1: 146–47; St. Clair to Captain Pipe, March 8, 1791, Indiana Historical Society, Northwest Territory Collection, MO367, box 1, folder 36, no. 6.

54. Proctor's narrative in *American State Papers, Class II,* 1: 149–65; National Archives (U.K.), C.O. 42/73: 175–87.

55. *Collections of the Michigan Pioneer and Historical Society,* 217–19.

56. Smith, *St. Clair Papers,* 2: 198.

57. Fitzpatrick, *Writings of George Washington,* 31: 320.

58. Guthman, *March to Massacre,* 202.

59. Smith, *St. Clair Papers,* 2: 21, 188; Nelson, "General Charles Scott," 219–20.

60. *American State Papers, Class II,* 1: 131–33.

61. Quaife, "A Picture of the First United States Army," 60.

62. Carter, *The Life and Times of Little Turtle,* 101.

63. Bond, *Correspondence of John Cleves Symmes,* 143.

64. Cutler to Sargent, Aug. 27, 1791, Winthrop Sargent Papers, reel 3: 256.

65. Wilkinson's report is in *American State Papers, Class II,* 1: 133–35 and in Smith, *St. Clair Papers,* 2: 233–39, and was reprinted in the *Connecticut Courant,* Oct. 10, 1791, 1.

66. Lytle, *The Soldiers of America's First Army,* 39–41.

67. Wilson, *Arthur St. Clair,* 144; St. Clair, *A Narrative,* 35.

68. Guthman, *March to Massacre,* 228; Winkler, *Wabash, 1791, 19–20.*

69. Weigley, *History of the United States Army,* 60; Risch, *Quartermaster Support of the Army,* 76–78.

70. Duffy, *The Military Experience,* 173–76.

71. *American State Papers, Class V,* 1: 36, 42.

72. Furlong, "Problems of Frontier Logistics," 148–50.

73. Knox to Butler, June 9, 1791, OSL, card 26, and in Smith, *St. Clair Papers,* 2: 216–17; *American State Papers, Class II,* 1: 188; *American State Papers, Class V,* 1: 36–39.

74. Guthman, *March to Massacre,* 207; Ferguson to St. Clair, June 25, 1791, OSL card 28, and in Smith, *St. Clair Papers,* 2: 223.

75. Knox to Butler, June 23, 1791, OSL, card 28.

76. Furlong, "Problems of Frontier Logistics"; Smith, *St. Clair Papers,* 2: 216, 241; *American State Papers, Class V,* 1: 37.

77. Knox to Duer, June 26, 1791, and July 2, 1791, Knox Papers.

78. Knox to Butler, July 7, 1791, OSL, cards 28–29.

79. St. Clair to Ludlow, Aug. 6, 1791, OSL, card 31; Smith, *St. Clair Papers,* 2: 246, 248.

80. Knox to Butler, July 21, Aug. 4, Aug, 11, Aug. 25, 1791, OSL, cards 30, 31, 32, 33; Smith, *St. Clair Papers,* 2: 232, 241.

81. Lytle, *Soldiers of America's First Army,* 51–52.

82. Quaife, "A Picture of the First United States Army," 44–60. Newman's manuscript journal is in Draper Mss. 4U: 101–31.

83. Smith, *St. Clair Papers,* 2: 124; Carter, *Territorial Papers,* 2: 216; Nelson, "General Charles Scott," 234.

84. [Sargent], "Winthrop Sargent's Diary," 242.

85. Denny, *Military Journal,* 170.

86. Keegan, *The Face of Battle*, 229; Duffy, *The Military Experience*, 96–114, Vegetius quote on 96. Marlantes, *What It Is Like to Go to War* explores the parallel experiences of modern soldiers.

87. St. Clair to Knox, Aug. 3, 1791, Knox Papers, 29–91.

88. Keegan, *Face of Battle*, 222.

89. Denny, *Military Journal*, 152–53.

90. Fischer, *A Well-Executed Failure*, 103.

91. St. Clair, *Narrative*, 5, 26; *American State Papers, Class V*, 1: 36–39.

92. [Sargent], "Winthrop Sargent's Diary," 241.

93. St. Clair to Knox, Sept. 18, 1791, OSL, card 34, and in Smith, *St. Clair Papers*, 2: 240–41.

94. Denny, *Military Journal*, 154–64; [Sargent], "Winthrop Sargent's Diary," 240–53; Quaife, "A Picture of the First United States Army," 60–73; Smith, *St. Clair Papers*, 2: 249–59; Wilson, *Journal of Capt. Daniel Bradley*, 19–28.

95. Duffy, *The Military Experience*, 160; Fischer, *A Well-Executed Failure*, 75.

96. "Extract of a letter from an Officer in the Western Army, Sept. 19," *Connecticut Courant*, Nov. 21, 1791, 3.

97. Quaife, "A Picture of the First United States Army," 64.

98. Quaife, "A Picture of the First United States Army," 64.

99. Quaife, "A Picture of the First United States Army," 71.

100. Denny, *Military Journal*, 127; Wilson, *Journal of Capt. Daniel Bradley*, 25.

101. Lytle, *Soldiers of America's First Army*, 78–79.

102. [Sargent], "Winthrop Sargent's Diary," 246.

103. Quaife, "A Picture of the First United States Army," 72.

104. St. Clair to Knox, Oct. 21, 1791, Knox Papers, 29–91.

105. Wilson, *Arthur St. Clair*, 116; Lytle, *Soldiers of America's First Army*, 80–81.

106. St. Clair to Knox, Nov. 1, 1791, Knox Papers, 29–91, and in Smith, *St. Clair Papers*, 2: 250.

107. Denny, *Military Journal*, 60; [Sargent], "Winthrop Sargent's Diary," 249.

108. St. Clair to Knox, Nov. 1, 1791, Knox Papers, 29–91.

109. [Sargent], "Winthrop Sargent's Diary," 250.

110. St. Clair to Knox, Nov. 1, 1791, Knox Papers, 29–91, and in Smith, *St. Clair Papers*, 2: 250.

111. St. Clair to Knox, Nov. 1, 1791, Knox Papers, 29–91, and in Smith, *St. Clair Papers*, 2: 250.

112. Denny, *Military Journal*, 162.

113. [Sargent], "Winthrop Sargent's Diary," 251.

114. St. Clair to Knox, Nov. 1, 1791, Knox Papers, 29–91; Smith, *St. Clair Papers*, 2: 249–51; *Connecticut Courant*, Dec. 26, 1791, 1.

115. *Collections of the Michigan Pioneer and Historical Society*, 331–34.

116. [Sargent], "Winthrop Sargent's Diary," 256.

117. Denny, *Military Journal*, 171.

118. St. Clair to Knox, Sept. 4, Oct. 21, 1791, Knox Papers, 29–91.

119. St. Clair to Knox, Oct. 21, 1791, Knox Papers, 29–91.

120. St. Clair, *Narrative*, 38, 132.

121. Denny, *Military Journal*, 171.

122. Wilson, "St. Clair's Defeat," 378–79; Draper Mss. 4U: 12.

123. [Sargent], "Winthrop Sargent's Diary," 253.

124. St. Clair to Knox, Jan. 22, 1792, OSL, card 37; Testimony of Captain Slough, OSL, card 39; Testimony of Lieut. Denny, OSL, card 40; Denny, *Military Journal*, 164; Smith, *St. Clair Papers*, 2: 266–67, 278; [Sargent], "Winthrop Sargent's Diary," 257; Guthman, *March to Massacre*, 236–37.

125. Smith, *St. Clair Papers*, 2: 263; St. Clair, *Narrative*, appendix 18.

126. St. Clair, *Narrative*, 111.

127. Winkler, *Wabash, 1791*, 52–53.

Chapter 4: The Indian Resistance Movement

1. Carter, *The Territorial Papers*, 2: 158–59; Smith, *The St. Clair Papers*, 2: 89.

2. Cutler and Cutler, *Life, Journals and Correspondence*, 1: 389; Jones, *A Journal of Two Visits*, 54.

3. Miller, *Ogimaag*; Kinietz and Voegelin, "Shawnee Traditions," 11–13, 17.

4. Hulbert and Schwarze, *David Zeiseberger's History*, 92–93, 100–103; O'Callaghan, *Documentary History of the State of New York*, 4:271 (Johnson).

5. White, *The Middle Ground*, 435, 441; Eid, " 'National' War among Indians of Northeastern North America," 145; Eid, "American Indian Military Leadership."

6. Smith, *St. Clair Papers*, 2: 303–4.

7. Cruikshank, *The Correspondence of Lieut. Governor John Graves Simcoe*, 2: 42.

8. Thwaites, *The Jesuit Relations*, 59: 129–31.

9. Quaife, *John Long's Voyages*, 61–62.

10. Klinck and Talman, *The Journal of Major John Norton*, 281–82.

11. Klinck and Talman, *Journal of Major John Norton*, 176.

12. Carter, *Territorial Papers*, 2: 362; Smith, *St. Clair Papers*, 2: 95–96.

13. Carter, *Territorial Papers*, 2: 245; Anson, *The Miami Indians*, 96, 105–6 (quote).

14. Tanner, "The Glaize in 1792," 16; Carter, *The Life and Times of Little Turtle*, 75–77; Johnston in Draper Mss. 11YY: 38; Quaife, "Henry Hay's Journal," 223.

15. Tanner, *Atlas of Great Lakes Indian History*, map. 18.

16. Fixico, "The Alliance of the Three Fires," 11.

17. Edmunds, *The Potawatomis*, 119; Anson, *The Miami Indians*, 109; Thornborough, *Outpost on the Wabash*, 159.

18. Sugden, *Blue Jacket*, 94; quote from Draper Mss. 23U: 88.

19. [Wells], "Indian History," 202.

20. Carter, *Life and Times of Little Turtle*, 44–45.

21. *American State Papers, Class II*, 1: 94; Carter, *Life and Times of Little Turtle*, 66, 81.

22. England in Cruikshank, *The Correspondence of Lieut. Governor John Graves Simcoe*, 2: 333–34; Adams quoted in Carter, *Life and Times of Little Turtle*, 4.

23. Sugden, *Blue Jacket*, 118–20; [Sargent], "Winthrop Sargent's Diary," 272; Knopf, *Anthony Wayne*, 532; Draper Mss. 4U: 166.

24. Sugden, *Blue Jacket*, 54; Calloway, *The Shawnees*, 87–88.

25. Quaife, *The Captivity of O. M. Spencer*, 89–92.

26. Sugden, *Blue Jacket*, especially 117–21.

27. [Wells], "Indian History," 203.

28. Quaife, *The Captivity of O. M. Spencer*, 28; *An Account of the Remarkable Occurrences in the Life and Travels of Col. James Smith*, 169.

29. Quoted in White, *Middle Ground*, 495.

30. Wells quoted in Hopkins, *A Mission to the Indians*, 66.

31. Calloway, *Crown and Calumet*; Allen, *His Majesty's Indian Allies*, ch. 4: Willig, *Restoring the Chain of Friendship*, ch. 1.

32. Nelson, *A Man of Distinction*; Horsman, *Matthew Elliott*.

33. Keating, *Rising Up from Indian Country*, 26–27, 35–36.

34. Hoffman, *Simon Girty*; Calloway, "Simon Girty"; Butterfield, *History of the Girtys*.

35. Carter, *Life and Times of Little Turtle*, 82–86; Hutton, "William Wells"; Gaff, "Three Men from Three Rivers," 152–53.

36. Smith, *Indian Woman and French Men*.

37. Sargent to St. Clair, Aug. 17, 1790, Ohio State Library, Arthur St. Clair Papers, 1788–1815 (hereafter OSL); Carter, *Territorial Papers*, 2: 301.

38. Denny, *Military Journal*, 145.

39. Carter, *Life and Times of Little Turtle*, 91; Thornborough, *Outpost on the Wabash*, 266.

40. National Archives (U.K.), C.O. 42/73: 27; *Collections of the Michigan Pioneer and Historical Society*, 24 (1895), 103, 105, 106, 109, 132.

41. C.O. 42/73; 31, 37; *Collections of the Michigan Pioneer and Historical Society*, 160; Sugden, *Blue Jacket*, 105.

42. Quaife, *Captivity of O. M. Spencer*, 92.

43. Tanner, "The Glaize in 1792," 15–39; Tanner, *Atlas of Great Lakes Indian History*, 88, map. 18.

44. C.O. 42/73: 37, 39–40, reprinted in "Information of Blue Jacket."

45. *American State Papers, Class II*, 1: 122.

46. "Journal of what happened at the Miamis and the Glaize."

47. *Collections of the Michigan Pioneer and Historical Society*, 246–47, 262.

48. *American State Papers, Class II*, 1: 196–97; *Collections of the Michigan Pioneer and Historical Society*, 277–79; Draper Mss. 4U: 203.

49. C.O. 42/83: 170–81.

50. Butterfield, *History of the Girtys*, 193.

51. *American State Papers, Class II*, 1: 198.

52. Mahon, "Anglo-American Methods of Indian Warfare," 259.

53. Smith, *St. Clair Papers*, 2: 89, 188, 193.

54. *An Account of the Remarkable Occurrences in the Life and Travels of Col. James Smith*, 161–72.

55. Kinietz and Voegelin, "Shawnee Traditions," 42.

56. Thwaites, *Early Western Journals*, 230–31.

57. Smith, *An Historical Account of the Expedition*, 44–45.

58. Johnston, *Recollections of Sixty Years*, 8.

59. *A Journal of the Adventures of Matthew Bunn*, 6, 9–10; *Collections of the Michigan Pioneer and Historical Society*, 132.

60. Copy of a letter from Capt. John Rogers, Dec. 19, 1791, *Connecticut Courant*, Dec. 26, 1791, 3.

61. *A Journal of the Adventures of Matthew Bunn*, 10.

62. [Sargent], "Winthrop Sargent's Diary," 272; Crackel, *The Papers of George Washington*, 10: 314.

63. Hopkins, *A Mission to the Indians*, 65; [Wells], "Indian History," 203 (1,133).

64. Klinck and Talman, *Journal of Major John Norton*, 177.

65. C.O. 42/89: 195.

66. Testimony of Mr. Barton in Testimonies of the Committee of Inquiry, OSL, card 39; *American State Papers, Class V,* 1: 37.

67. Diary of Zeisberger, 2: 201, 216, 222; *Collections of the Michigan Pioneer and Historical Society,* 330.

68. C.O. 42/89: 35; *Collections of the Michigan Pioneer and Historical Society,* 329–30.

69. Miller, *Ogimaag,* 119; Klinck and Talman, *Journal of Major John Norton,* 177.

70. Karl Marlantes laments the lack of such spiritual preparation in the modern American army and in his own experience in Vietnam: "Warriors must touch their souls because their job involves killing people" (*What It Is Like to Go to War,* 44). "Soldiers stand in most need to be very holy men because they may be taken away very suddenly," said one minister in a sermon during the English Civil War. Carlton, *This Seat of Mars,* 154.

71. *American State Papers, Class II,* 1: 243.

72. "Indian Account, Of the unfortunate action of the 4th Nov. received via Pittsburgh," *New-Hampshire Gazette and General Advertiser,* March 7, 1792.

73. Draper Mss. 4U: 166.

74. Winthrop Sargent Papers, reel 3: 404.

75. "Story of George Ash," *Cincinnati Chronicle and Literary Gazette,* Nov. 7, 1829.

76. "Story of George Ash"; Klinck and Talman, *Journal of Major John Norton,* 178.

77. Klinck and Talman, *Journal of Major John Norton,* 178; C.O. 42/89: 195.

78. *Collections of the Michigan Pioneer and Historical Society,* 336.

Chapter 5: The Battle with No Name

1. Quoted in Black, *The Battle of Waterloo,* 98–99; also Carlton, *This Seat of Mars,* 164.

2. Marlantes, *What It Is Like to Go to War,* xi.

3. Keegan, *The Face of Battle,* 47, 172–77, 297–98.

4. Wright, *Those Who Have Borne the Battle,* 15.

5. Denny, *Military Journal,* 170.

6. [Sargent], "Winthrop Sargent's Diary," 259.

7. St. Clair's pen-and-ink drawing showing the deployment of his troops at the time of the battle is in the Indiana Historical Society, Northwest Territory Collection, MO 367, box 1, folder 35, map 001. Ebenezer Denny reproduced his map of the encampment and battleground in *Military Journal.* Winthrop Sargent's sketches are in Winthrop Sargent Papers, reel 1: 400, 421; his description of the disposition of troops is in "Winthrop Sargent's Diary," 256. Winkler, *Wabash, 1791,* 58–59, 62–63, provides detailed diagrams of the battle.

8. "St. Clair's Defeat: Robert Bradshaw's Narrative," Draper Mss. 4U: 143.

9. Examination of the officer of the day in Testimonies of the Committee of Inquiry, Ohio State Library, Arthur St. Clair Papers, 1788–1815 (hereafter OSL), card 39.

10. Smith, *The St. Clair Papers,* 2: 263; [Sargent], "Winthrop Sargent's Diary," 258; Winthrop Sargent Papers, reel 1: 360; "Extract from a letter from a

Gentleman…, Nov. 8, 1791," *Columbian Centinel*, Dec. 28, 1791, 3; "St. Clair's Defeat: Robert Bradshaw's Narrative," Draper Mss. 4U: 143.

11. Lytle, *The Soldiers of America's First Army*, 93, 295; Carter, *The Life and Times of Little Turtle*, 106 (Oldham's relationship to Wells).

12. St. Clair, *A Narrative*, 221.

13. Schoolcraft, *History of the Indian Tribes*, 6: 336.

14. Wilson, "St. Clair's Defeat," 379–80; Draper Mss. 4U:13.

15. [Sargent], "Winthrop Sargent's Diary," 259.

16. "Extract from a letter from Capt. John H. Buell, Nov. 8, 1791," *Connecticut Courant*, Dec. 19, 1791, 3.

17. Smith, *St. Clair Papers*, 2: 266.

18. Denny, *Military Journal*, 165–66; Wilson, *Journal of Capt. Daniel Bradley*, 29.

19. O'Callaghan, *Documentary History of the State of New York*, 4:271 (Johnson); Thwaites, *Early Western Journals*, 231.

20. Duffy, *The Military Experience*, 239–54.

21. Lytle, *Soldiers of America's First Army*, 94, 96, 101; Draper Mss. 4U: 13 ("Bellys"; 90 minutes); Darke to Washington, Nov. 9, 1791, Knox Papers, 30: 12.

22. Robert Bradshaw's Narrative, Draper Mss. 4U: 143.

23. St. Clair later stated he had four horses killed in the battle, three of them his private property, for which he claimed compensation, and a fourth "that belonged to the public." Indiana Historical Society, Northwest Territory Collection, MO367, box 1, folder 37: 1; box 2, folder 4: 10.

24. Smith, *St. Clair Papers*, 2: 263.

25. Darke to Washington, Nov. 9, 1791, Knox Papers, 30: 12; Denny, *Military Journal*, 166.

26. Quaife, *The Captivity of O. M. Spencer*, 25.

27. Smith, *St. Clair Papers*, 2: 264; [Sargent], "Winthrop Sargent's Diary," 260.

28. "St. Clair's Defeat," in Howe, *Historical Collections of Ohio*, 2: 227–28.

29. [Sargent], "Winthrop Sargent's Diary," 266.

30. Denny, *Military Journal*, 168.

31. [Sargent], "Winthrop Sargent's Diary," 269.

32. [Sargent], "Winthrop Sargent's Diary," 260.

33. *Columbian Centinel*, Jan. 7, 1792, 3.

34. "St. Clair's Defeat," in Howe, *Historical Collections of Ohio*, 2: 227.

35. Testimony of Captain Slough in Testimonies of the Committee of Inquiry, OSL, card 39; Klinck and Talman, *The Journal of Major John Norton*, 178;. Quaife, *Captivity of O. M. Spencer*, 25; Sword, *President Washington's Indian War*, 188, 191.

36. Denny, *Military Journal*, 167.

37. Draper Mss. 4U:13; Darke to Washington, Nov. 9, 1791, Knox Papers, 30: 12; Bond, "Memoirs of Benjamin Van Cleve," 26–27. "The maxim of Scipio, that a golden bridge should be made for a flying enemy, has been much commended," wrote the Roman Vegetius. "For when they have room to escape they think of nothing but how to save themselves by flight, and the confusion becoming general, great numbers are cut to pieces." Quoted in Duffy, *The Military Experience*, 258.

38. Denny, *Military Journal*, 168; [Sargent], "Winthrop Sargent's Diary," 261–62.

39. Lytle, *The Soldiers of America's First Army*, 215.

40. "St. Clair's Defeat," in Howe, *Historical Collections of Ohio*, 2: 228–29.

41. Lytle, *Soldiers of America's First Army*, 71; Bond, "Memoirs of Benjamin Van Cleve," 27.

42. "St. Clair's Defeat," in Howe, *Historical Collections of Ohio*, 2: 230.

43. Robert Bradshaw's Narrative, Draper Mss. 4U: 143–44.

44. Duffy, *Military Experience*, 257; Carlton, *This Seat of Mars*, 168–69; Ferguson, "Prisoner Taking and Prisoner Killing."

45. *American State Papers, Class II*, 1: 137; Smith, *St. Clair Papers*, 2: 262–64; St. Clair to Knox, Nov. 9, 1791, OSL, card 35.

46. St. Clair to Knox, Nov. 9, 1791, OSL, card 35 and in Smith, *St. Clair Papers*, 2: 265, 270; St. Clair, *Narrative*, 28.

47. Testimony of Mr. Barton in Testimonies of the Committee of Inquiry, OSL, card 39.

48. Wilson, *Journal of Capt. Daniel Bradley*, 34.

49. Hopkins, *A Mission to the Indians*, 133–34.

50. [Sargent], "Winthrop Sargent's Diary," 265; Winthrop Sargent Papers, reel 3: 276–77, 284.

51. *Collections of the Michigan Pioneer and Historical Society*, 365.

52. "Indian Account, Of the unfortunate action of the 4th Nov. received via Pittsburgh," *New-Hampshire Gazette and General Advertiser*, March 7, 1792; Quaife, *Captivity of O. M. Spencer*, 26; "Narrative of John Brickell's Captivity Among the Delaware Indians," 54; Klinck and Talman, *Journal of Major John Norton*, 178.

53. *Collections of the Michigan Pioneer and Historical Society*, 24 (1895), 420–21.

54. Duffy, *Military Experience*, 259–60.

55. Winthrop Sargent Papers, reel 3: 404; Testimony of Mr. Barton in Testimonies of Committee of Inquiry, OSL, card 39.

56. *American State Papers, Class II*, 1: 243.

57. "Indian Account, Of the unfortunate action of the 4th Nov."

58. [Sargent], "Winthrop Sargent's Diary," 254, 263; Sargent's Orderly Book, Nov. 9, 1791; Winthrop Sargent Papers, reel 1.

59. Owens, *Mr. Jefferson's Hammer*, 16.

60. [Sargent], "Winthrop Sargent's Diary," 255.

61. Darke to Washington, Nov. 9, 1791, Knox Papers 30: 12.

62. Denny, *Military Journal*, 171–74; Winthrop Sargent Papers, reel 3: 274, 282; Quaife, *Captivity of O. M. Spencer*, 27; [Sargent], "Winthrop Sargent's Diary," 269.

63. Buell, *The Memoirs of Rufus Putnam*, 329.

64. *Dunlap's American Daily Advertiser*, June 19, 1793, 2–3.

65. Quaife, *Captivity of O. M. Spencer*, 96.

66. St. Clair, *Narrative*, 128.

67. St. Clair, *Narrative*, 128; Winthrop Sargent Papers, reel 3: 404.

68. National Archives (U.K.), C.O. 42/89: 193; *Collections of the Michigan Pioneer and Historical Society*, 336.

69. [Wells], "Indian History," 203.

70. Klinck and Talman, *Journal of Major John Norton*, 178.

71. [Sargent], "Winthrop Sargent's Diary," 262, 272; Winthrop Sargent Papers, reel 3: 306; Carter, *The Territorial Papers*, 2: 382 ("very inconsiderable").

72. Draper Mss. 4U: 166.

73. Testimony of Mr. Barton in Testimonies of the Committee of Inquiry, OSL, card 39.

74. "Indian Account, Of the unfortunate action of the 4th Nov."

75. "Story of George Ash," *Cincinnati Chronicle and Literary Gazette*, Nov. 7, 1829.

76. Carter, *Life and Times of Little Turtle*, 107.

77. Winthrop Sargent Papers, reel 3: 327–31; [Sargent], "Winthrop Sargent's Diary," 271–72.

CHAPTER 6: RECRIMINATIONS AND REVERSAL

1. Nov. 9–27, 1791, Ohio State Library, Arthur St. Clair Papers, 1788–1815 (hereafter OSL), card 35.

2. St. Clair to Knox, Nov. 9, 1791, OSL, card 35 and in Smith, *The St. Clair Papers*, 2: 262–67.

3. St. Clair to Knox, Nov. 17, 1791, and same to Knox(?) private, Nov. 17, 1791, OSL, card 35.

4. St. Clair to Knox, Nov. 24, 1791, OSL, card 36 and in Smith, *St. Clair Papers*, 2: 269; Knox to St. Clair, Dec. 23, 1791, OSL, card 36.

5. Denny, *Military Journal*, 174–75.

6. Denny, *Military Journal*, 175–77.

7. Reported in Lossing, *The Pictorial Field Book of the War of 1812*, 49–50.

8. Quoted in Anderson, *Crucible of War*, 106.

9. Draper Mss. 4U: 166.

10. John Rogers to Gov. Henry Lee, Nov. 26, 1791, Draper Mss. 4U: 153–54.

11. Boyd et al., *The Papers of Thomas Jefferson*, 22: 384, 415.

12. *American State Papers, Class II*, 1: 136.

13. "Melancholy Account Respecting the Western Army"; Walsh, "The Defeat of Major General Arthur St. Clair," 122–23.

14. Jacobs, *The Beginning of the U.S. Army*, 123, provides a partial listing of the newspapers.

15. *Connecticut Courant*, Dec. 19, 1791, 3; *Columbian Centinel*, Dec. 17 and 19, 1791; *Connecticut Gazette*, Dec. 22, 1791, 2.

16. *Gentleman's Magazine* 71 (1792), 175.

17. Wallace, *Thirty Thousand Miles with John Heckewelder*, 261.

18. David Sayles to Hon. Benjamin Bourne, Jan. 1, 1792, Indiana Historical Society, Northwest Territory Collection, MO367, box 1, folder 37, no. 1.

19. After the Lakota and Cheyenne destroyed Custer's Seventh Cavalry at the Battle of the Little Bighorn in 1876 and the Zulus annihilated a British army column at Isandhlwana in 1879, each of the stunned imperial nations conducted an official investigation and brought their military might to bear with increased urgency to complete the subjugation of the tribes. See Gump, *The Dust Rose Like Smoke*.

20. St. Clair to Knox, Nov. 24, 1791, OSL, card 36, and in Smith, *St. Clair Papers*, 2: 271.

21. Darke to Washington, Nov. 9, 1791, Knox Papers, 30: 12; Smith, *St. Clair Papers*, 2: 270; Sargent's Orderly Book, Oct. 31–Dec. 8, 1791, in Winthrop

Sargent Papers, reel 1: 393–94; Proceedings of a General Court Martial held at Fort Washington for the trial of Major John F. Hamtramck, OSL, card 36.

22. Symmes to St. Clair, Sept. 8, 1791, OSL, card 34; Draper Mss. 3WW: 93, 97; Bond, *The Correspondence of John Cleves Symmes*, 144, 156, 158.

23. St. Clair to Knox(?), Nov. 17, 1791, OSL, card 35; St. Clair to Washington, March 26, 1792, OSL, card 38 and in Smith, *St. Clair Papers*, 2: 282–83.

24. St. Clair to Brown, Nov. 12, 1791, OSL, card 35; Smith, *St. Clair Papers*, 2: 265; St. Clair, *A Narrative*, 54–55, 148.

25. Smith, *St. Clair Papers*, 2: 277.

26. Imlay, *A Topographical Description of the Western Territory*, 245–46.

27. "St. Clair's Defeat: Robert Bradshaw's Narrative" and Ensign Charles Wells's account, both in Draper Mss. 4U: 142; 147.

28. *Boston Gazette*, Jan. 2, 1792, 2 (Anti-Pizaro letter).

29. Cruikshank, *The Correspondence of Lieut. Governor John Graves Simcoe*, 1: 98.

30. *Carlisle Gazette, and the Repository of Western Knowledge*, Feb. 15, 22, and 29, 1791.

31. Lewis, *St. Clair's Defeat, a Poem*; *St. Clair's Defeat: A New Song*, copy in the American Antiquarian Society, Worcester, Massachusetts; "Monody to the memory of the young heroes, who fell at the Miami, under general St. Clair," *American Museum, or Universal Magazine*, Dec. 2, 1792, 10–12.

32. St. Clair to Major Edmund Butler, March 3, 1792, OSL, card 38; Smith, *St. Clair Papers*, 2: 267n, 280–82; St. Clair, *Narrative*, 55–56.

33. *Carlisle Gazette, and the Repository of Western Knowledge*, Feb. 29, 1791; St. Clair to Major Edmund Butler, March 3, 1792, OSL, card 38; Smith, *St. Clair Papers*, 2: 267n, 280–82; St. Clair, *Narrative*, 55–56; *Connecticut Courant*, Jan. 30, 1791, 2–3 (Butler's defenders).

34. Chernow, *Washington*, 667.

35. For example, *Boston Gazette*, Feb. 13, 1792, 102.

36. Walsh, "The Defeat of Major General Arthur St. Clair," chs. 4–5.

37. Walsh, "The Defeat of Major General Arthur St. Clair," 205.

38. St. Clair to Washington, March 26, 1792, Feb. 24 (draft), March 26 (formal letter), March 31, 1792, OSL, card 38; St. Clair to Washington, Apr. 7, 1792, OSL, card 40; Smith, *St. Clair Papers*, 2: 279, 283–86; Fitzpatrick, *The Writings of George Washington*, 32: 12–13, 15–16; *Connecticut Courant*, Apr. 23, 1792, 1; *American Museum, or Universal Magazine*, June 3, 1792, 85–88.

39. Smith, *St. Clair Papers*, 2: 286–87.

40. Chalou, "St. Clair's Defeat, 1792"; Currie, "The First Congressional Investigation."

41. Smith, *St. Clair Papers*, 2: 300.

42. Knox to St. Clair, Dec. 23, 1791, OSL, card 36; St. Clair to Fitzsimmons, Jan. 23, 1792, OSL card 37, and in Smith, *St. Clair Papers*, 2: 278–79.

43. Fitzpatrick, *Writings of George Washington*, 32: 15.

44. The testimonies of the committee of inquiry are in OSL, cards 38–40. The committee's report is in *American State Papers, Class V*, 1: 36–39; St. Clair, *Narrative*, 59–79; and, with extracts from testimonies, Smith, *St. Clair Papers*, 2: 286–99.

45. *American State Papers, Class V*, 1: 39, 41–44; also reprinted in St. Clair, *Narrative*, 155–73.

46. Carter, *The Territorial Papers*, 2: 398.

47. St. Clair, *Narrative*.

48. *American State Papers, Class II*, 1: 198.

49. Extract from a letter from Lansingburg, Sept. 1, *Connecticut Courant*, Oct. 1, 1792, 3.

50. Knox to St. Clair, Jan, 7, 1792, Indiana Historical Society, Northwest Territory Collection, MO367, box 1, folder 37, no. 7.

51. Griffin, *American Leviathan*, 216.

52. *American State Papers, Class II*, 1: 215–17, 222–24.

53. Fitzpatrick, *Writings of George Washington*, 31: 442, 32: 2, 6.

54. Cruikshank, *The Correspondence of Lieut. Governor John Graves Simcoe*, 1: 29–30, 67, 100–101, 114, 151, 170, 173–74; National Archives (U.K.), C.O. 42/89: 47–50.

55. C.O. 42/89: 193; *Collections of the Michigan Pioneer and Historical Society*, 336–37.

56. C.O. 42/90: 154, 172; *Collections of the Michigan Pioneer and Historical Society*, 366, 401–2; Cruikshank, *The Correspondence of Lieut. Governor John Graves Simcoe*, 1: 157 (quote).

57. Wilson, *Journal of Capt. Daniel Bradley*, 44.

58. *American State Papers, Class II*, 1: 226, 228–29, 231, 236, 245, 249.

59. *American State Papers, Class II*, 1: 227.

60. *American State Papers, Class II*, 1: 230.

61. Buell, *The Memoirs of Rufus Putnam*, 118–20, 257–67, quote on 265; *American State Papers, Class II*, 1: 233–36.

62. *American State Papers, Class II*, 1: 243; Burnet, *Notes on the Early Settlement of the North-Western Territory*, 129–31.

63. Wallace, *Thirty Thousand Miles with John Heckewelder*, 271.

64. The treaty and proceedings are in Buell, *The Memoirs of Rufus Putnam*, 335–67; Edmunds, "Nothing Has Been Effected."

65. Boyd et al., *The Papers of Thomas Jefferson*, 22: 389; Cruikshank, *The Correspondence of Lieut. Governor John Graves Simcoe*, 1: 132.

66. *American State Papers, Class II*, 1: 199; Prucha, *The Sword of the Republic*, 28.

67. "Organization of the Army in 1792," in *American State Papers, Class V*, 1: 40–41; Knopf, *Anthony Wayne*, 13 (overhauled quote); Weigley, *History of the United States Army*, 92; Bergman, *The American National State*, 53–55.

68. Unger, *"Mr. President,"* 138–39, 237.

69. Gaff, *Bayonets in the Wilderness*, 23–24.

70. Knopf, *Anthony Wayne*, 67.

71. Cruikshank *The Correspondence of Lieut. Governor John Graves Simcoe*, 1: 131 ("Stain").

72. Burnet, *Notes on the Early Settlement of the North-Western Territory*, 133.

73. Quoted in Gaff, *Bayonets in the Wilderness*, 71.

74. Sugden, *Blue Jacket*, 130.

75. *American State Papers, Class II*, 1: 243 (May); Butterfield, *History of the Girtys*, 203 (Cornplanter).

76. Cruikshank, *The Correspondence of Lieut. Governor John Graves Simcoe*, 1: 218.

77. *American State Papers, Class II*, 1: 322.

78. Cruikshank, *The Correspondence of Lieut. Governor John Graves Simcoe*, 1: 222.

79. Cruikshank, *The Correspondence of Lieut. Governor John Graves Simcoe*, 1: 218–29; Coates, "A Narrative of an Embassy to the Western Indians from the Original Manuscript of Hendrick Aupaumut," 118.

80. Cruikshank, *The Correspondence of Lieut. Governor John Graves Simcoe*, 1: 243.

81. Klinck and Talman, *The Journal of Major John Norton*, 180.

82. Harvey, *History of the Shawnee Indians*, 98.

83. Cruikshank, *The Correspondence of Lieut. Governor John Graves Simcoe*, 2: 34–35, 68–69, 86, 99–100, 102, 105.

84. Cruikshank, *The Correspondence of Lieut. Governor John Graves Simcoe*, 2: 1–35, contains details of the talks that spring and summer. American accounts are in Lincoln, "Journal of a Treaty" and *The New American State Papers*, 4: 120–45.

85. Knopf, *Anthony Wayne*, 230.

86. Cruikshank, *The Correspondence of Lieut. Governor John Graves Simcoe*, 1: 355.

87. Horsman, "The British Indian Department." For divisions, see Joseph Brant's "Journal of Proceedings at the General Council held at the foot of the Rapids of the Miamis," May 1793, in Cruikshank, *The Correspondence of Lieut. Governor John Graves Simcoe*, 2: 5–17.

88. The Indian message to the commissioners and the commissioners' response are in Cruikshank, *The Correspondence of Lieut. Governor John Graves Simcoe*, 2: 17–24, and in *New American State Papers*, 4: 139–41.

89. *New American State Papers*, 4: 144.

90. Heckewelder's comment in Wallace, *Thirty Thousand Miles with John Heckewelder*, 319.

91. Boyd et al., *The Papers of Thomas Jefferson*, 27: 450.

92. Howe, *Historical Collections of Ohio*, 2: 232.

93. C.O. 42/98: 104–5; Cruikshank, *The Correspondence of Lieut. Governor John Graves Simcoe*, 2: 149–50.

94. "Diary of an officer at the Glaize," National Archives Canada, Claus Family Papers, MG 19, F1, reprinted in Cruikshank, *The Correspondence of Lieut. Governor John Graves Simcoe*, 5: 90–94 and as "The Diary of an Officer," 638, 641.

95. Wooster, *The American Military Frontiers*, 14 (sublegions); Grenier, *The First Way of War*, 199–200 (without fear).

96. Howard, "The Battle of Fallen Timbers," 39.

97. Nelson, *A History of Jonathan Alder*, 109.

98. Wayne's report in *American State Papers: Class II*, 2: 491.

99. Klinck and Talman, *Journal of Major John Norton*, 186.

100. *American State Papers: Class II*, 2: 490.

101. Cruikshank, *The Correspondence of Lieut. Governor John Graves Simcoe*, 3: 8.

102. Keating, *Rising Up from Indian Country*, 38.

103. *American State Papers, Class II*, 2: 579.

104. The treaty and proceedings are in *American State Papers, Class II*, 2: 562–83. The treaty with the full list of signatories is in Kappler, *Indian Affairs*, 2: 39–45.

105. White, *The Middle Ground*, 494.

106. Bergmann, *The American National State*, 129.

107. Slaughter, *The Whiskey Rebellion*; Hogeland, *The Whiskey Rebellion*.

108. Cayton, "Radicals in the 'Western World,'" 88; Cayton, "'Separate Interests' and the Nation-State."

EPILOGUE

1. Carter, *The Territorial Papers*, 2: 470.

2. Nelson, *A History of Jonathan Alder*, 16–17, 117.

3. Wood, *Empire of Liberty*, 152–53.

4. Shannon, "'This Unpleasant Business.'"

5. Bond, *The Correspondence of John Cleves Symmes*, 174–75.

6. Carter, *Territorial Papers*, 2: 552–57; Rohrbough, *The Land Office Business*, 18–19.

7. Linklater, *Measuring America*, 141–42.

8. Linklater, *Measuring America*, 143, 148.

9. Hinderaker, *Elusive Empires*, 249.

10. St. Clair, *A Narrative*, vii.

11. Smith, *The St. Clair Papers*, 2: 482.

12. Brown, "Arthur St. Clair and the Establishment of U.S. Authority in the Old Northwest," 39.

13. Denny, *Military Journal*, 28–30.

14. Bond, *Correspondence of John Cleves Symmes*, 301–3.

15. John Cleves Symmes Papers, Draper Mss. WW3: 2.

16. Owens, *Mr. Jefferson's Hammer*.

17. Knopf, *Anthony Wayne*, 532; Sugden, *Blue Jacket*, 119.

18. Mann, "The Silenced Miami," Harrison quoted on 401; Well's pledge, Dec. 9, 1796, Indiana Historical Society, Northwest Territory Collection, MO367, box 2, folder 17.

19. Carter, *Life and Times of Little Turtle*, 158; Gaff, "Three Men from Three Rivers," 148.

20. Corner, *The Autobiography of Benjamin Rush*, 240–41; Pearson, "Medical Diplomacy and the American Indian," 106.

21. Carter, *Life and Times of Little Turtle*, 4–6.

22. Volney, *View of the Climate and Soil*, 405, 408–9.

23. Volney, *View of the Climate and Soil*, 432–34.

24. Carter, *Life and Times of Little Turtle*, 161–64 (alcohol quote on 163); Pearson, "Medical Diplomacy and the American Indian," 108; McHenry to Little Turtle, May 30, 1800, and McHenry to Wells, Dec. 24, 1801, Indiana Historical Society, Northwest Territory Collection, MO367, box 3, folder 5, nos. 24, 30.

25. Hutton, "William Wells"; Edmunds, "'Evil Men Who Add to Our Difficulties'"; Thornborough, *Letter Book of the Indian Agency at Fort Wayne*, 12–18, 46–48; Sugden, *Tecumseh*, 49–50 (Shane).

26. Johnston, *Recollections of Sixty Years*, 19–20; Gaff, "Three Men from Three Rivers," 149.

27. Wallace, *Jefferson and the Indians*, 232–33.

28. Sugden, *Blue Jacket*, 208.

29. Sugden, *Tecumseh*, 379.

30. Calloway, *The American Revolution in Indian Country*; Benn, *The Iroquois in the War of 1812*; Hauptman, *Between Two Fires*.

31. Dunlay, *Wolves for the Blue Soldiers*; Van De Logt, *War Party in Blue*.

32. Krouse, *North American Indians in the Great War*.

33. Bernstein, *American Indians and World War Two*.

34. Rosier, *Serving Their Country*.

35. Holm, *Strong Hearts, Wounded Souls*.

36. As a parallel illustration, the Black Leggings tipi that serves as a war memorial commemorating Kiowa military service combines images of nineteenth-century warfare, when the Kiowa fought *against* the United States, with insignias and depictions of Kiowa service *in* the U.S. armed forces in the twentieth and twenty-first century. See Jordan and Swan, "Painting a New Battle Tipi." My thanks to Michael Jordan for this.

Bibliography

Manuscripts

British Museum
Papers of Sir Frederick Haldimand (Additional Manuscripts 21661–21892)

Indiana Historical Society
Northwest Territory Collection, 1721–1825, www.ulib.iupui.edu/digitalscholarship

Massachusetts Historical Society
Henry Knox Papers (microfilm)
Winthrop Sargent Papers (microfilm)
Timothy Pickering Papers (microfilm)

National Archives (formerly Public Record Office), Kew, England
Colonial Office Records, Class 42 (C.O.42)

National Archives Canada
"Diary of J. C., an officer at the Glaize," Claus Family Papers, MG 19, F1

Ohio State Library
Arthur St. Clair Papers, 1788–1815. Microform: 119 microcards.

Wisconsin State Historical Society
Lyman Draper Manuscripts (microfilm):
U: Frontier Wars Papers, 1789–1792
W: Josiah Harmar Papers
WW: John Cleves Symmes Papers

Newspapers and Magazines

The American Museum, or Universal Magazine (Philadelphia)
Boston Gazette and Country Journal
Carlisle (Pa.) Gazetteer, and the Western Repository of Knowledge

Cincinnati Chronicle and Literary Gazette
Columbian Centinel (Boston)
Connecticut Courant (Hartford)
Connecticut Gazette
Massachusetts Spy (Worcester)
New Hampshire Gazette and General Advertiser

PRINTED PRIMARY SOURCES

An Account of the Remarkable Occurrences in the Life and Travels of Col. James Smith, during his Captivity with the Indians (1799). Reprinted as *Scoouwa: James Smith's Indian Captivity Narrative*. Columbus: Ohio Historical Society, 1978.

American State Papers: Documents, Legislative and Executive, of the Congress of the United States. Class II. Indian Affairs. Selected and edited by Walter Lowrie and Matthew St. Clair Clarke. 2 vols. Washington, DC: Gales and Seaton, 1832.

American State Papers: Documents, Legislative and Executive, of the Congress of the United States. Class V: Military Affairs. Selected and edited by Walter Lowrie and Matthew St. Clair Clarke. Vol. 1. Washington, DC: Gales and Seaton, 1832.

"At a Meeting of the Directors and Agents of the OHIO COMPANY, held at the Bunch of Grapes Tavern in Boston, Aug. 29, 1787." *Early American Imprints*, Series 1, no. 20602.

Bond, Beverley W., ed. *The Correspondence of John Cleves Symmes*. New York: Macmillan, 1926.

Bond, Beverley W., Jr., ed. "Memoirs of Benjamin Van Cleve." *Quarterly Publication of the Historical and Philosophical Society of Ohio* 17 (Jan.–June 1922): 1–71.

Boyd, Julian P., et al., eds. *The Papers of Thomas Jefferson*. 40 vols. Princeton, NJ: Princeton University Press, 1950–.

Buell, Rowena, ed. *The Memoirs of Rufus Putnam and Certain Official Papers and Correspondence*. Boston: Houghton Mifflin, 1903.

Bunn, Matthew. *A Journal of the Adventures of Matthew Bunn, A Native of Brookfield, Massachusetts*. Providence, RI: Printed for the author, 1796.

Burnet, Jacob. *Notes on the Early Settlement of the North-Western Territory*. Cincinnati, OH: Derby, Bradley, 1847.

Carter, Clarence Edwin, ed. *The Territorial Papers of the United States*. 28 vols. Vol. 2: *The Territory Northwest of the River Ohio, 1787–1803*. Washington, DC: Government Printing Office, 1934.

Coates, B. H., ed. "A Narrative of an Embassy to the Western Indians from the Original Manuscript of Hendrick Aupaumut." *Memoirs of the Historical Society of Pennsylvania* 2 (1827), part 1: 61–131.

Collections of the Michigan Pioneer and Historical Society. 40 vols. Lansing: Michigan Historical Commission, 1876–1929, Vol. 24 (1895).

"Contests with the Indians: St. Clair's Campaign." *Western Review and Miscellaneous Magazine* 3, no. 1 (1820): 58–62.

"The Contract of the Ohio Company with the Honorable Board of Treasury of the United States of America." Oct. 27, 1787. *Early American Imprints*, Series 1, no. 20604.

Crackel, Theodore J., ed. *The Papers of George Washington: Digital Edition.* Presidential Series. Charlottesville: University of Virginia Press, Rotunda, 2008.

Cruikshank, Ernest A., ed. *The Correspondence of Lieut. Governor John Graves Simcoe, with Allied Documents Relating to His Administration of the Government of Upper Canada.* 5 vols. Toronto: Ontario Historical Society, 1923–31.

Cruikshank, Ernest A., ed. "The Diary of an Officer in the Indian Country, 1794." *American Historical Magazine* 3 (1908), 639–43.

Cutler, William Parker, and Julia Perkins Cutler, eds. *Life, Journals and Correspondence of Rev. Manasseh Cutler, LL.D.* 2 vols. Cincinnati, OH: Robert Clarke, 1888.

Denny, Ebenezer. *Military Journal of Major Ebenezer Denny: An Officer in the Revolutionary and Indian Wars.* Philadelphia: J. B. Lippincott, 1859.

Fitzpatrick, John C., ed. *The Writings of George Washington.* 39 vols. Washington, DC: Government Printing Office, 1931–44.

Heart, Jonathan. "A Letter to Benjamin Smith Barton." *Transactions of the American Philosophical Society* 3 (1793): 214–22.

Heckewelder, John. *History, Manners, and Customs of the Indian Nations Who Once Inhabited Pennsylvania and the Neighboring States.* 1876. New York: Arno Press, 1971.

Hopkins, Gerard T. *A Mission to the Indians, from the Indian Committee of Baltimore Yearly Meeting, to Fort Wayne, in 1804.* Philadelphia: T. Ellwood Zell, 1862.

Howe, Henry. *Historical Collections of Ohio.* 2 vols. Cincinnati, OH: C. J. Krehbiel, 1908.

Hulbert, Archer Butler, ed. *The Records of the Original Proceedings of the Ohio Company.* 2 vols. Marietta, OH: Marietta Historical Commission, 1917.

Hulbert, Archer Butler, and William Nathaniel Schwarze, eds. *David Zeiseberger's History of the North American Indians.* 1910; Lewisburg, PA: Wennawoods, 1999.

Imlay, Gilbert. *A Topographical Description of the Western Territory of North America... In a series of letters to a friend in England.* New York: Samuel Campbell, 1793.

"Indian Account, Of the unfortunate action of the 4th Nov. received via Pittsburgh." *New-Hampshire Gazette and General Advertiser,* March 7, 1792.

"Information of Blue Jacket." *Collections of the Michigan Pioneer and Historical Society* 24 (1895): 135–38.

Johnston, John. *Recollections of Sixty Years on the Ohio Frontier.* 1915. Van Buren, OH: Eastern Frontier / R. E. Davis, 2001.

Jones, David. *A Journal of Two Visits made to some Nations of Indians on the West Side of the River Ohio, in the Years 1772 and 1773.* Burlington, VT: Isaac Collins, printer, 1774.

"Journal of what happened at the Miamis and the Glaize with the Ouias & Piconns, 1791." *Collections of the Michigan Pioneer and Historical Society* 24 (1895): 220–23.

Journals of the Continental Congress, 1774–1789. 34 vols. Washington, DC: Library of Congress, 1904–37.

Kappler, Charles J., comp. *Indian Affairs: Laws and Treaties.* Vol. 2: *Treaties.* Washington, DC: Government Printing Office, 1904.

Klinck, Carl F., and James J. Talman, eds. *The Journal of Major John Norton, 1816.* Toronto: Champlain Society, 1970.

Knopf, Richard C., ed. *Anthony Wayne: A Name in Arms. The Wayne-Knox-Pickering-McHenry Correspondence.* Pittsburgh: University of Pittsburgh Press, 1960.

Labaree, Leonard, et al., eds. *Papers of Benjamin Franklin.* 40 vols. New Haven, CT: Yale University Press, 1959–.

Lewis, Eli. *St. Clair's Defeat, a Poem.* Harrisburg, PA: Allen and Wyeth, 1792.

Lincoln, Benjamin. "Journal of a Treaty held in 1793, with the Indian Tribes northwest of the Ohio by Commissioners of the United States." *Collections of the Massachusetts Historical Society,* 3rd series, 5 (1836): 109–76.

"Melancholy Account Respecting the Western Army." Broadside, Boston, Dec. 19, 1791. Early American Imprints, Series 1, no. 23214.

Merrell, James H., ed. *The Lancaster Treaty of 1744.* Boston: Bedford/St. Martin's, 2008.

Minutes of Debates in Council on the banks of the Ottawa River, November 1791 Said to be held there by the Chiefs of the several Indian Nations, who defeated the Army of the United States, on the 4th of that Month. Philadelphia: William Young, 1792.

"Narrative of John Brickell's Captivity Among the Delaware Indians." *American Pioneer: A Monthly Periodical* 1 (1842): 43–56.

Nelson, Larry L., ed. *A History of Jonathan Alder: His Captivity and Life with the Indians.* Akron, OH: University of Akron Press, 2003.

The New American State Papers: Indian Affairs, 1789–1860. 13 vols. Wilmington, DE: Scholarly Resources, 1972.

O'Callaghan, E. B., ed. *Documentary History of the State of New York.* 4 vols. Albany, NY: Weed, Parsons, 1849.

The Proceedings of a Court of Inquiry, Held at the Special Request of Brigadier General Josiah Harmar, to Investigate his Conduct as Commanding Officer of the Expedition against the Miami Indians, 1790. Philadelphia: John Fenno, 1791.

Quaife, Milo M., ed. *The Captivity of O. M. Spencer.* New York: Citadel Press, 1968.

Quaife, Milo M., ed. "Henry Hay's Journal from Detroit to the Miami River." *Proceedings of the Wisconsin State Historical Society for 1914* (Madison, 1915): 208–61.

Quaife, Milo M., ed. *John Long's Voyages and Travels in the Years 1768–1788.* Chicago: R. R. Donnelley and Sons, 1922.

Quaife, Milo M., ed. "A Picture of the First United States Army: The Journal of Captain Samuel Newman." *Wisconsin Magazine of History* 2 (Sept. 1918): 40–73.

The Remarkable Adventures of Jackson Johonnet, of Massachusetts, Who served as a Soldier in the Western Army, in the Massachusetts Line, in the Expedition under General Harmar, and the Unfortunate General St. Clair. Containing an Account of his Captivity, Sufferings, and Escape from the Kickapoo Indians. Written by Himself. Boston: Samuel Hall, 1793.

Rogers, Robert. *Journals of Robert Rogers.* London, 1765.

[Sargent, Winthrop]. "Winthrop Sargent's Diary while with General Arthur St. Clair's Expedition against the Indians." *Ohio Archaeological and Historical Society Publications* 33 (1924): 237–82.

Smith, Dwight L., ed. *The Western Journals of John May, Ohio Company Agent and Business Adventurer*. Cincinnati: Historical and Philosophical Society of Ohio, 1961.

Smith, William. *An Historical Account of the Expedition against the Ohio Indians in the year MDCCLXIV*. Philadelphia, 1766.

Smith, William Henry, ed. *The St. Clair Papers: The Life and Public Services of Arthur St. Clair... with his Correspondence and Other Papers*. 2 vols. Cincinnati, OH: Robert Clarke, 1881.

St. Clair, Arthur. *A Narrative of the Manner in which the Campaign against the Indians, in the Year One Thousand Seven Hundred and Ninety-one, was Conducted, under the Command of Major General Arthur St. Clair*. Philadelphia, 1812.

"Story of George Ash." *Cincinnati Chronicle and Literary Gazette*, Nov. 7, 1829.

Sullivan, James, et al., eds. *The Papers of Sir William Johnson*. 14 vols. Albany: University of the State of New York, 1921–65.

Thornborough, Gayle, ed. *Letter Book of the Indian Agency at Fort Wayne 1809–1815*. Indianapolis: Indiana Historical Society, 1961.

Thornborough, Gayle, ed. *Outpost on the Wabash, 1787–1791: Letters of Brigadier General Josiah Harmar and Major John Francis Hamtramck and other letters and documents selected from the Harmar Papers in the William L. Clements Library*. Indianapolis: Indiana Historical Society, 1957.

Thwaites, Reuben G., ed. *Early Western Journals, 1748–1765*. 1904. Lewisburg, PA: Wennawoods, 1998.

Thwaites, Reuben G., ed. *The Jesuit Relations and Allied Documents*. 71 vols. Cleveland, OH: Burrows Brothers, 1896–1901.

Vaughan, Alden T., gen. ed. *Early American Indian Documents: Treaties and Laws, 1607–1789*. 20 vols. Vol. 18: *Revolution and Confederation*. Bethesda, MD: University Publications of America, 1994.

Volney, C. F. *View of the Climate and Soil of the United States of America: to which are added some accounts of Florida, the French Colony on the Scioto, certain Canadian Colonies, and the Savages or Natives*. Translated from the French. London: J. Johnson, 1804.

Wallace, Paul A., ed. *Thirty Thousand Miles with John Heckewelder, or Travels Amoung the Indians of Pennsylvania, New York & Ohio in the 18th Century*. 1958; Lewisburg, PA: Wennawoods, 1998.

[Wells, William]. "Indian History. From the Manuscript of Mr. William Wells." *Western Review and Miscellaneous Magazine* 2, no. 4 (1820): 201–4.

Wilson, Frazer E., ed. *Journal of Capt. Daniel Bradley*. Greenville, OH: Frank H. Jobes and Son, 1935.

Wilson, Frazer E., ed. "St. Clair's Defeat, as Told by an Eye-Witness." *Ohio Archaeological and Historical Society Publications* 10 (1901–2): 378–80.

Secondary Sources

Alford, Thomas Wildcat. *Civilization and the Story of the Absentee Shawnees*. Norman: University of Oklahoma Press, 1939.

Allen, Robert S. *His Majesty's Indian Allies: British Indian Policy in the Defence of Canada, 1774–1815*. Toronto: Dundurn Press, 1992.

Anderson, Fred. *Crucible of War: The Seven Years War and the Fate of Empire in British North America, 1754–1766*. New York: Knopf, 2000.

Anderson, Fred, and Andrew Cayton. *The Dominion of War: Empire and Liberty in North America, 1500–2000.* New York: Penguin, 2005.

Anson, Bert. *The Miami Indians.* Norman: University of Oklahoma Press, 1970.

Barnes, Celia. *Native American Power in the United States, 1783–1795.* Madison, NJ: Fairleigh Dickinson University Press, 2003.

Barr, Daniel P., ed. *The Boundaries between Us: Natives and Newcomers along the Frontiers of the Old Northwest Territory, 1750–1850.* Kent, OH: Kent State University Press, 2006.

Barr, Daniel P., *A Colony Sprung from Hell: Pittsburgh and the Struggle for Authority on the Western Pennsylvania Frontier, 1744–1794.* Kent, OH: Kent State University Press, 2014.

Bellfy, Phil. *Three Fires Unity: The Anishnaabeg of the Lake Huron Borderlands.* Lincoln: University of Nebraska Press, 2011.

Benn, Carl. *The Iroquois in the War of 1812.* Toronto: University of Toronto Press, 1998.

Bergman, William H. *The American National State and the Early West.* Cambridge: Cambridge University Press, 2012.

Bernstein, Alison R. *American Indians and World War Two: Towards a New Era in Indian Affairs.* Norman: University of Oklahoma Press, 1991.

Bhabha, Homi K. *Nation and Narration.* London: Routledge, 1990.

Black, Jeremy. *The Battle of Waterloo.* New York: Random House, 2010.

Blight, David W. *Beyond the Battlefield: Race, Memory, and the American Civil War.* Amherst: University of Massachusetts Press, 2002.

Brooks, Lisa. *The Common Pot: The Recovery of Native Space in the Northeast.* Minneapolis: University of Minnesota Press, 2008.

Brown, Jeffery P. "Arthur St. Clair and the Establishment of U.S. Authority in the Old Northwest." In *Builders of Ohio: A Biographical History*, ed. Warren Van Tine and Michael Pierce. Columbus: Ohio State University Press, 2003, 26–40.

Butterfield, Consul Willshire. *History of the Girtys.* Cincinnati, OH: Robert Clarke, 1890.

Calloway, Colin G. *The American Revolution in Indian Country.* Cambridge: Cambridge University Press, 1995.

Calloway, Colin G. *Crown and Calumet: British-Indian Relations, 1783–1815.* Norman: University of Oklahoma Press, 1987.

Calloway, Colin G. *The Shawnees and the War for America.* New York: Viking/Penguin, 2007.

Calloway, Colin G. "Simon Girty: Interpreter and Intermediary." In *Being and Becoming Indian: Biographical Studies of North American Frontiers*, ed. James A. Clifton. Chicago: Dorsey Press, 1989, 38–58.

Carlton, Charles. *This Seat of Mars: War and the British Isles, 1485–1746.* New Haven, CT: Yale University Press, 2011.

Carroll, Brian D. "'Savages' in the Service of Empire: Native American Soldiers in Gorham's Rangers, 1744–1762." *New England Quarterly* 85 (2012): 383–429.

Carter, Harvey Lewis. *The Life and Times of Little Turtle.* Urbana: University of Illinois Press, 1987.

Cayton, Andrew R. L. *The Frontier Republic: Ideology and Politics in the Ohio Country, 1780–1825.* Kent, OH: Kent State University Press, 1986.

Cayton, Andrew R. L. "Radicals in the 'Western World': The Federalist Conquest of Trans-Appalachian North America." In *Federalists Reconsidered*, ed. Doron Ben-Atar and Barbara B. Oberg. Charlottesville: University of Virginia Press, 1998, 77–96.

Cayton, Andrew R. L. " 'Separate Interests' and the Nation-State: The Washington Administration and the Origins of Regionalism in the Trans-Appalachian West." *Journal of American History* 79 (1992): 39–67.

Cayton, Andrew R. L., and Stuart D. Hobbs, eds. *The Center of a Great Empire: The Ohio Country in the Early Republic*. Athens: Ohio University Press, 2005.

Chalou, George C. "St. Clair's Defeat, 1792." In *Congress Investigates, 1792–1974*, ed. Arthur M. Schlesinger Jr. and Roger Burns. New York: Chelsea House, 1975, 1–18.

Chernow, Ron. *Washington: A Life*. New York: Penguin, 2010.

Chet, Guy. *Conquering the American Wilderness: The Triumph of European Warfare in the Colonial Northeast*. Amherst: University of Massachusetts Press, 2003.

Corner, George W., ed. *The Autobiography of Benjamin Rush*. Princeton, NJ: Princeton University Press, 1948.

Coss, Edward J. *All for the King's Shilling: The British Soldier under Wellington, 1808–1814*. Norman: University of Oklahoma Press, 2010.

Crocker, Thomas E. *Braddock's March*. Yardley, PA: Westholme, 2009.

Currie, James T. "The First Congressional Investigation: St. Clair's Military Disaster of 1791." *Parameters: U.S. Army War College Quarterly* 20 (Dec. 1990): 95–102.

Dowd, Gregory Evans. *A Spirited Resistance: The North American Indian Struggle for Unity, 1745–1815*. Baltimore: Johns Hopkins University Press, 1992.

Duffy, Christopher. *The Military Experience in the Age of Reason, 1715–1789*. New York: Barnes and Noble, 1987.

Dunlay, Thomas W. *Wolves for the Blue Soldiers: Indian Scouts and Auxiliaries with the United States Army, 1860–90*. Lincoln: University of Nebraska Press, 1982.

Edel, Wilbur. *Kekionga! The Worst Defeat in the History of the U.S. Army*. Westport, CT: Praeger, 1997.

Edmunds, R. David. " 'Evil Men Who Add to Our Difficulties': Shawnees, Quakers, and William Wells, 1807–1808." *American Indian Culture and Research Journal* 14 (1990): 1–14.

Edmunds, R. David. "Nothing Has Been Effected: The Vincennes Treaty of 1792." *Indiana Magazine of History* 74 (March 1978): 23–35.

Edmunds, R. David. *The Potawatomis: Keepers of the Fire*. Norman: University of Oklahoma Press, 1978.

Eid, Leroy V. "American Indian Military Leadership: St. Clair's 1791 Defeat." *Journal of Military History* 57 (Jan. 1993): 71–88.

Eid, Leroy V. " 'National' War among Indians of Northeastern North America." *Canadian Review of American Studies* 16 (Summer 1985): 125–54.

Eid, Leroy V. " 'The Slaughter Was Reciprocal': Josiah Harmar's Two Defeats, 1790." *Northwest Ohio Quarterly* 65 (Spring 1993): 51–67.

Ellis, Joseph J. *American Creation: Triumphs and Tragedies at the Founding of the Republic*. New York: Knopf, 2007.

Ellis, Joseph J., *Founding Brothers: The Revolutionary Generation*. New York: Random House, 2000.

Ferguson, Niall. "Prisoner Taking and Prisoner Killing in the Age of Total War: Towards a Political Economy of Military Defeat." *War in History* 11, no. 2 (2004): 148–92.

Fischer, Joseph R. *A Well-Executed Failure: The Sullivan Campaign against the Iroquois, July–September, 1779.* Columbia: University of South Carolina Press, 1997.

Fixico, Donald L. "The Alliance of the Three Fires in Trade and War, 1630–1812." *Michigan Historical Review* 20 (Fall 1994): 1–23.

Friedenberg, Daniel M. *Life, Liberty, and the Pursuit of Land: The Plunder of Early America.* Buffalo, NY: Prometheus Books, 1992.

Furlong, Patrick J. "Problems of Frontier Logistics in St. Clair's 1791 Campaign." In Selected Papers from the 1983 and 1984 George Rogers Clark Trans-Appalachian Frontier History Conferences. http://www.nps.gov/history/history/online_books/gero/papers/1983-1984/sec6.htm.

Gaff, Alan D. *Bayonets in the Wilderness: Anthony Wayne's Legion in the Old Northwest.* Norman: University of Oklahoma Press, 2004.

Gaff, Donald H. "Three Men from Three Rivers: Navigating between Native and American Identity in the Old Northwest Territory." In *The Boundaries between Us: Natives and Newcomers along the Frontiers of the Old Northwest Territory, 1750–1850*, ed. Daniel P. Barr. Kent, OH: Kent State University Press, 2006, 143–60.

Grenier, John. *The First Way of War: American War Making on the Frontier, 1607–1814.* Cambridge: Cambridge University Press, 2005.

Griffin, Patrick. *American Leviathan: Empire, Nation, and the Revolutionary Frontier.* New York: Hill and Wang, 2007.

Griffin, Patrick. "Reconsidering the Ideological Origins of Indian Removal: The Case of the Big Bottom 'Massacre.'" In *The Center of a Great Empire: The Ohio Country in the Early Republic*, ed. Andrew R. L. Cayton and Stuart D. Hobbs. Athens: Ohio University Press, 2005, 11–35.

Gump, James O. *The Dust Rose Like Smoke: The Subjugation of the Zulu and the Sioux.* Lincoln: University of Nebraska Press, 1994.

Guthman, William H. *March to Massacre: A History of the First Seven Years of the United States Army, 1784–1791.* New York: McGraw-Hill, 1970.

Harvey, Henry. *History of the Shawnee Indians.* Cincinnati: Ephraim Morgan and Sons, 1855.

Hauptman, Laurence M. *Between Two Fires: American Indians in the Civil War.* New York: Free Press, 1995.

Hinderaker, Eric. *Elusive Empires: Constructing Colonialism in the Ohio Valley, 1673–1800.* Cambridge: Cambridge University Press, 1997.

Hoffman, Phillip W. *Simon Girty, Turncoat Hero.* Franklin, TN: American History Imprints, 2008.

Hogeland, William. *The Whiskey Rebellion: George Washington, Alexander Hamilton, and the Frontier Rebels Who Challenged America's Newfound Sovereignty.* New York: Scribner, 2006.

Holm, Tom. *Strong Hearts, Wounded Souls: Native American Veterans of the Vietnam War.* Austin: University of Texas Press, 1996.

Horsman, Reginald. "The British Indian Department and the Abortive Treaty of Lower Sandusky, 1793." *Ohio Historical Quarterly* 70 (1961): 189–213.

Horsman, Reginald. *Expansion and American Indian Policy, 1783–1812.* Norman: University of Oklahoma Press, 1992.

Horsman, Reginald. *Matthew Elliott, British Indian Agent.* Detroit: Wayne State University Press, 1964.

Howard, Dresden W. "The Battle of Fallen Timbers as Told by Chief Kin-Jo-I-No." *Northwest Ohio Quarterly* 20 (1948): 37–49.

Hurt, R. Douglas. "John Cleves Symmes and the Miami Purchase." In *Builders of Ohio: A Biographical History,* ed. Warren Van Tine and Michael Pierce. Columbus: Ohio State University Press, 2003, 114–25.

Hurt, R. Douglas. *The Ohio Frontier: Crucible of the Old Northwest, 1720–1830.* Bloomington: Indiana University Press, 1996.

Hutton, Paul A. "William Wells: Frontier Scout and Indian Agent." *Indiana Magazine of History* 74 (1978): 183–222.

Irving, Washington. *Life of Washington.* New York: G. P. Putnam, 1863.

Jacobs, James Ripley. *The Beginning of the U.S. Army, 1783–1812.* Princeton, NJ: Princeton University Press, 1947.

Jordan, Michael Paul, and Daniel C. Swan. "Painting a New Battle Tipi: Public Art, Intellectual Property, and Heritage Construction in a Contemporary Native American Community." *Plains Anthropologist* 56, no. 219 (2011): 195–213.

Keating, Ann Durkin. *Rising Up from Indian Country: The Battle of Fort Dearborn and the Birth of Chicago.* Chicago: University of Chicago Press, 2012.

Keegan, John. *The Face of Battle.* New York: Viking, 1976.

Kelman, Ari. *A Misplaced Massacre: Struggling over the Memory of Sand Creek.* Cambridge, MA: Harvard University Press, 2013.

Kelsay, Isabel Thompson. *Joseph Brant, 1743–1807: Man of Two Worlds.* Syracuse, NY: Syracuse University Press, 1984.

Kinietz, Vernon, and Erminie W. Voegelin, eds. "Shawnee Traditions: C. C. Trowbridge's Account." *Occasional Contributions from the Museum of Anthropology of the University of Michigan* 9 (1939), 1–71.

Kohn, Richard H. *Eagle and Sword: The Federalists and the Creation of the Military Establishment in America, 1783–1802.* New York: Free Press, 1975.

Kopper, Kevin Patrick. "Arthur St. Clair and the Struggle for Power in the Old Northwest, 1763–1803." PhD diss., Kent State University, 2005.

Krouse, Susan Applegate. *North American Indians in the Great War.* Lincoln: University of Nebraska Press, 2007.

Larkin, Jack. *The Reshaping of Everyday Life, 1790–1840.* New York: Harper and Row, 1988.

Linklater, Andro. *Measuring America: How the United States Was Shaped by the Greatest Land Sale in History.* New York: Penguin/Plume, 2003.

Lossing, Benson. *The Pictorial Field Book of the War of 1812.* New York: Harpers, 1868.

Lytle, Richard M. *The Soldiers of America's First Army.* Lanham, MD: Scarecrow Press, 2004.

Mahon, John K. "Anglo-American Methods of Indian Warfare, 1676–1794." *Mississippi Valley Historical Review* 45 (1958–59), 254–75.

Malone, Patrick M. *The Skulking Way of War: Technology and Tactics among the New England Indians.* Lanham, MD: Madison Books, 1991.

Mann, Rob. "The Silenced Miami: Archaeological Evidence for Miami-British Relations, 1795–1812." *Ethnohistory* 46 (1999): 399–427.

Marlantes, Karl. *What It Is Like to Go to War*. New York: Atlantic Monthly Press, 2011.

McConnell, Michael N. *A Country Between: The Upper Ohio Valley and Its Peoples, 1724–1774*. Lincoln: University of Nebraska Press, 1992.

McGlinchey, Frazier Dorian. "'A Superior Civilization': Appropriation, Negotiation, and Interaction in the Northwest Territory, 1787–1795." In *The Boundaries between Us: Natives and Newcomers along the Frontiers of the Old Northwest Territories, 1750–1850*, ed. Daniel P. Barr. Kent, OH: Kent State University Press, 2006, 118–42.

Miller, Cary. *Ogimaag: Anishinaabeg Leadership, 1760–1845*. Lincoln: University of Nebraska Press, 2010.

Miller, Francis W. *Cincinnati's Beginnings: Missing Chapters in the Early History of the City and the Miami Purchase; chiefly from hitherto unpublished documents*. Cincinnati, OH: Peter G. Thompson, 1880.

Millett, Allan R., Peter Maslowski, and William B. Feis. *For the Common Defense: A Military History of the United States from 1607 to 2012*. 3rd ed. New York: Free Press, 2012.

Nelson, Larry L. *A Man of Distinction among Them: Alexander McKee and British-Indian Affairs along the Ohio Country Frontier, 1754–1799*. Kent, OH: Kent State University Press, 1999.

Nelson, Paul David. "General Charles Scott, the Kentucky Mounted Volunteers, and the Northwest Indian Wars, 1784–1794." *Journal of the Early Republic* 6 (Fall 1986): 219–51.

Nichols, David Andrew. *Red Gentlemen and White Savages: Indians, Federalists, and the Search for Order on the American Frontier*. Charlottesville: University of Virginia Press, 2008.

Odom, William M. "Destined for Defeat: An Analysis of the St. Clair Expedition of 1791." *Northwest Ohio Quarterly* 65 (Spring 1993): 68–93.

Onuf, Peter S. *Statehood and Union: A History of the Northwest Ordinance*. Bloomington: Indiana University Press, 1987.

Owens, Robert M. *Mr. Jefferson's Hammer: William Henry Harrison and the Origins of American Indian Policy*. Norman: University of Oklahoma Press, 2007.

Pearson, J. Diane. "Medical Diplomacy and the American Indian: Thomas Jefferson, the Lewis and Clark Expedition, and the Subsequent Effects on American Indian Health and Public Policy." *Wicazo Sa Review* 19 (2004): 105–30.

Prucha, Francis Paul. *The Sword of the Republic: The United States Army on the Frontier, 1783–1846*. Bloomington: Indiana University Press, 1969.

Richter, Daniel K. *Trade, Land, Power: The Struggle for Eastern North America*. Philadelphia: University of Pennsylvania Press, 2013.

Risch, Erna. *Quartermaster Support of the Army: A History of the Corps, 1775–1939*. Washington, DC: Center of Military History, 1989.

Rohrbough, Malcolm J. *The Land Office Business: The Settlement and Administration of American Public Lands, 1789–1837*. New York: Oxford University Press, 1968.

Roosevelt, Theodore. "St. Clair's Defeat." *Harper's New Monthly Magazine* 92, no. 549 (1896): 387–403.

Rosier, Paul C. *Serving Their Country: American Indian Politics and Patriotism in the Twentieth Century*. Cambridge, MA: Harvard University Press, 2011.

Schoolcraft, Henry Rowe. *History of the Indian Tribes of the United States: Their Present Condition and Prospects, and a Sketch of Their Ancient Status.* 6 vols. Philadelphia: Lippincott, Grambo, 1851–57.

Schutt, Amy C. *Peoples of the River Valleys: The Odyssey of the Delaware Indians.* Philadelphia: University of Pennsylvania Press, 2007.

Shannon, Timothy J. "The Ohio Company and the Meaning of Opportunity in the American West, 1786–1795." *New England Quarterly* 64 (1991): 393–413.

Shannon, Timothy J. " 'This Unpleasant Business': The Transformation of Land Speculation in the Ohio Country, 1787–1820." In *The Pursuit of Public Power: Political Culture in Ohio, 1787–1861,* ed. Jeffery P. Brown and Andrew L. Cayton. Kent, OH: Kent State University Press, 1994, 15–30.

Silver, Peter. *Our Savage Neighbors: How Indian War Transformed Early America.* New York: Knopf, 2008.

Slaughter Thomas P. *The Whiskey Rebellion: Frontier Epilogue to the American Revolution.* New York: Oxford University Press, 1986.

Smith, Susan Sleeper. *Indian Woman and French Men: Rethinking Cultural Encounter in the Western Great Lakes.* Amherst: University of Massachusetts Press, 2001.

Sugden, John. *Blue Jacket, Warrior of the Shawnees.* Lincoln: University of Nebraska Press, 2000.

Sugden, John. *Tecumseh: A Life.* New York: Henry Holt, 1997.

Sword, Wiley. *President Washington's Indian War: The Struggle for the Old Northwest, 1790–1795.* Norman: University of Oklahoma Press, 1985.

Szatmary, David. *Shay's Rebellion: The Making of an Agrarian Insurrection.* Amherst: University of Massachusetts Press,.

Tanner, Helen H., ed. *Atlas of Great Lakes Indian History.* Norman: University of Oklahoma Press, 1987.

Tanner, Helen H. "The Glaize in 1792: A Composite Indian Community." *Ethnohistory* 25 (1978): 15–39.

Taylor, Alan, *The Divided Ground: Indians, Settlers, and the Northern Borderland of the American Revolution.* New York: Knopf, 2006.

Taylor, Alan. *Liberty Men and Great Proprietors: The Revolutionary Settlement on the Maine Frontier.* Chapel Hill: University of North Carolina Press, 1990.

Unger, Harlo Giles. *"Mr. President": George Washington and the Making of the Nation's Highest Office.* New York: Da Capo Press, 2013.

Van De Logt, Mark. *War Party in Blue: Pawnee Scouts in the U.S. Army.* Norman: University of Oklahoma Press, 2010.

Wallace, Anthony F. C. *Jefferson and the Indians: The Tragic Fate of the First Americans.* Cambridge, MA: Harvard University Press, 1999.

Walsh, William Patrick. "The Defeat of Major General Arthur St. Clair, November 4, 1791: A Study of the Nation's Response." PhD diss., Loyola University of Chicago, 1977.

Warren, Stephen. *The Worlds the Shawnees Made: Migration and Violence in Early America.* Chapel Hill: University of North Carolina Press, 2014.

Weigley, Russell F. *History of the United States Army.* Bloomington: Indiana University Press, 1984.

White, Richard. *The Middle Ground: Indians, Empires, and Republics in the Great Lakes Region, 1650–1815.* Cambridge: Cambridge University Press, 1991.

White, Richard. *Railroaded: The Transcontinentals and the Making of America.* New York: Norton, 2011.

Wilson, Frazer E. *Arthur St. Clair, Rugged Ruler of the Old Northwest.* Richmond, VA: Garret and Massie, 1944.

Willig, Timothy D. *Restoring the Chain of Friendship: British Policy and the Indians of the Great Lakes, 1783–1815.* Lincoln: University of Nebraska Press, 2008.

Winkler, John F. *Wabash, 1791: St. Clair's Defeat.* Botley, England: Osprey, 2011.

Wood, Gordon S. *Empire of Liberty: A History of the Early American Republic, 1789–1815.* New York: Oxford University Press, 2009.

Wood, Gordon S. *The Idea of America: Reflections on the Birth of the United States.* New York: Penguin, 2011.

Wooster, Robert. *The American Military Frontiers: The United States Army in the West, 1783–1900.* Albuquerque: University of New Mexico Press, 2010.

Wright, James. *Those Who Have Borne the Battle: A History of America's Wars and Those Who Fought Them.* New York: Public Affairs, 2012.

Index

A page number in *italics* indicates an illustration.

"Act for making farther and more effectual
    Provision for the Protection of the Frontiers
    of the United States" (1792), 142–43
An Act Raising a Second Regiment to the
    Military Establishment of the United
    States...(1791), 71
Adams, John, 22, 100–101
adoptions, 124. *See also* captives and hostages;
    Wells, William (Miami) *and other adoptees*
Afghanistan War, 164
Africans, 16
agriculture
    American and Indian compared, 31
    federal land sales and, 155
    federal policy and, 15, 25, 33, 37, 39, 73, 141
    Little Turtle on, 159
    population size and, 16
    See also whiskey tax
Albany Congress (1754), 12
Alder, Jonathan, 150, 153
Algonquian confederation, 13
Allegheny River and Valley, 26, *41*, 139
alliances, Indian
    British and, 12, 13, 17, 18, 30
    calumets and, 96
    French and, 32
    Indian definition of, 13
    Knox on, 138
    relocations and, 26
    Spanish and, 8, 18
    See also confederacies/unity, Indian; Covenant
        Chain *and other alliances*
American Eagle, 59–60

Ames, Fisher, 60, 70
Amherst, Jeffery, 52
Anishinaabeg, 13. *See also* Ojibwas (Chippewas);
    Ottawas (Odawas); Potawatomis
Armstrong, John, 132
Articles of Confederation (U.S.), 7, 11, 36
artillery, 77, 78–79, *118*, 119–20, 125, 126, 142, 143
Ash, George, 113, 128
assimilation, 163
Auglaize River and Valley, 29, 104, 106, 149, 150, 151
Aupaumut, Hendrick (Mahican), 141, 145, 147
Austrian army, 126
authority, Indian, 6, 12, 13, 94
authority, St. Clair's, 53
authority, U.S. federal
    Congressional investigation and, 136
    education and, 15
    expansion and, 7, 35, 37, 38
    land and, 36, 73
    over frontier whites, 7, 24, 35, 152
    over Indians, 25
    over U.S. Army, 20, 22, 53
    slavery and, 24
    U.S. Constitution and, 7, 11, 22, 25
    Washington and, 35, 73, 152
    See also protection

Ball, Henry, 127
Baltimore, 16, 130, 159
"banditti," 34, 35, 63, 106, 152
bark houses, 32
Battle of Agincourt (1415), 124
Battle of Culloden (1746), 124

Battle of Fontenay (1745), 5
Battle of Malplaquet (1709), 5
Battle of Point Pleasant (1774), 27
Battle of Prague (1757), 126
Battle of the Little Bighorn (1876), 6, 131, 138,
  179n19
Battle of the Somme (1916), 8, 82
Battle of the Thames (1813), 157, 162
Battle of Zorndorf (1758), 5
Battle with No Name (Battle on the Wabash)
  (St. Clair's Defeat)
  as anomaly, 162
  battlefield reclaimed by U.S., 148
  casualties and losses at, 3, 127–28
  deployments, 113–114, 116–17, *118*, 176n7
  description of, 3, 116–26
  forgetting of, 6, 10, 152
  importance of, 5–6
  tactics and, 110, 119–21
  timing of, 9–10, 113
  Washington on, 139
  See also Battle with No Name, aftermath of;
    blame for St. Clair's defeat; Indian army;
    U.S. Army
Battle with No Name, aftermath of
  Congressional investigations and, 135–39
  immediate, 126–27
  Indians and, 138–42, 145–52
  long-term effects of, 5–6
  reactions to reports, 131–35
  reports of Battle, 24, 129–31
  U.S. Army and, 5–6, 142–45
  U.S. authority and, 152
  See also blame for St. Clair's defeat
bayonet charges, 120–21
Bedinger, George, 116, *118*
Big Bottom Massacre (1791), 69
Big Cat (Delaware), 32, 105, 125
Big Knives, 63
Big Miami Treaty (Treaty of Fort Finney) (1786),
  43–46, 95, 122
Big Tree (Seneca), 73
Billy (Owatanon), 127–128
Black Hoof (Shawnee), 151, 160
Black Leggings tipi, 184n36
blame for St. Clair's defeat
  Congressional investigation and, 8, 136–37
  by Knox, 137
  of Knox, 134
  of militias, 10, 67–68
  murders at Gnadenhütten and, 131
  of officers, 132
  of provisioning, 137
  of soldiers, 3, 4, 7–8, 9
  of St. Clair, 132–33, 134, 136, 137, 155

  of training and discipline, 8, 136, 137–38
  of Washington, 134
Blue Jacket (Waweyapiersenwaw) (Shawnee)
  at Battle, 113–14
  British and, 105–6
  Gamelin and, 63
  Indian confederacy/unity and, 138, 145, 149
  later life and death of, 160, 162
  as leader, 101, 108, 111, 138, 150
  Little Turtle and, 157
  Treaty at Fort Finney and, 44
  Treaty of Greenville and, 151
  Wayne and, 151
  as white, 101
Board of Treasury (Continental Congress), 46,
  48, 49, 51
Boston, 16
Boudinot, Elias, 55
boundaries, 10
Bouquet, Henry, 109, 110
Bowdoin, James, niece of, 53
Brackett's Tavern meetings, 46, 51
Braddock's defeat
  blame for, 7
  compared to St. Clair's, 124–25, 162
  described, 4
  Indian tactics and, 110
  veterans of, 73, 75, 77
  Washington on, 130
  weather and terrain and, 83
Bradley, Daniel, 83, 119, 124–25
Bradshaw, Robert, 117, 120, 123
Brady, Mrs., 80–81
Brant, Joseph (Thayendanegea) (Mohawk)
  as absent from battle, 114
  on Indian army strength, 112
  on Indian Battle-deployment, 113–14
  Indian unity and, 107, 108
  on land, 33
  literacy of, 9
  on Muskingum River as boundary, 147
  Northwest Confederacy and, 96–97
  portrait of, 97
  Rapids of the Maumee council and, 146, 147, 148
  Sandusky council and, 30–31, 167n43
  Treaty of Fort Harmar and, 58
  Washington/Knox and, 140
Brickell, John, 32, 125
Britain and the British (also England and the
  English)
  betrayal of Indians by, 150
  Blue Jacket and, 105–106
  Brant and, 96
  captured papers and, 125
  in census, 16

Fallen Timbers and, 150
Gamelin and, 63
S. Girty and, 103
Heckewelder on, 148
Indian barrier state and, 139
Indian perceptions of, 30, 98
Indian resistance and, 18–19, 20, 85, 102–6,
    107–8, 112, 127, 138, 139–40, 149, 162
invasion of Ohio and, 65–66, 68
Miamis and, 85, 97–98, 104
presence in Indian country of, 17–18, 28
Proctor and, 74
tactics and, 61, 62
trade and, 28, 29, 66, 99, 103, 104–5, 118,
    139, 152
on Treaty of Fort Harmar, 59
U.S. relations, 5, 95, 139, 152
Zulus and, 179n19
See also Battle of the Thames (1813) *and other
    battles;* Braddock's defeat; Europeans; Jay
    Treaty; McKee, Alexander *and other British
    men;* Peace of Paris (1783); Treaty of Fort
    Stanwix (1768)
Brownstown Council (1786), 45
Brumley, Captain, 112
Buckongahelas (Delaware), 100, 102, 105, 108,
    113–14, 145, 151, 160
Buell, John, 119
Bunch of Grapes tavern meetings, 45, 50, 51
Bunn, Matthew, 111
Butler, Edward and Thomas, 77, 134
Butler, Richard
    Harmar and, 67
    invasion of Ohio and, 72, 77, 80, 83, 85, 86, 92
    letter to *Gazette* and, 133–34
    portrait of, *43*
    Shawnees and, 43, 122
    on tents, 78
    as treaty commissioner, 42, 43, 44
    wounding of, 121, 122
Butler's battalion, 106, 116, 117, *118*, 120

Cahokia (Illinois), 32
calumet pipes, 95–96, 106
Canada, 52, 96, 108, 117, 138, 139, 145, 162. *See also*
    Britain and the British (also England and
    the English); Simcoe, John Graves *and other
    British in Canada*
Canadian militia/volunteers, 4, 107
Canasatego (Onondaga), 12
capitalism, 40, 45, 52
Captain Johnny (Kekewepelethy) (Shawnee), 42,
    43–44, 105, 106
Captain Pipe (Hopocan) (Delaware), 74
captives and hostages

Indian intelligence and, 111
    on Indian leadership, 101, 102
    on Indian poverty, 140
    on Indian resistance, 107
    interculturality and, 32–33, 103–4
    invasion of Ohio and, 75, 76
    Kekionga and, 29
    treaties and, 44
    women and children, 123, 127
    See also adoptions; Spencer, Oliver *and other
        captives*
Carey, Mathew, 24
Carleton, Guy, 148
Carlisle Gazette (newspaper), 133–34
Carrington, Edward, 48
casualties
    Battle with No Name and, 3, *43*, 119, 127–28,
        129–30
    Braddock's defeat and, 4
    invasion of Ohio and, 60, 67, 75, 85
    newspapers and, 24
    retreats and, 124
cattle, 87–88
cavalry, 143
Cayton, Andrew, 50, 152
Cayugas, 12, 26, 31, *41*, 114, 128. *See also* Iroquois
    (Iroquois Confederacy/League) (Six Nations)
    (Five Nations); Mingoes
census of 1790, 15–16
Charleston, 16
Chene, Antoine (Anthony Shane), 104, 159, 162
Cherokees
    as "banditti," 63
    Brant and, 31
    British expeditions against, 62
    the Glaize council and, 145
    Indian unity and, 45, 108, 138, 146
    St. Clair and, 63
    Treaty of Fort Stanwix and, 37 *See also*
        Chickamaugas
Cheyennes, 6, 179n19
Chicago, 151, 160
Chickamaugas, 105
Chickasaws, 89, 91, 126–27, 146, 162
chief, 94
children, 127
children, Indian, 141
Chillicothe (Shawnee town), 27, 66
Chippewas. *See* Ojibwas
Choctaws, 146, 163
Cincinnati, 56, 69, 154, 155
citizenship, 163
"civilization," 53, 60, 123–24, 141
Civil War, U.S., 162
Claiborne, William C., 156

Clark, Abraham, 135
Clark, George Rogers, 42, 43, 44
Clark, John, 116
Clark's Battalion, 117, *118*, 120, 122
Cleveland, 155
confederacies/unity, Indian
  Battle aftermath and, 140
  British and, 149, 150
  challenges to, 33
  described, 6–7, 12–14, 26–31, 95
  expansion and, 6, 13
  Fort Finney Treaty and, 42–43
  Indian preparations and, 106
  invasion of Ohio and, 63
  Knox on, 74, 138
  Ohio country and, 29–30, 31
  Ohio River as boundary and, 97–98, 142, 146
  Shawnees and, 145, 146
  St. Clair and, 34, 35, 58, 59, 63, 74, 93, 106, 108
  Tecumseh and, 101
  Tenskwatawa and, 161
  treaties and, 42–43, 45
  U.S. federal government and, 13, 45, 59, 63, 140–42, 46, 147, 157
  See also alliances, Indian; councils, Indian; Northwest Confederacy *and other confederacies;* resistance movement, Indian
Confederation Congress, 19, 25, 38. *See also* Continental Congress
confederation/union, U.S.
  challenges to, 11–12, 13–14, 33
  A. Hamilton's plans and, 23
  land and, 36
  the press and, 24
  slavery and, 24–25
  U.S. Army and, 19–23
  U.S. expansion and, 15–19, 25–26, 33
  whiskey tax and, 23–24
Congressional investigations, 5, 8, 24, 82, 112, 135–39
Connecticut, 19, 23, 36, *41*, 80
Connecticut soldiers, 19, 80, 130, 131
Conoys, 105, 108, 145
consensus, 93–94, 95
Constantin-François (Comte de Volney), 158
Contepas (Shawnee), 106
Continental Army, 19, 21, 40, 52, 78. *See also* Revolutionary War (War of Independence); veterans of Revolutionary War
Continental Congress, 39–40. *See also* Board of Treasury; Confederation Congress; Northwest Ordinance of 1787
Continental money, 45–46, 51
contractors. *See* provisioning and contractors
Coocoochee (Mohawk), 105
Cornplanter (Seneca), 58, 73, 145

councils, Indian, 59, 94, 105, 108, 127–28, 138, 145, 147, 149, 150. *See also* Brownstown council (1786) *and other councils*
court of inquiry, 67
Covenant Chain, 12
Creek Confederacy, 13
Creeks, 27, 31, 108, 138, 145, 146. *See also* McGillivray, Alexander (Creek)
Cumberland, Duke of, 124
currency, 15
Custer, George Armstrong, 6, 138, 179n19
Cutler, Manasseh, 37, 46, 47, *47*, 48–52, 54, 76

Darke, Joseph, 121
Darke, William
  at Battle, 116, 117, 120–21
  on Battle, 7, 119, 122, 127
  First Regiment of Levies and, 77
  Hamtramck and, 131
  Harmar and, 67
  invasion of Ohio and, 90
  on Washington, 134
Dayton (Ohio), 151
Dayton, Jonathan, 55, 56, 57, 58, 151
Delaware (state), 135
Delawares
  attacks on, 132
  Brant and, 31
  casualties, 128
  deployment in Battle of, 113–14
  famine and, 139
  the Glaize council and, 145
  Gnadenhütten slaughter and, 99
  Harmar's attack and, 104
  Indian unity and, 45, 74, 108, 146
  language of, 44
  map of lands, *41*
  "Miami towns" and, 98
  Northwest Confederacy and, 97
  Ohio country and, 26
  raiding parties of, 69
  St. Clair and, 63, 108
  Treaty of Fort Harmar and, 58, 59
  Treaty of Greenville and, 151
  See also Big Cat *and other Delawares*
Denny, Ebenezer
  on Butler, 72
  on Indian tactics, 119
  invasion of Ohio and, 71–72
  journals of, 83–90
  on Kekionga, 104
  on Kentucky volunteers, 82
  later years and death of, 156
  on losses, 127
  on Moluntha, 44

on provisioning, 87, 89
on retreat, 122
St. Clair's report and, 128–29
on treaties, 58–59
on U.S. Army, 7, 64, 82, 90, 116
on warning signs, 91
Denny's wife and children, 156
desertions
effects of, 90
journal entries and, 80, 81, 85, 86–87, 88, 89
Oldham's men, 82
Potawatomi, 113
Detroit, 18, 28, 32, 75, *84*, 85, 102, 103
Detroit Council (1760), 13
Detroit Council (1786), 168n29
diplomacy, 6, 74. *See also* peace
discipline. *See* training and discipline, Indian;
training and discipline, U.S.
domestic debt, 23
Doughty, John, 19, 106
dragoons, 116, 122, 142, 143, 149
drinking and liquor, 80–81, 124–25, 125–26, 133, 159
drunkenness, 80–81
DuCoigne, Jean Baptiste (Kaskaskia), 141
Duer, William, 46–48, 49, 52, 78, 79, 134, 137, 154
Duke of Wellington, 8, 115
Dunlap's Station, 69
Du Quania (Six Nations), 114

eastern elites, 18–19, 33, 36
eastern frontier, 16
eastern woodland societies, 94
economic factors, 18. *See also* capitalism; land;
trade; whiskey tax
Eel River, 27, *41*, 76
Egushaway (Ottawa), 99, 100, 138, 151
Eliot, John, 61–62
Elliott, Matthew, 103, 104, 108, 140, 147, 162
Ellis, Joseph, 15
empire, American, 6, 35, 36, 37, 39, 46, 54, 60, 131.
See also expansion, U.S.
England. *See* Britain and the British
England, Richard, 100
epidemics, 16, 26, 30
Europeans
land as commodity and, 38
Ohio country and, 27
private contractors and, 77
savagery and, 124
Scioto Company and, 52
See also France and the French *and other
Europeans*
executive privilege, 5, 136
expansion, U.S.
Battle with No Name and, 5

British support *versus*, 30, 139
confederation/union of states and, 15–19, 25–26, 33
federal authority and, 7, 35, 37, 38
Indian unity and, 6, 13
Indian War and, 33–34
interculturality and, 33
land companies and, 9–10
national debt and, 38
Northwest Ordinance and, 25, 50
See also empire, American; land; Northwest
Ordinance of 1787 *and other legislation;* Ohio
River as boundary

Fallen Timbers (1794), *84*, 150
famines, 30, 62
farming. *See* agriculture
Faulkner, William, 116
Federalists, 23
Ferguson, William, 64, 77, 78–79, 86, 119–20, 126
Fifth British Regiment, 112
First American Regiment, 19–20. *See also* militias
First Gulf War, 164
First (Infantry) Regiment, 60, 77, 89, 92, 124
First Regiment of levies, 77, 82. *See also* levies
Fitzsimmons, Thomas, 135, 137
Five Nations. *See* Iroquois
Florida, 152
Ford, Mahlon, 120
foreign affairs, 14
foreign capitalist interests, 52
forgetting, 165n18
Fort Dearborn evacuation, 160
Fort Defiance, 149
Fort Duquesne, 4
Fort Finney, *84. See also* Treaty of Fort Finney
(1786)
Fort Hamilton, *84*
Fort Harmar, *41*, *84. See also* Treaty of Fort
Harmar (1789)
Fort Jefferson, *84*, 86, 88, 124, 126
Fort McIntosh. *See* Treaty of Fort McIntosh (1785)
Fort Miamis, *84*, 148, 150
Fort Niagara, 74
Fort Pitt, 19, 71, 77
Fort Recovery, 148, 149
forts, U.S., 151. *See also* Fort Miamis *and other forts*
Fort Stanwix. *See* Treaty of Fort Stanwix (1768)
Fort Washington
Battle aftermath and, 126
described, 56
illustration, *57*
Indians and, 69, 75
map, *84*
Newman's troops and, 80
St. Clair's campaign and, 71, 76, 78

Fort Wayne, 150, 159
Fowler, Jacob, 121, 122
Fowler, Theodosius, 78
Foxes, 104, 145
France and the French
  American War of Independence and, 4
  army organization of, 142–43
  British and, 102
  Fort Duquesne and, 4
  Indian alliances and, 32
  Le Gris's town and, 99
  Miamis and, 97–98
  national debt and, 23
  Ohio country and, 32
  Scott's expedition and, 75
  tactics and, 62
  trade and, 29, 99, 104
  See also Europeans; French and Indian War;
    Volney, Constantin-François, Comte de *and*
    other Frenchmen
Franklin, Benjamin, 12, 15
Freeman, Comfort and Lucy, 16
French and Indian War, 27, 46, 52, 62
French Canadians, 103
French Revolution, 30
frontier whites, 7, 16–17, 19, 24, 35, 42, 138–39, 152.
  See also settlers
Frothingham, Ebenezer, 67
funding the military, 22–23
fur trade, 31, 32

Gage, Thomas, 4
Gaither, Henry, 116, *118*
Gamelin, Antoine, 63, 100
Georgia, 17, 23
Germans, 16
Gibson, George, 67, 77
Giles, William Branch, 135
Girty, George and James, 103
Girty, Simon
  artillery spoils and, 126
  Indian alliances/resistance and, 108, 162
  on Indian army strength, 112
  Indians and, 32, 33, 103, 104, 107, 145
  later life and death of, 162
the Glaize, 29, 68, 69, *84*, 105, 106
the Glaize council, 145
Gnadenhütten slaughter, 99, 131
Gorham's Rangers, 62
gout, 53, 88, 126, 153, 158, 160
government, Indian, 94
Graham, Mrs., 80
"the Great Carrying Place," 27–28
Great Lakes, 18, 27–28

Great Lakes Indians, 126. *See also* Ojibwas
  (Chippewas); Ottawas (Odawas);
  Potawatomis
Great Miami River, *41*, 69, *84*, 86, 154
guns and weapons, 61, 78–79, 94, 107, 109, 121.
  See also artillery
Guthman, William, 22
Guyasuta (Seneca), 13

Hague Convention, 124
Haldimand, Frederick, 61
Half Town (Seneca), 73
Hamilton, Alexander, 5, 22, 23, 47–48, 57, 68, 134,
  135–36
Hamilton, Robert, 133
Hammond, George, 142
Hamtramck, John, 65, 66, 67, 74, 77, 89, 124, 128,
  131, 150
hangings, 88
Hannah (Captain), *118*
Hardin, John, 66–67, 100, 141
Harmar, Josiah
  on Chillicothes, 27
  congressional testimony of, 82
  Denny and, 71–72, 82
  First American Regiment and, 19
  Fort Washington and, 56
  on Kentucky volunteers, 82
  Miamis and, 100
  portrait of, *65*
  M. Scott and, 75
  on Treaty of Fort Harmar, 59
  W. Wells and, 103
Harmar's defeat (1790)
  agriculture and, 73
  Battle compared to, 125
  blame for, 67–68
  described, 64–67
  Hardin and, 141
  Heckewelder on, 131
  Indian resistance of, 101, 102, 103, 104–5, 106–7
  map, *84*
  M. Scott and, 75
  settlers' perception of, 138
  speculators and, 68–69, 76
  St. Clair on, 108–9
  training and, 143
Harrison, William Henry, 126, 156–57
Hastings, Mary, 80
Hay, Henry, 29
Heart, Jonathan, 36, 53, *57*, 77, 85, 116, 120–21
Heart's son, 85, 87
Heckewelder, John, 30, 31, 131, 142, 148, 153
heroism, 8

Hodgdon, Samuel, 78, 79, 80, 85, 136, 137
horsemen, *118*, 122, 124
horses, 87–88, 89, 120, 125, 127, 177n23
horses stolen, 85, 86, 91
hostages. *See* captives and hostages
Hunt, Abner, 69
hunting, 31, 159
Huron River, 31
Hurons, 31, 45, 113
Hutchins, Thomas, 39

identities, 10, 24
Illinois country, 32, 50, 154, 156
Imlay, Gilbert, 132
Indiana, 50, 99, 151, 154, 156
Indian army
    multiculturalism and, 93
    preparation of, 112, 116
    provisioning and, 109, 111, 140
    rate of travel of, 113
    size of, 91–92, 108–9, 111–13, 136, 138 *See also*
        Battle with No Name (Battle on the
        Wabash) (St. Clair's Defeat); leadership,
        Indian; resistance movement, Indian; tactics,
        Indian; training and discipline, Indian
Indian nations map, *41*
Indian perceptions, 68, 124, 167n47
Indian policy, 24–25, 133, 134
Indian raids, 22, 149
    invasion of Ohio and, 63, 69
    Kekionga and, 29
    Kentuckians and, 81
Indians
    as fighters for U.S., 162–63, 184n36
    number of, 90
    population figures, 26–27, 30, 98–99, 106, 139
    social and political structures, 93–95, 108
        See also confederacies/unity, Indian; Indian
        army; Little Turtle *and other Indians;*
        resistance movement, Indian; women, Indian
Indian Trade and Intercourse Act (1790), 35
Indian wars
    cost of, 25–26
    criticisms of, 133
    expansion and, 33–34
    versus land purchase, 25, 95
    of the West, 163
    See also protection, U.S. federal
infantry, 22, 142
intelligence, 111, 144. *See also* scouts, Indian; scouts
    for Americans
interculturality (multiculturalism), 32, 33, 93,
    102–4, 105
invasion of Ohio

    blame for losses of, 68
    Denny on, 71–72
    Hardin and, 66–67
    Harmar and, 64–69, 82
    Indian raids and, 69–71
    Jefferson on, 72–73
    Knox and, 63–64, 72, 74–75, 83
    map of, *84*
    provisions for, 77–80
    Scott's expedition and, 75–76
    Six Nations and, 73–74
    soldiers and, 80–82, 90
    St. Clair and, 82–83, 90–92
    tactics and, 61–62
    Washington and, 9–10, 61, 64, 73, 80, 83, 171n49
    Wilkinson's raid and, 76–77
    See also Battle with No Name; Wayne's
        invasion
Iraq War, 164
Irishmen, 16, 102
Ironside, George, 103, 105
Iroquois (Iroquois Confederacy/League)
    (Six Nations) (Five Nations)
    background, 12–13
    at Battle, 114, 122
    Brownstown Council (1786) and, 45
    campaigns against, 62, 73, 83
    the Glaize council and, 145
    Knox on, 138
    Miami village and, 105
    Northwest Confederacy and, 96, 97
    Rapids of the Maumee Council and, 146, 148
    Sandusky Council (1783) and, 31
    St. Clair and, 59, 63
    Treaty of Fort Harmar and, 58, 59
    Treaty of Fort Stanwix and, 27, 37, 97
    U.S. federal government and, 73–74, 140–41
    World War II and, 163
    See also Brant, Joseph (Thayendanegea)
        (Mohawk) *and other leaders;* Cayugas;
        Mohawks; Oneidas; Onondagas; Senecas;
        Tuscaroras
Irwin, Thomas, 91, 117
Isandhlwana (1879), 179n19

Jay Treaty (1794), 152
Jefferson, Thomas
    on Battle with No Name, 5, 142
    on census, 16
    on centralization, 23
    Congressional investigation and, 136
    on expansion, 35, 39
    invasion of Ohio and, 72–73
    land claims and, 38

Jefferson, Thomas (*continued*)
  land policy and, 156
  Little Turtle and, 159
  Marietta mounds map and, 53
  national debt and, 23, 72–73
  on peace negotiations, 148
  reports of Battle and, 130
  Sargent and, 156
  on standing army, 142
  St. Clair and, 155
  on Washington, 15
Jenner, Edward, 159
Johnson, William, 27, 94, 119
Johnston, John, 98, 159, 160
Jones, David, 94

Kaskaskia (Illinois), 32
Kaskaskias, 141
Kaweahatta (The Porcupine) (Miami), 32
Keegan, John, 82, 115
Kekewepelethy (Captain Johnny) (Shawnee), 42,
  43–44
Kekionga (Miami village)
  attacks on, 66, 67, 75, 104
  Fort Wayne and, 150, 159
  Indian resistance and, 98
  interculturality and, 27–29, 103
  maps, *29, 41, 84*
  Miami leadership and, 75, 98–99
  mistaken by St. Clair, 92
  orders from Knox and, 72
  Shawnees and, 44
Kennan, William, 123
Kentucky
  Battle deployment of, *118*
  Harmar and, 56
  land speculation and, 132, 154
  peace and, 58, 74–75
  population of, 16
  raids on, 99
  separatist tendencies of, 17
Kentucky militia (volunteers), 27, 44, 64–65, 67,
  76, 77, 81–82, 85, 116–17, 130–31, 141, 149.
  See also Oldham, William; Scott, Charles
  and other members
Kentucky River, *41*, 75, 154
Kethtippecanunk (Tippecanoe), 75
Kickapoo River, *41*
Kickapoos
  Chickasaws and, 89
  Gamelin and, 63
  Indian resistance and, 106, 108
  Northwest Confederacy and, 96, 97, 98
  Putnam and, 141
  Scott's expedition and, 75

  villages of, 99
  Wilkinson's expedition and, 76
King Philip's War, 61
King Philip (Metacom) (Wampanoag), 13
kinship, 93–94, 95
Kinzie, John, 103, 151, 160
Kiowas, 184n36
Kirk, William, 159
Kishkalwa (Shawnee), 27, *28*
Kittanning attack (1756), 132
Knox, Henry
  background, 20
  Battle reports and, 129
  on Battle with No Name, 5
  blame by, 137
  blamed, 134
  Brant and, 140
  Congressional investigation and, 135–36
  correspondence with St. Clair, 24
  Cutler and, 52
  Dayton and, 56
  death of, 153
  Duer and, 52, 78
  on expansionism, 9–10
  on S. Girty, 145
  images, *21*
  on Indian alliances, 138
  on Indian army strength, 108
  Indian policy and, 25
  invasion of Ohio and, 63, 64, 65–66, 67, 80, 83
  Ohio Company and, 48
  peace and, 72, 73–74, 140–141
  provisioning and, 78, 79, 80
  U.S. Army and, 20, 21, 22, 71, 142–143, 166n23
  on Washington, 15
Knox, William, 78
Korean War, 164
Kosciusko, Thaddeus, 158

Lake Champlain, 18
Lake Nations, 146. *See also* Ojibwas; Ottawas;
  Potawatomis
Lake Ontario, 18
Lakotas, 179n19
land
  as commodity, 38
  cost/prices of, 39, 48, 51, 55, 57, 153, 154, 155,
  168n51
  Indian contempt and, 123
  Indian unity and, 33
  Indian wars and, 25, 95
  Miami River purchases, 151
  newspapers on, 133
  Peace of Paris and, 17, 36, 46, 61, 148
  Treaty of Greenville and, 153

U.S. federal policy and, 24–25, 141, 234
U.S. federal sales of, 39, 153–55
See also agriculture; expansion, U.S.; Northwest
    Ordinance of 1787 *and other legislation;* right
    of conquest; speculators; surveys and
    surveyors
land companies, 35, 36–37, 40, *41. See also* Ohio
    Company of Associates; Scioto Company;
    speculators
Land Ordinance (1785), 39, 48
L'Anguille, 76
leadership, Indian, 6–7, 13, 75, 94–95, 98–103, 113–14.
    See also Blue Jacket; Brant, Joseph; Little
    Turtle
Lear, Tobias, 130
Lee, Arthur, 42, 51
Lee, Henry, 130
Le Gris (Miami), 29, 98–99
levies
    background, 71, 77, 82, 83
    at Battle, 27, 116
    blamed, 10
    Darke on losses of, 127
    terms of service and, 71, 86, 87, 88, 89, 90, 126
    See also U.S. Army
Lewis, Eli, 133
Limestone River, 56
Lincoln, Benjamin, 146
Linklater, Andro, 40
liquor and drinking, 29, 80–81, 124–25, 125–26,
    133, 159
Little Miami River, *41, 84*
Little Turtle (Mishikinaakwa) (Miami) and his
    warriors
    at Battle, 113–14, 125
    Indian resistance/unity and, 98, 105, 108
    on Kekionga, 28
    later life and death of, 157–60
    as leader, 100–102, 125, 150, 157
    number of warriors of, 111–12
    portrait of, *110*
    Treaty of Greenville and, 151
Livingston, Walter, 51
Logan, Benjamin, 44
log cabins, 31–32
logistical problems, 8
Losantiville, 55, 56
Louisburg, 52
Ludlow, Israel, 151

Madison, James, 23
Mahicans, 141, 145
Maine, 16, 52, 78
Manifest Destiny, 6
Mannitoos, 107

Manwangopath (Sweet Breeze) (Miami), 103–4
Marietta (Ohio), 53–54, 154, 155
Marlantes, Karl, 115, 173n86, 176n70
Maryland, 12, 23, 36, 105, 130, 135
Maryland soldiers, 77, 111, 116
Massachusetts, 23, 36, 51, 52, 135. *See also* Putnam,
    Rufus *and other people from Massachusetts*
Massachusetts recruits, 80
material culture, 32
Maumee River and Valley
    Battle and, 3
    British and, 102, 103, 107, 127, 140, 148
    famine and, 30
    Indian villages, and, 26, 27, 29, 102, 140
    map, *41*
    Northwest Confederacy and, 98–99, 104
    Wayne's invasion and, 148, 149, 150, 151
    See also Harmar's defeat; Rapids of the
        Maumee council
May, William, 112, 125–26, 145
McDowell, 123
McGillivray, Alexander (Creek), 17
McHenry, James, 159
McKee, Alexander
    background, 103
    Battle aftermath and, 139
    British support and, 45, 68, 103, 106, 107, 108
    the Glaize council and, 145
    on Indian losses, 128
    later life and death of, 162
    loss of Ohio and, 162
    on peace, 139
    Rapids of Maumee council and, 147
    Shawnees and, 148
    on Six Nations, 114
    on Treaty of Fort Harmar, 58
    on Wayne's invasion, 150
McKee, Thomas, 107
McKenzie, Margaret, 103
McKnight, Mary, 127
Meadow, Polly, 127
Measuring America (Linklater), 40
Mekoches (Shawnees), 42–43
Mercer, John, 135
Messquakenoe (Painted Pole) (Shawnee),
    145–46, 160
Metacom (King Philip) (Wampanoag), 13. *See
    also* King Philip's War
Métis, 103
Miami Confederacy. *See* Northwest Confederacy
Miami Purchase (Symmes Purchase), 55–56, 57,
    68–69, 132
Miami River and Valley, 26, *41*, 56, 145, 151
Miami River council (1788), 98
Miami River council (1792), 141

Miamis
   British and, 85
   captives and, 103
   Cornplanter and, 73
   deployment in Battle of, 113–14
   famine and, 139
   the Glaize council and, 145
   Harmar's attack and, 104
   Indian army strength and, 113
   Indian confederacies/unity and, 45, 59, 74, 96,
      97–98, 107, 108, 146
   invasion of Ohio and, 65, 66, 67, 102
   Kekionga fort and, 72
   Knox's orders and, 140
   Ohio country and, 26–27
   planned attack on, 92
   Proctor and, 74
   Six Nations and, 63
   St. Clair and, 63, 90–91
   Treaty of Greenville and, 151
   warnings by, 108
   western tribes and, 63
   See also Kekionga (Miami village); Little
      Turtle *and other Miamis;* Piankeshaws;
      Weas
"Miami towns," 98–99, 104, 107, 146
Michigan, 50
military historians, 6
military warrants, 39–40, 50, 55
militia acts, 71, 143, 152
militias
   attacks on Delawares, 99
   at Battle, 3, 90, 116–117, *118*, 119, 121
   blamed for defeats, 10, 66–68, *131*
   discontent/desertions of, 86, 87, 89
   Harmar and, 64–65
   Knox's plan and, 22, 166n23
   regulars *versus*, 66–67, 87, 133, 142, 143
   standing army *versus*, 19–21, 22
   St. Clair and, 53, 72
   tactics/training of, 62, 64–65
   U.S. Congressional legislation and, 71, 143, 152
   See also Kentucky militia *and other state
      militias*
Miller, Catherine (Redheaded Nance), 123
Mingoes, 12, 26, 31, *41*, 114, 128. *See also* Iroquois
   (Iroquois Confederacy/League) (Six
   Nations) (Five Nations)
(Mishikinaakwa) (Miami). *See* Little Turtle
Mississauga Ojibwas, 117
Mississippi River, 17, 18, 19, 23, 145, 152
Mohawks, 12, 108. *See also* Brant, Joseph
   (Thayendanegea) *and other Mohawks;*
   Iroquois (Iroquois Confederacy/League)
   (Six Nations) (Five Nations)

Moluntha (Shawnee), 44
Moravian Indian communities, 31, 131
Morgan, John, 133–34
Morris, Robert, 77
Mott, Corporal, 123
multiculturalism (interculturality), 32, 33, 93,
      102–4, 105
Muskingum River and Valley
   as boundary, 96–97, 145, 146, 147
   Indian attacks and, 69
   map, *84*
   Ohio company and, 53, 55
   myths, 6, 9, 138

Nanticokes, 105, 108, 145
Napoleon's Imperial Guard, 8, 116
*Narrative of the Manner in which the Campaign
      against the Indians…was Conducted…*
      (St. Clair), 137
national debt/national bank, 22–23, 36, 38, 46, 49,
      70, 72–73, 134
national defense, 14
naturalization, 14
Navajo code talkers, 163
New England, 13, 60, 69–70. *See also* King Philip's
      War; Maine *and other states;* Putnam, Rufus
      and other New Englanders
New Hampshire, 51
New Hampshire Rangers, 62
New Jersey, 19, 55, 56, 69, 135
New Jersey levies/militia, 19, 77
Newman, Samuel, 80–81, 83–90, 85, 87, 88, *118*, 121, 123
Newman's son, 85, 121
New Mexico, 13
New Salem, 31
newspapers and other press, 5, 24, 71, 130–131,
      133–35, 138
New York City, 16, 17
New York militia, 19
New York state, 36, 153
Niagara, 18, 140
North Carolina, 12, 14, 17, 77, 135
Northwest Confederacy (Miami Confederacy)
      (Wabash Confederacy)
   after Battle, 138, 141, 149–50, 151, 161
   Indian resistance movement and, 96–105
   interculturality and, 93
   land and, 6, 33
   leadership of, 6–7, 99
   members of, 96
   Miamis and, 98, 104
   St. Clair on, 59, 93
   See also confederacies/unity, Indian; Shawnees
      and other members
Northwest Ordinance of 1787, 25, 48–51, 64, 148

Northwest Territory, 16, 22, 25, 139. *See also* Northwest Ordinance of 1787
Norton, John (Mohawk Scots Cherokee), 96, 97, 112, 113, 122, 125, 128, 150

Odawas. *See* Ottawas
officers, U.S.
    Battle and, 119–20, 120–21
    blame and, 132
    Braddock's campaign and, 4
    Darke on, 127
    in defeat, 126
    militia *versus* army, 142
    preparation of, 7
    regular army and, 22
    retreat and, 122
    veterans as, 13, 71
Ohio, 10, 18, 19, 26–27, 36–37, 50, 153
Ohio Company of Associates
    "civilization" and, 53
    contracts and, 51–52
    Cornplanter and, 73
    corporate structure of, 45–46
    cost per acre and, 51, 168n51
    federal land sales and, 154
    Harmar and, 56
    lands of, *41*, 55
    Northwest Ordinance and, 48–50, 49
    protection of land and, 60
    Putnam on, 70
    regional differences and, 166n11
    Scott's success and, 76
    St. Clair and, 52
    See also land companies
Ohio River, 16, 28, *41*, *84*
Ohio River as boundary
    Blue Jacket on, 63
    Brant and, 96–97
    Indian unity and, 97–98, 142, 146
    Northwest Ordinance and, 51
    number of settlers north of, 153
    Rapids of the Maumee Council and, 147–48
    treaties and, 27, 42, 43, 58, 61
Ojibwas (Chippewas)
    Battle deployment of, 124
    Brant and, 31
    the Glaize council and, 145
    Indian resistance/confederacies/unity and, 13, 45, 72, 96, 99, 106, 108, 149
    lands of, *41*, 99
    leaders of, 100
    Muskingum River as boundary and, 146
    Treaty of Fort Harmar and, 58–59
    troop strength and, 113
Oldham, William, 77, 81, 91–92, 117

Old Northwest, 10
Omees, 67
Oneidas, 12. *See also* Iroquois (Iroquois Confederacy/League) (Six Nations) (Five Nations)
Onondagas, 12. *See also* Iroquois (Iroquois Confederacy/League) (Six Nations) (Five Nations)
Onuf, Peter, 38
Operation Desert Storm, 164
Ordinance of 1785, 154
Osgood, Samuel, 49, 51
Ottawas (Odawas)
    attack on Fort Recovery, 149
    Brant and, 31
    casualties, 128
    deployment in Battle of, 114
    the Glaize council and, 145
    Harmar's attack and, 105
    Indian alliances/unity and, 13, 45, 96, 106, 108
    invasion of Ohio and, 66
    Kekionga fort and, 72
    leaders of, 100
    map of lands, *41*
    Muskingum River as boundary and, 146
    Ohio country and, 26
    Treaty of Fort Harmar and, 58, 59
    Treaty of Greenville and, 151
    See also Egushaway *and other Ottawas*
Ouiatenon (Wea village), 75, 76–77
Owatanons, 127

Pacanne (Miami), 98, 157
Painted Pole (Messquakenoe) (Shawnee), 145–46, 160
panics, financial, 153
Parsons, Samuel H., 40, 43, 46, 52, 53, 94
Patterson, Thomas, 116, *118*
peace
    Blue Jacket and, 151, 160
    Brant and, 96
    calumets and, 96
    Cornplanter and, 73
    expansion and, 14, 19, 42, 74, 134
    Jefferson and, 72–73, 148
    Kentucky and, 58, 74–75
    Knox and, 72, 73–74, 140–41
    Little Turtle and, 157
    Little Turtle on, 150
    McKee and, 147
    McKee on, 139
    Pacanne and, 98
    Putnam and, 141–42
    Red Jacket on, 145
    Simcoe on, 147

peace (*continued*)
  squatters and, 40
  St. Clair and, 62–64, 92
  Wayne on, 146–47
  See also Ohio River as boundary; standing
    army; treaties
Peace of Paris (1783), 17, 36, 61, 148
Peccan (Pacanne) (Miami), 98, 157
Pendrick, Margaret, 127
Penn, William, 167n47
Pennsylvania, 16, 17, 36, 138–39, 153, 154, 167n47.
    See also Fitzsimmons, Thomas *and other*
    Pennsylvanians; Philadelphia
Pennsylvania soldiers, 19, 64, 77, 116, 122
Peshewa (Jean Baptiste Richardville), 98
Philadelphia
  arrival of Battle news at, 5, 129, 130
  as capital, 23
  Indian visits to, 73, 140, 141, 142, 146, 157, 158, 160
  magazines, 24
  population and, 16
  speculators and, 40
  supplies and, 78
Piankeshaws (Miamis), *41*, 45, 63, 66, 68, 98,
    106, 141
Pickering, Timothy, 74, 146
Pierce (Sergeant), 81
Piestewa, Lori (Hopi), 164
Pinckney, Thomas, 152
Piomingo (Chickasaw), 89, 91, 126
Piqua (village), 27
Pittsburgh, 16, 81, 138–39, 154
political and social structures, Indian, 93–95, 108
political parties, 5, 135
Polly (Wyandot), 106
Pond, Peter, 140
Pontiac (Ottawa), 13
Pontiac's War (1763), 27
population figures
  census of 1790 and, 15–16
  Indian, 26–27, 30, 98–99, 106, 139
  Northwest Ordinance and, 50
  Ohio and, 153
The Porcupine (Kaweahatta) (Miami), 32
Potawatamis
  Muskingum River as boundary and, 146
Potawatomis
  attacks by, 160
  Brant and, 31
  deserters, 113
  the Glaize council and, 145
  Indian alliances/unity and, 13, 45, 96, 108, 149
  map of lands, *41*
  Treaty of Fort Harmar and, 58, 59
  Treaty of Greenville and, 151

  villages of, 99
  See also Anishinaabeg
prayers, 109–10, 112, 120
presidential powers, 143. *See also* executive privilege
prisoners, 76, 81, 111, 124. *See also* Spencer, Oliver
    and other prisoners
Proctor, Thomas, 73–74, 75
prophet (Tenskwatawa) (Shawnee), 157, 161
prostitutes, 87
protection, U.S. federal
  expansion of army and, 71
  forts and, 53, 56, 72, 152
  frontier perceptions of, 19, 42, 138–39
  funding and, 22
  Miami villages and, 72
  southern perceptions of, 152
  speculators and, 42, 55–57, 60, 69, 70, 76
  unity of states and, 19, 60
  U.S. Congressional legislation and, 142
  Washington on, 14, 25
  See also authority, U.S. federal; U.S. Army
provisioning and contractors
  battle losses and, 4, 125
  blamed, 3, 137
  Continental Army experience and, 78
  of Indians, 107, 109, 111, 112, 141
  Knox/Hamilton contractor fraud and, 5
  St. Clair's army and, 77–80, 85, 87, 88, 89, 116
  U.S. Army and, 22
public credit, 15, 23
Public Land Act (1800), 155, 156
Pueblo peoples, 13
Putnam, Rufus, 46, 52, 53, 60, 69–70, 95, 141–42, 154

quartermaster general, 79–80, 137. *See also*
    Continental Army
Quebec, 52

Randolph, Beverly, 146
Randolph, Edmund, 136
ranges, townships and sections, 39
Rapids of the Maumee council, 146–48
rations, 87, 89
Redheaded Nancy (Catherine Miller), 123
Red Jacket (Seneca), 145, 146
regional strains, 16–17, 166n11
regulars
  Indian resistance and, 68
  militia *versus*, 66–67, 87, 133, 142, 143
  number of, 64, 65, 67, 71, 116, 149
  retreats and, 66–67, 116
  Washington on, 64, 143
  See also U.S. Army
Republicans, 135
resistance movement, Indian

British and, 102–3, 104, 105–6, 107, 108, 112, 138, 139–40, 148, 162
Indian leaders and, 99–103, 113–14
Indian monitoring and, 106, 111
interculturality and, 102–4, 105
invasion of Ohio and, 95–96, 106–8
"Miami towns" and, 98–99
Northwest Confederacy and, 96–105
prayers and, 109–10
social and political structures and, 93–95
St. Clair on, 108–9, 111
See also confederacies/unity, Indian; Indian army
retreats, 3, 4, 66–67, 115–16, 120, 122–26, 177n37
Revolutionary War (War of Independence)
Clark and, 43
Indians/British allies and, 13, 31, 32, 101, 103, 140, 162
Knox and, 20
land claims and, 36
officer experience and, 7, 19, 71, 73, 77, 80
Putnam and, 46
quartermaster and, 78
soldiers and, 7
St. Clair and, 53, 137
tactics and, 4, 62
See also Continental Army; veterans of Revolutionary War
Rhea, Thomas, 107, 108
Rhode Island, 12, 131
Richardville, Jean Baptiste (Peshewa), 98, 157
riflemen, *118*, 142
right of conquest, 42
Rio Grande Valley, 13
Rogers, Robert, 62
Royal American Regiment, 46
Rush, Benjamin, 11, 158

Saginaws, 106
Sandusky, Sandusky River and Valley, 30, *84*, 97
Sandusky Council (1783), 30, 31
Sandusky Council (1793), 146–48, 167nn42, 43
Sargent, Rowena, 77
Sargent, Winthrop
as acting governor, 155
background, 52, 77
on Battle, 116, 117, 119, 121, 122, 128
on Chickasaws, 89, 126–27
on Congressional investigation, 135–36
on Darke, 121
on encampment, 90
on Indians, 104, 117, 128
journal entries and, 83–90
on Kentucky militia, 64–65, 67, 76, 81–82
later years and death of, 155–56

on losses, 125
on officers, 126
Ohio Company and, 46, 51–52
on prospects, 89
on women, 127
Sauks, 104, 145
scalpings by Americans, 66, 75, 150
scalpings by Indians, 28, 29, 69, 75, 89
at Battle, 121, 122, 125, 126
fear of, 124
of Hardin/Truman, 141
myths and, 9
St. Clair on, 117
Schoolcraft, Henry Rowe, 117
Scioto Company, *41*, 49, 52, 60, 154. *See also* land companies
Scioto River, 26, *41*, *84*
Scipio, maxim of, 177n37
scorched-earth campaigns, 62, 66, 68, 73–77, 83, 103, 150
Scotch-Irish, 16
Scotland, 52
Scots, 16, 102, 103, 124
Scott, Charles and his raid, 74–75, 81, 107, 108, 149
Scott, Merritt and Samuel, 75
scouts for Americans, 88–89, 92, 132–33, 139, 143, 144, 146, 162
scouts, Indian
for Americans, 143, 144, 146, 162–63
Braddock and, 4
effectiveness of, 111, 113
journal entries and, 86, 89
St. Clair on, 91, 92, 117
Tecumseh as, 161
U.S. legislation and, 143
See also Piomingo (Chickasaw)
Second (Infantry) Regiment, 71, 72, 77, 106, 116, 120–21
Second Regiment of levies, 77, 83, 86. *See also* levies
Sedgwick, Theodor, 135, 137
Seiten, General, 126
Senecas, 13, 26, *41*, 66, 103, 146. *See also* Cornplanter *and other Senecas;* Iroquois (Iroquois Confederacy/League) (Six Nations) (Five Nations)
settlers
British *versus* American, 30
eastern elites and, 18
federal authority and, 7, 24, 35, 152
federal sales of land and, 155
killing of Indians and, 74
Little Turtle and, 160
Northwest Ordinance and, 50

settlers (*continued*)
  perception of land and, 33
  Rapids of the Maumee council and, 147–48
  St. Clair's defeat and, 132, 133
  traders *versus*, 32, 42
  union of states and, 17
  veterans as, 37, 45–46
  whiskey tax and, 24
  See also agriculture; frontier whites; land; Ohio
    River as boundary; protection; speculators;
    squatters
Seven Nations (Canada), 145
Seven Ranges (Ohio), 39, *41*
Shane, Anthony (Antoine Chene), 104, 159, 162
Shawnees (Shawanese) (Shawonons)
  as "banditti," 63
  Brant and, 31
  British and, 96
  R. Butler and, 43, 122
  captives and, 127
  casualties, 128
  division of, 160
  famine and, 139
  Gamelin and, 63
  the Glaize council and, 145
  government and, 94
  Harmar and, 100
  Harrison and, 157
  Indian unity and, 42–43, 45, 59, 74, 97, 106–7, 108, 146
  interculturality and, 104
  invasion of Ohio and, 66, 70
  language of, 44
  lead in battle of, 113–14
  map of lands, *41*
  McKee and, 103
  "Miami towns" and, 98
  Northwest Confederacy and, 97, 98
  Ohio country and, 26, 27
  Rapids of the Maumee council and, 146
  resistance and, 105
  St. Clair and, 63
  Symmes and, 59–60
  Treaty at Fort Harmar and, 59–60, 170n84
  Treaty of Fort Stanwix and, 37
  Treaty of Greenville and, 151
  warnings by, 108
  See also Blue Jacket *and other Shawnees;*
    Chillicothe
Shaylor, Joseph and son, 85
Simcoe, John Graves, 95, 147, 148
Sioux, 6
Six Nations. *See* Iroquois
slaves and slavery, 16, 24–25, 33, 50, 171
Slough, Jacob, 92, 122, 134
smallpox and inoculations, 30, 158, 159

Smith, James, 109, 111
Smith, John, 105
Smith, William, 110
Snake (Shawnee), 105
Snowden, Jonathan, 116
social and political structures, Indian, 93–95, 108
soldiers, U.S.
  blamed, 3, 4, 82
  blaming of, 3, 4, 7–8
  invasion of Ohio and, 64
  militia *versus* army, 142
  pay of, 22
  preparation of, 7
  regular army and, 22
  Washington and, 37
  See also levies; militias; regulars; training and
    discipline, U.S.; U.S. Army
songs and yells, Indian, 112, 113, 117, 148, 164
the South, 23
South Carolina, 23, 53
southern Indians, 138, 140. *See also* Cherokees *and
    other southern tribes*
Southwest Territory, 17, 152
Spain and the Spaniards, 5, 13, 17, 18, 23, 130, 146,
    152, 163. *See also* Europeans
Sparks, Richard, 89
speculators
  Battle with No Name and, 153
  empire and, 36
  federal protection and, 19
  Harmar's failure and, 76
  Maine and, 78
  methods of, 39–40
  national bank and, 23
  risks and, 57
  U.S. Congress and, 35–40, 46, 49–50, 51, 55, 56, 57
  U.S. federal government and, 9, 35, 70, 132, 154
  See also land companies; Symmes, John Cleves
    and other speculators
Spencer, Oliver, 101, 102, 105, 120, 125, 127
spiritual preparation, 109–10, 112, 113, 176n70
squatters, 19, 35, 36, 38–39, 40, 56, 70
standing army, 19–21, 22, 137–38, 142
State of the Union addresses, 14
states, 22, 50. *See also* Virginia *and other states*
St. Clair, Arthur
  background, 52–53, 58, 71
  on Battle, 119, 120
  at Battle with No Name, 120, 121, 122, 124
  blamed, 132–33, 134, 136, 137, 155
  British and, 65–66, 68
  on R. Butler, 134
  Cincinnati and, 56
  Congressional investigation and, 135, 136, 137
  Cornplanter and, 73

correspondence of, 24
Delawares and, 108
drawing of deployment, 176n7
expansionism of, 9
health of, 76, 88, 89, 90
horses of, 177n23
on Indian army, 90–92, 108–9, 119
on Indian losses, 127–28
on Indian scouts, 117
Indian unity and, 59, 74, 93, 108, 109
journals of, 83–90
Kentuckians and, 81, 85
Knox's orders and, 72
land purchase by, 151
later years and death of, 155
levies and, 88
Northwest Ordinance and, 48
Ohio Company and, 46
portrait, 54
preparations for invasion of Ohio and, 62–64
on provisioning of Indians, 111
provisions and, 79–80, 87
rejoins the army, 86
reports of Battle and, 129, 131
on Sargent, 77
Symmes and, 56–57
treaties and, 58
on U.S. Army, 21
victory claims and, 67
warning signs and, 82–83, 91
Washington on, 130
Wyandots and, 74, 108
See also invasion of Ohio; Treaty of Fort
    Harmar (1789)
St. Clair, Phoebe and Peg, 62
St. Clair's Defeat. *See* Battle with No Name
    (Battle on the Wabash) (St. Clair's Defeat)
"St. Clair's Defeat" (Lewis), 133
Steedman, William, 140
Steele, John, 135
Steubenville (Ohio), 155
Stiles, Ezra, 53
St. Joseph River, 26, 27, 41, 99
St. Lawrence area, 18
St. Marys River, 26, 27, 41, 91
Stroud, 32
Stuart, Gilbert, 158
Sullivan, John and his campaign (1779), 62, 73, 83
surrender, 124
surveys and surveyors, 19, 39, 48, 154. *See also*
    Sargent, Winthrop *and other surveyors*
survivors, 132–33, 138
Sweet Breeze (Manwangopath) (Miami), 103–4
Sweringen, Marmaduke van, 101
Sylvly (Captain), 112

Symmes, Anna, 156
Symmes, John Cleves
    blame of soldiers by, 7
    land claims of, 41, 55, 69
    later life and death of, 156
    Miami Purchase and, 68–69, 131–32
    Shawnees and, 59–60
    as speculator, 37, 55–57, 154, 156
    St. Clair and, 131, 137
Symmes Purchase (Miami Purchase), 55–56, 57,
    68–69, 132

tactics, Indian, 60, 61–62, 68–69, 110, 113–14, 116,
    119, 132
tactics, U.S., 4, 62, 143, 150
Tarhe (Wyandot), 151
taxes, 23, 24, 33, 36, 152, 156
Tecumseh (Shawnee), 101, 111, 151, 157, 159, 161–62
Tennessee, 16, 17
Tenskwatawa (Shawnee prophet), 157, 161
Thayendanegea (Mohawk). *See* Brant, Joseph
"Thirteen Fires" (U.S.), 14
Three Fires confederation, 13, 96, 99, 149
Ticonderoga, 53
timing of battles, 150
Tippecanoe (Kethtippecanunk) (town), 75, 157
tobacco, 106
torture, 69, 123–24, 128
townships, 39, 50, 154
trade and traders
    Americans and, 42
    British and, 18, 28, 66, 68, 99, 103, 104–5, 118,
        139, 152
    Fort Washington and, 56, 83
    Indian confederacies and, 12
    Indian resistance and, 103, 104–5, 108, 149
    interculturality and, 29, 32–33, 104, 105
    invasion of Ohio and, 66, 68
    Jay Treaty and, 152
    Miamis and, 26–28
    union of U.S. and, 17
    See also Butler, Richard *and other traders;* fur
        trade; Indian Trade and Intercourse Act
        (1790); Kinzie, John *and other traders;*
        whiskey tax
training and discipline, Indian, 72, 108–9, 119, 126
training and discipline, U.S.
    during Battle, 115–16, 121
    blame and, 8, 136, 137–38
    Custer and, 138
    defeat and, 126
    Fallen Timbers and, 150
    Knox on, 22, 72
    militia *versus* regular army, 121
    Newman on, 80–81

training and discipline, U.S. (*continued*)
  Sargent on, 116
  St. Clair on, 82, 132
  Washington on, 14
  Wayne's invasion and, 149
treaties
  Buckongahelas and, 160
  calumets and, 96
  Constitution and, 35
  Delawares and, 99
  Indian sophistication about, 61
  Indian unity and, 45
  land and, 36, 42
  See also Treaty of Greenville (1795) *and other treaties*
Treaty of Fort Finney (Big Miami Treaty) (1786), 43–46, 95, 122
Treaty of Fort Harmar (1789), 58–59, 70
Treaty of Fort McIntosh (1785), 42, 44, 95
Treaty of Fort Stanwix (1768), 27, 37, 61
Treaty of Greenville (1795), 151, 153, 157, 160
Treaty of Hopewell (1786), 89
Treaty of Lancaster (1744), 12
Treaty of Vincennes (1793), 141–42
Truman, Alexander, 116, 122, 141
Turner, Samuel, 111, *118*
Tuscaroras, 12. *See also* Iroquois (Iroquois Confederacy/League) (Six Nations) (Five Nations)
Tyler, John, 157

union of states. *See* confederation/union, U.S.
unity, Indian. *See* confederacies/unity, Indian
U.S. Army
  Battle aftereffects on, 5–6, 142–45
  establishment of, 12, 19–24
  history of, 131
  Indian service in, 162–64, 184n36
  Jefferson on, 72–73
  protection of lands and, 42
  rate of travel of, 83, 86, 89, 90
  reorganization of, 142–45
  size of, 19–20, 22, 71, 90, 116, 149
  U.S. Congress and, 19–22, 71, 142–43
  Washington on, 14
  See also Battle with No Name (Battle on the Wabash) (St. Clair's Defeat); Butler's battalion *and other battalions;* First American Regiment *and other regiments;* levies; militias; officers; regulars; soldiers, U.S.; standing army; tactics, U.S.; training and discipline, U.S.; *specific state levies, militias and regulars*
U.S. Congress
  Indian citizenship and, 163
  Indian perceptions of, 95
  land and, 25–26, 35–40, 42, 45, 51, 154–55
  protection and, 142
  provisioning and, 77
  reaction to defeat of, 130, 133, 135
  slavery and, 24
  Southwest Territory and, 17
  speculators and, 35–40, 46, 49–50, 51, 55, 56, 57
  St. Clair and, 53, 58
  U.S. Army and, 19–22, 71, 142–43
  Vincennes Treaty and, 142
  See also Ames, Fisher *and other congressmen;* congressional investigations; militia acts; Public Land Act *and other legislation;* Washington, George, presidential addresses and messages of
U.S. Constitution
  armed forces and, 20
  federal authority and, 7, 11, 22, 25
  Indian affairs and, 35
  militias and, 143
  presidency and, 15
  slavery and, 24
  union of states and, 11–12
U.S. Department of the Interior, 25
U.S. federal government
  effects of battle on, 5–6
  Indian confederacies/unity and, 13, 45, 59, 63, 140–42, 146, 147, 157
  Indian wars and, 19
  land policy and, 24–25, 141
  land sales of, 39, 153–55
  protection and, 18, 138–39
  speculators and, 9, 35, 70, 132, 154
  See also Knox, Henry *and other officials;* presidential powers; protection, U.S. federal; U.S. Congress

Van Cleve, Benjamin and John, 69, 122, 123
Vegetius Renatus, Publius Flavius, 82, 177n37
Vermont, 16, 17
veterans of Revolutionary War
  land bounties and, 36, 37, 39–40, 45–46, 48
  as speculators, 35–36, 40, 52
  U.S. officers as, 13, 71
victors, 6, 9
Victory with No Name. *See* Battle with No Name (Battle on the Wabash) (St. Clair's Defeat)
Vietnam War, 164, 176n70
Vincennes, 32, 65, 98, 130
Vincennes Treaty, 141–42
Vining, John, 135, 137
Virginia and Virginians
  Battle of Point Pleasant and, 27
  Canasatego and, 12

debt and, 23
Indian perceptions of, 167n47
land and, 36, 154
military warrants and, 55
population and, 16, 153
protection and, 139
Washington and, 37
See also Giles, William Branch *and other Virginians*
Virginia Battalion (levies), 77, 87, 88, 90, 116. *See also* levies
Virginia Military District, 36
Volney, Constantin-François, Comte de (French), 158–59

Wabash Confederacy. *See* Northwest Confederacy
Wabash (Ouabash) Indians
as "banditti," 63
Cornplanter and, 73
Indian unity and, 59
Kekionga fort and, 72
Pacanne and, 98
peace offers and, 64, 140
Putnam and, 141
St. Clair and, 91
Wilkinson's expedition and, 76
Wabash River and Valley
French traders and, 32
Indian population of, 27, 98–99, 106
maps, 41, 84, 118
mistaken for St. Mary's, 92
Scott and Wilkinson and, 107
Scott's expedition and, 75
Wampanoags, 13
wampum, 43–44, 95, 96, 98, 107, 146
Wapacomegat (Mississauga Ojibwa), 117
war chiefs, 94
War Department, 20, 25
war medicine, 109–10
War of 1812, 162
War of Independence. *See* Revolutionary War
Washington, George
on armed forces, 21, 22
army reorganization and, 142–43
Battle reports and, 129–30
blamed, 134
Blue Jacket/Painted Pole and, 160
Braddock's defeat and, 4
Brant and, 140
census and, 16
Congressional investigation and, 136
on expansion, 35
Harmar and, 64, 67
on Indian land, 25, 139

invasion of Ohio and, 9–10, 61, 64, 73, 80, 83, 171n49
Knox and, 20
Little Turtle and, 158, 160
on loss of men, 139
mortality of, 15
national debt and, 23
on peace, 14, 74
popular history and, 10
presidential addresses and messages of, 14, 34, 130, 131
protection and, 139
Putnam and, 46, 69–70
Senecas and, 73
as speculator, 36, 37, 38, 134
St. Clair and, 24, 53, 71, 130, 135, 137
on union of states, 18
Vincennes Treaty and, 142
warnings about, 146
Whiskey Rebellion and, 152
See also executive privilege
Waterloo, 8, 115, 116
Waweyapiersenwaw (Shawnee). *See* Blue Jacket
Wayne, Anthony, 101, *144*, 145, 146–47, 152, 153, 157
Wayne's invasion, 143–51, 162
weapons. *See* guns and weapons
Weas (Miamis)
attacks on, 74–75, 76–77
Gamelin and, 63
Indian resistance/unity and, 45, 106
Miami leadership and, 75, 98
Putnam and, 141
villages of, 75, 76–77, 99
weather, 85, 86, 87–88, 89, 90, 113, 139
weights and measures, 15
Wellington, Duke of, 8, 115
Wells, Hayden, 117
Wells, Samuel, 117, 128
Wells, William (Miami)
adoption by Miami of, 32
at Battle, 119
on Indian army strength, 111–12
on Indian leaders, 100, 102
on Indian losses, 128
Indian resistance and, 32, 103–4
as interpreter, 141, 151
later life and death of, 158, 159, 160, *161*
Little Turtle and, 100, 101, 157, 158, 159
Wells's wives and baby, 76, 103–4
Welshmen, 102
Western Reserve, 36
West Point, 19
What It Is Like to Go to War (Marlantes), 115, 173n86, 176n70
Whiskey Rebellion, 152